Studying Human Rights

Studying Human Rights draws on key theories and methods from the social sciences to develop a framework for the systematic study of human rights problems. It argues that solid empirical analysis of human rights problems rests on examining the observable practices from state and non-state actors that constitute human rights violations to provide plausible explanations for their occurrence and deeper understanding of their meaning.

Such explanation and understanding draws on the theoretical insights from rational, structural, and cultural approaches in the social sciences. This book includes:

- an outline of the scope of human rights;
- the terrain of key actors that have an impact on human rights;
- a summary of social science theories, methods and measures for studying human rights;
- a separate treatment of global comparative studies, truth commissions, and human rights impact assessment.

Studying Human Rights is the first book to use the synthesis of social science approaches to studying human rights, and its quantitative and qualitative approach provides useful insights. This book makes a unique contribution to the extant literature on human rights and is an invaluable tool for both scholars and practitioners in this area.

Todd Landman served as Co-Director of the Human Rights Centre (2003–2005) and is a Reader in the Department of Government at the University of Essex. His recent publications include *Protecting Human Rights: A Comparative Study* (Georgetown University Press, 2005) and *Issues and Methods in Comparative Politics* (Routledge, 2000, 2003).

Studying Human Rights

Todd Landman

Routledge
Taylor & Francis Group

LONDON AND NEW YORK

First published 2006
by Routledge
2 Park Square, Milton Park, Abingdon, Oxon OX14 4RN

Simultaneously published in the USA and Canada
by Routledge
270 Madison Avenue, New York, NY 10016

Routledge is an imprint of the Taylor & Francis Group

© 2006 Todd Landman
Cover image by Kim Barclay

Typeset in Garamond 3 by
Keystroke, Jacaranda Lodge, Wolverhampton
Printed and bound in Great Britain by
TJ International Ltd, Padstow, Cornwall

British Library Cataloguing in Publication Data
A catalogue record for this book is available from the British Library

Library of Congress Cataloging in Publication Data
A catalog record for this book has been requested

ISBN10: 0–415–32604–4 (hbk)
ISBN10: 0–415–32605–2 (pbk)

ISBN13: 9–78–0–415–32604–9 (hbk)
ISBN13: 9–78–0–415–32605–6 (pbk)

Contents

Illustrations

Figures

Tables

Preface and acknowledgements

This book has been inspired by a series of key events throughout my own academic career as a political scientist. My undergraduate studies at the University of Pennsylvania from 1984 to 1988 were dominated by a focus on Latin America when South America was dominated by prolonged periods of military authoritarian rule (most notably Argentina, Brazil, Chile, Paraguay, and Uruguay) and Central America was undergoing extreme and violent civil conflict, which had been coupled with US interventionism either on the side of governments fighting Communist subversion (as in El Salvador and Honduras) or supporting anti-Communist movements seeking to overthrow their governments (as in the case of the Contras in Nicaragua). It was also a time when students were mobilizing on campus against the University's hierarchy to disinvest in South Africa to protest against the human rights abuses being committed under the auspices of the apartheid system. These political developments and events had grave consequences for the human rights of thousands of innocent people and had a politicizing effect on me throughout my studies at Penn. While pursuing an MA in Latin Studies at Georgetown University between 1988 and 1990, my student job in the library's audio-visual department found me being asked to reproduce photos for the Presidential Commission investigating the murder of six Jesuit priests, their cook, and her daughter on the morning of 16 November 1989 at the Central American University in El Salvador. Again, my shock and moral outrage at and abhorrence of these acts continued to motivate my academic studies and solidified my commitment to the promotion and protection of human rights.

My pursuit of a further master's degree (Boulder) and PhD (Essex) in political science was driven in part by a quest to explain and understand how such events take place through the application of the tools of the social sciences. My time at Boulder provided an excellent background in the philosophy, paradigms, theories, and methods of the social sciences, while my time at Essex has fortified my understanding of the field of human rights and how political science can make a difference to their promotion and protection. Having taught on the various human rights options and core courses that make up the MA in the Theory and Practice of Human Rights, and after having developed the Undergraduate Programme in Human Rights, I have seen how the same quest for explanation and understanding has over the years motivated countless students who have come to Essex and gone on to work in the field of human rights. My own research agenda has been framed around general discussions of social scientific methods as applied to politics (Landman 2002, 2003); questions of human rights measurement, impact assessment and evaluation of human rights NGOs, cross-national comparison, and the political science of human rights (Landman 2002, 2004, 2005a; Landman and Häusermann 2003; Landman and Abraham 2004); and a specific set of systematic inquiries on the variable protection over time and across space of citizenship rights (Foweraker and Landman 1997) and human rights (Landman 2005b).

Studying Human Rights ties together these different strands from my personal experiences and my professional work as a political scientist of human rights and offers students, scholars and practitioners a framework for analysing human rights problems from a non-legal perspective. It draws on key theories and methods from the social sciences to develop a framework for the systematic study of human rights problems. It argues that solid empirical analysis of human rights problems rests on examining the *observable practices* from state and non-state actors that constitute human rights violations, and then applying the theories and methods from the social sciences to provide plausible explanations for their occurrence and provide deeper understanding of their meaning. Such explanation and understanding draws on the theoretical insights from rational, structural, and cultural approaches in the social sciences combined with different kinds of quantitative and qualitative methods. The book outlines the scope of human rights, the terrain of key actors that have an impact on human rights; summarizes dominant social science theories, methods, and measures for studying human rights; and then provides separate treatment and discussion of global comparative studies, truth commissions, and human rights impact assessment. Overall, the book contributes to the literature on human rights by moving beyond the philosophical search for an agreed set of foundations and uses the international law of human rights as a useful way of delineating the core content of those human rights categories and dimensions subject to systematic social scientific analysis.

As ever, no such book is wholly produced without the benefit of the various insights, ideas, arguments, and caveats from my colleagues at Essex and around the world. At Essex, I would like to thank Kevin Boyle, Michael Freeman, Joe Foweraker, David Howarth, Aletta Norval, Hugh Ward, Albert Weale, David Sanders, Paul Hunt, Nigel Rodley, Diana Morales, Anat Barsella, Tom Sorell, and Sheldon Leader. Outside Essex, I would like to thank Attracta Ingram, Horst Fischer, Neil Mitchell, David Cingranelli, Darren Hawkins, Jack Donnelly, Bert Lockwood, Sumner Twiss, Patrick Ball, Paola Cesarini, Shareen Hertel, Claudia Dahlerus, Dan Goldstein, Thomas Wolnick, and the various members of the Human Rights Section of the American Political Science Association.

I would also like to thank the European Commission for its funding of the project on measuring democracy, good governance and human rights; the Ministry of Foreign Affairs of the Netherlands for funding the evaluation and assessment of nine human rights organizations; the International Centre for Transitional Justice for funding the project on the use of information management systems in truth commissions; Capacity Building International in Germany (InWent) for supporting my work on human rights measurement; and Minority Rights Group International for its project on evaluating and assessing its programme on the Council of Europe's Framework Convention for the Protection of National Minorities.

I give special and personal thanks to Dave Smith, Leigh Amos, and Lily and Flora Amos-Smith, Malcolm and Sibel Latchman, and Paul, Gemma, and Oliver Mackman. I extend warm and heartfelt thanks to my family in the US: Laura, Drew, Kate, and Hank Landman. By way of thanks for their constant love and support, I dedicate this book to my family in the UK: Sophia Laura Landman, Melissa Collier and Oliver Heginbotham.

Todd Landman
Colchester, Essex

Introduction
Studying human rights

The field of human rights has long been dominated by the discipline of law (Freeman 2001: 123; 2002b: 77–78), which has been dedicated to studying (and in part advancing) the normative evolution in the promotion and protection of human rights. The public international law of human rights has concentrated on the legal processes that affect the nature of state sovereignty, the degree of state obligations, the structure, function, and scope of the UN and regional systems and mechanisms established to protect human rights, and the justifiability of an increasing number of human rights that have become formally protected through the proliferation of international treaties. Alongside the long history of the commitment of law to study and advance the struggle for human rights, disciplines within the social sciences have overcome their own tendency to marginalize human rights and have grappled with a large variety of human rights problems, puzzles, and contradictions that have characterized the modern struggle for greater protection of human rights. Indeed the political sociology of the struggle for citizenship rights pre-dates work on the modern human rights movement, while political science research has included global, small-N, and case-study analysis of the determinants of human rights protection, the analysis of foreign aid and human rights, the effect of globalization on human rights, the transmission of international human rights norms to the domestic level, and the politics of transitional justice in post-authoritarian and post-conflict countries, among many other substantive topics (see Landman 2002, 2005a). Anthropology, long seen to be diametrically opposed to human rights (see Freeman 2002a, 2002b), has re-asserted its commitment to providing deep understanding of human rights problems that overcome its natural aversion to cross-cultural generalizations and the universality of concepts (Messer 1993). Moreover, rights-based approaches to development have brought economics 'back in' to the study of human rights as the international development policy agenda seeks to integrate human rights concerns into large- and small-scale aid and technical assistance programmes (see Human Rights Council of Australia 1995; Chapter 8 this volume).

While the social sciences have not eclipsed law in the field of human rights, there is now more than ever an increasing space and need for systematic social scientific research and analysis to expand our knowledge about the social, economic, and political conditions within which the promotion and protection of human rights is made possible and over which significant struggles for human rights are fought. Much of the international discourse on human rights is replete with declarations and normative claims that many human rights scholars and practitioners translate (un)wittingly into empirical claims, which in many instances may lead to policy decisions that adversely affect the protection of human rights. Such discourse has sought to transcend the historical development of human rights, which draws on the longer history of citizenship rights and claims that all rights are indivisible, mutually reinforcing, and interdependent. Such language, for example, appears throughout the 1993 Vienna Declaration and Programme of Action, which as Boyle (1995: 81) concedes, sits uncomfortably with many social scientists since much empirical analysis has yet to be done that confirms the existence of 'mutually reinforcing and interdependent' relationships between and among the different types of human rights. Mere declaration and iteration may have a tendency to reify such relationships, but in the absence of systematic analysis on the degree to which these relationships exist, such claims remain largely baseless. Thus, foreign aid, developmental assistance and programmes, and actions by the 'international community' that are often heavily influenced by such claims may be made in haste or at the service of ideological and political agendas, which in the end may have the perverse effect of undermining the promotion and protection of human rights.

It is thus paramount for students of human rights to have the necessary conceptual frameworks and methodological tools to approach problems in the field of human rights in a scholarly and critical fashion, and it is the aim of this volume to provide such a framework for sound social scientific analysis of human rights. In order to realize this aim the volume is designed to (1) map the complex terrain of contemporary human rights, including their overall scope and the ways in which they can be promoted, protected, and defended; (2) provide a social scientific framework for studying human rights, including dominant paradigms of social theory, varieties of social scientific methods, and the ways in which human rights can be measured and compared; and (3) illustrate how social scientific analysis has been and can be applied to a selection of typical problems and research areas confronting the field of human rights, including global comparative analysis on the determinants of rights violations, the social science of truth commissions, and human rights impact assessment. The volume's conclusion ties these different elements of the book together and argues how greater systematic study of human rights can help in the struggle for their continued promotion and greater protection.

Social science and human rights

In 1971, Alisdair MacIntyre asked 'Is a science of comparative politics possible?' Ten years later, John McCamant (1981) asked 'Are the "tools of the trade" of the social scientist appropriate to the study of human rights?' Twenty years after this question was posed, Michael Freeman asked 'Is a political science of human rights possible?' These perennial questions about the scientific nature of social inquiry and its applicability to the study of human rights are the central concerns of this volume. In short, this volume asks, 'Is a social science of human rights possible?' MacIntyre's (1971: 171–172) answer to his own question claims that a general science of political action is not impossible, but faces serious obstacles, particularly in making cross-cultural *law-like generalizations* akin to the 'covering laws' in the natural sciences. In similar fashion, Freeman (2001: 127–128) does not reject out of hand a political science of human rights, but highlights two fundamental problems. On the one hand, he argues that there is an unresolved tension or 'philosophical contradiction' between the positivistic foundations of behavioural social science and normative values of human rights. On the other hand he argues that the rise of social science in the 19th century sought to displace philosophy and political theory with economics and sociology and so rejected any notion of human rights. The solution for MacIntyre (1971) is to lower expectations for making comparative inferences that seek universal applicability, while the solution for Freeman (2001: 139) is to reject scientific and legal positivism and to pursue a political science of human rights that is 'neither narrow nor rigid'.

This present volume provides an answer to its own question that is much less sceptical than the answers provided by either MacIntyre or Freeman, and is broadly in line with McCamant who argues that there is a great need for social scientific analysis of human rights problems. My own answer is thus a qualified 'yes' and is based on five important assumptions. First, the volume is grounded in the assumption that the goal of empirical social science is *explanation* and *understanding* of observed social phenomena (see also Landman 2000a, 2003). For the substantive focus of this volume, such observable social phenomena comprise a virtually infinite variety of human rights *practices* that provide the evidentiary base upon which social scientific analysis can take place. These human rights practices include both *negative* and *positive* actions of state and non-state actors that have a bearing on the individual and collective enjoyment of all human rights (see Chapter 2). Such a typology of negative and positive dimensions of rights protection and rights provision is crucial to the ways in which human rights can be measured and analysed through qualitative and quantitative means (see Chapter 5; and Landman 2004). Moreover, certain analytical techniques have been developed over the years that can provide reasonable estimates of certain types of *unobservable* human rights practices that can also form the universe of evidence for secondary social scientific analysis (see Chapter 7; and Ball *et al.* 1994; Ball, Spirer and Spirer 2000; Ball, Asher, Sulmont and Manrique 2003). In addition to these observable and unobservable human rights practices, there is an equally infinite variety of events, actors, interests, structures, societal features (e.g. class, gender, race, ethnicity) and outcomes that may have direct and indirect impacts on the promotion and protection of human rights that are equally subject to social scientific analysis.

Second, the volume argues that cross-cultural generalizations are an essential and inherent feature of human rights research since the international law of human rights sets a universal ideal standard against which country performances and cultural contexts are compared (see Landman 2002), and it is entirely possible to make cross-cultural generalizations *if certain basic rules of social science inquiry are observed*. The framework developed throughout the book is based on a general commitment to a 'logic of inference' that drives all good social scientific analysis. Making inferences involves 'using facts we know to learn something about facts we do not know' (King *et al.* 1994: 119 après J. S. Mill; see also Couvalis 1997). There is an inseparable link between evidence and inference, while there is a direct trade-off between the strength of the inferences that are made and the number of observations that are used to make them. Strong and general inferences are made possible from examination of a wide range of observations over space and time, such as individual nation states, regions, sub-national units, or individual human beings. A smaller number of observations limits the explanatory nature of the inferences that are drawn, but may increase our understanding of a particular human rights problem. The choice that a social scientist makes about the number, type, and quality of observations under investigation will necessarily affect the types and strength of inferences that can be drawn about a particular human rights problem (see Chapter 4).

Third, despite such notable examples as the Michels 'iron law of oligarchy' (Michels 1959; see also Zald and Ash 1966; Kriesi 1996: 156), 'Duverger's law' on the correspondence between electoral systems and party systems (Duverger 1951), and the 'dyadic peace' between democracies (Levy 2002), this volume readily concedes that there are few 'laws' in the social sciences and that generalizations will always and everywhere carry with them *varying degrees of uncertainty*. But it is crucial to understand that there are strategies for the proper application of social theories and methods that can *reduce the presence of uncertainty* and so enhance the usefulness of the generalizations that are made (see King, Keohane and Verba 1994). Measurement error, indeterminate research designs, problems of case selection, and misspecification of explanatory models affect the degree to which social scientists can make generalizations in their research (see Chapter 4). And it is the problems with and differences across such factors that explain what may appear to be mixed results of social scientific research on human rights.

Fourth, the whole volume is based on the fundamental assumption that the social scientific analysis of human rights problems can take place in the absence of agreed philosophical foundations for their existence (Landman 2005a). Efforts in philosophy and normative political theory have long sought to establish the definitive foundations for the existence of human rights through various appeals to God, nature, and reason (see e.g. Finnis 1980; Waldron 1984; Ingram 1994; Jones 1994; Donnelly 2003). These traditions in rights theories and their attempts to argue for the existence of human rights have variously been criticized by utilitarians as *nonsense* (Waldron 1987), communitarians as *fantasy* (MacIntyre 1984), Marxists as *bourgeois* (Marx 1978a: 26–52), and (some) postmodernists as *relative* (Rorty 1993), such that there has been a cumulative scepticism that has undermined rather than fortified the quest for foundations (Mendus 1995; Donnelly 2003: 18–21). Human rights are nonsense to utilitarians since any notion of human rights might actually undermine the achievement of the greatest happiness for the greatest number of people within a given context. For MacIntyre (1984: 69), belief in the existence of human rights is like the belief in unicorns and witches. For Marx, human rights were simply legal protections for the further empowerment of the propertied classes. For some postmodernists, fixing human rights is impossible since human rights discourse itself is one of many social constructions and does not enjoy any foundational or hegemonic position, and even within the field of human rights, there is no way to adjudicate among the various contentious foundational claims to their existence.

A popular response to such scepticism has been to take a pragmatic turn by sidestepping the need for philosophical foundations for human rights and making legal and political claims about their existence and the need for their protection. Legal claims focus on the proliferation of human rights norms since the 1948 Universal Declaration (see Chapters 1 and 2) and emphasize the global consensus on the content of human rights that has been achieved within dominant international fora, such as the various regular and special meetings within the United Nations system for the promotion and protection of human rights. Such a claim cites the participation of over a hundred nation states in such fora, which in many cases has led to the promulgation of formal declarations and the setting of international standards, as clear evidence of this global consensus on the core content of human rights (McCamant 1981: 534; Freeman 2001: 132). Such formal declarations offer a 'language of commitment' about human rights that can be used to carry out advocacy strategies for their further promotion and protection (Boyle 1995: 81), but for a social science of human rights the language of commitment establishes a useful baseline from which to operationalize human rights concepts for systematic analysis (see McCamant 1981: 546, 551; Adcock and Collier 2001; Landman and Häusermann 2003; see also Chapter 1 this volume).

The second pragmatic response to the absence of agreed foundations for human rights involves making political claims about how rights may both constrain and facilitate human behaviour. Some scholars see human rights as important means to achieving certain ends, such as social claims for institutionalized protection (Turner 1993), as bulwarks against the permanent threat of human evil (Mendus 1995: 23–24), as necessary legal guarantees for the exercise of human agency (Ignatieff 2001), or as an important political lever for the realization of global justice (Falk 2000). In this way, human rights are not held in some metaphysical suspended animation, but are practical tools used to limit the worst forms of human behaviour while creating conditions for the protection of human dignity. For empirical social scientists interested in studying human rights problems, such a pragmatic turn represented by these legal and political claims has allowed scholars to bypass the quest for foundations and to use the content found in the international law of human rights as a useful starting point for their research.

Finally, the volume argues that the positivistic heritage of modern social science is less problematic for studying human rights than Freeman contends. While strict positivists may eschew making ethical judgements and may well want to pursue 'value-free' scientific research, social scientists of human rights, consistent with Max Weber (1991b: 143–149), can carry out research on topics that have been *influenced* by values but the research process itself should not have been so influenced. In contrast to Galtung (1977), this approach is not to conflate the normative and empirical, but to use the tools of empirical analysis to research real-world problems that have normative importance (McCamant 1981: 534). Moreover, to ignore the actual practice of human rights violations carried out by state and non-state actors for some notion of objective scientific purism would have precluded a large body of research in social science carried out since the 1960s, such as the comparative work on political violence (e.g. Gurr 1968, 1970; Hibbs 1973), social protest and social mobilization (e.g. Marshall 1963; Tilly 1978; Piven and Cloward 1977; Foweraker and Landman 1997), and state repression (see Lichbach 1987; Davenport 2000).

There are numerous analogous areas of research in the social sciences where there have not been agreed philosophical foundations about a particular object of inquiry. For example, there are no agreed foundations for the existence of democracy, yet political scientists have studied democracy and democratic performance since the days of Aristotle. There are no agreed philosophical foundations for the existence of the market, yet economists have developed theories and methods to analyse and predict individual and collective economic behaviour. It is also the case that new legal developments may add dimensions to existing understandings and categories of human rights (such as rape as a war crime or domestic violence as a human rights violation), which can then lead to further empirical research on such practices. Such research efforts may define the scope of human rights that is to be studied, but will not make larger appeals to the philosophical foundations for their existence.

In sum, this book is grounded in an ontology of human rights that moves beyond definitive and agreed philosophical foundations and focuses on human rights practices delineated by reference to the extant international law of human rights, which is itself a product of the history of the struggle for human rights. Epistemologically, the book is grounded in the general understanding that such observable human rights practices and related social phenomena are subject to robust analysis and empirical testing that allow scholars to make reasoned, informed, and intelligent analytical statements useful for the promotion and protection of human rights. Methodologically, the book is committed to providing the necessary tools for maximizing inferences about particular human rights problems and puzzles that have been subjected to systematic social scientific analysis. In this way, the framework developed in this book makes possible progressive and incremental gains in knowledge about the promotion and protection of human rights in the world.

Structure of the book

Against this background defence of the possibility of a social science of human rights, the book is structured to develop the necessary theoretical and methodological tools to carry out social scientific analysis of human rights problems. Chapter 1 outlines the scope of human rights, including their different categories (civil, political, economic, social, cultural, and solidarity) and dimensions (positive and negative). While charting the genealogy of human rights, one accepts that there have been chronological generations of rights, but that in their current manifestation, such a history does not privilege one set of rights over another. Moreover, the chapter makes clear that all sets of rights have positive and negative dimensions such that in some way the realization of human rights will always be in part dependent on the fiscal capacity of states. Chapter 2 reviews the main international, regional, and domestic key actors that have a direct and indirect bearing on human rights. Using the notion of 'organizational field' (Di Maggio and Powell 1983), the chapter maps out these different actors, comprising public, private non-profit, and private for-profit organizations at the domestic and international levels of analysis.

The next three chapters move beyond these general exercises in mapping the scope and organizational terrain of human rights to consider theories, methods, and measures for studying human rights problems. Chapter 3 examines rationalist, structuralist, and culturalist empirical theories at the domestic and international levels and considers how they apply to the study of human rights. It evaluates them through an examination of their assumptions, explanatory logic, and the types of testable propositions they make about the protection of human rights. Chapter 4 outlines the main social scientific methods available for studying human rights, including qualitative, quantitative and mixed methods. The discussion includes the examination of an epistemological continuum in the social science that ranges from deep hermeneutic and 'thickly descriptive' (Geertz 1973) approaches to formal nomothetic and deductive approaches, as well as across the degree to which these different approaches privilege evidence over inference (see Almond 1996; Landman 2003). Chapter 5 illustrates how and why to measure human rights, including measures of rights in principle (*de jure*), rights in practice (*de facto*), and as outcomes of public policies designed to enhance or realize the protection of human rights. The chapter identifies serious lacunae in our efforts to measure human rights and over-reliance on standards-based scales of civil and political rights.

Chapters 6 to 8 show how the theories and methods of the social sciences can be applied to human rights problems. Chapter 6 shows how global comparative studies have tried to identify a series of explanations for the global variation in human rights protection and to examine a number of important related factors, including foreign aid, the presence of multinational capital, and the impact of international human rights law. The chapter also discusses the limitations of this kind of analysis, including a narrow focus on civil and political rights, a fairly high level of abstraction and generality of findings, and an over-reliance on crude measures of human rights. Chapter 7 shows how social science methods have been used to enhance the work of truth commissions established after periods of conflict, authoritarian rule, and foreign occupations. The chapter argues that one of the main tasks of truth commissions represents a classic social scientific problem, namely estimating and explaining an elusive but finite number of human rights violations for a given context during a given period of time. Chapter 8 shows how the logic of inference that forms the basis of all good social scientific research is useful in developing a framework for human rights impact assessment. The chapter develops a typology of human rights impact assessment based on the intersection of their different forms (i.e. direct and indirect) and timing (i.e. *ex ante* and *ex post*) and then shows the complexity of determining the impact of specific policies of governments or programmes of organizations on a particular human rights situation. It concludes by examining the ways in which quantitative and qualitative analysis can be used to estimate the different *contribution* and *attribution* of human rights policies and programmes on the human rights situation.

Finally, Chapter 9 concludes the book with a main summary of the key insights and main contributions that the book makes to furthering our knowledge about human rights problems and how greater application of systematic social scientific analysis is vital for their ultimate realization in the world. It is recommended that the book be read in the order in which it has been presented even though many of the chapters can serve as 'stand-alone' contributions to particular debates in the field. Every effort has been made to provide useful cross-referencing between chapters where appropriate. Each chapter contains a list for further reading, while Chapter 5 contains a list of web sites for accessing and downloading popular forms of human rights data. It is hoped that the book presents a useful framework for analysing human rights problems from a social scientific perspective.

1 The scope of human rights

In their contemporary manifestation, human rights are a set of individual and collective rights that have been formally promoted and protected through international and domestic law since the UN Declaration of Human Rights in 1948. Arguments, theories, and protections of such rights, however, have been in existence for much longer (see e.g. Claude 1976; Foweraker and Landman 1997: 1–45; Freeman 2002b: 14–54; Ishay 2004; Woodiwiss 2005), but since the UN Declaration, the evolution of their express legal protection has grown rapidly. Today, there are numerous international treaties on human rights promulgated since the UN Declaration to which an increasingly large number of nation states are a party (see below), while the language of human rights increasingly pervades our moral, legal, and political vocabulary to such an extant that many have claimed we now live in an 'age of rights' (see Bobbio 1996). Indeed, the development of a human rights doctrine has changed the ways in which nation states act towards each other at the international and regional levels, and the ways in which governments, individuals and groups interact at the domestic level. These new types of action and interaction cover a broad range of areas, including political rights, civil rights, social, economic, and cultural rights, as well as questions of poverty and the distribution of socio-economic resources. Politically and legally, both the sovereignty and pursuit of power-based national interest has become increasingly checked by the application of international, regional, and national human rights norms and practices (Landman 2005b). This chapter provides an overview of the current categories of human rights that make up the field and maps the breadth and depth of the international and regional systems for their protection by looking at the degree to which nation states in the world formally participate in these systems through ratification of human rights treaties. The chapter concludes by considering whether the world has reached the limits of specifying new human rights in need of protection and whether key actors with prime responsibility for their promotion and protection (see Chapter 2) should now concentrate their energies on the full implementation and enforcement of human rights.

Categories and dimensions of human rights

The collection of human rights protected by international law draws on a longer tradition of rights from philosophy, history, and normative political theory and now includes three sets or categories of rights that have become useful shortcuts for talking about human rights among scholars and practitioners in the field, and will be used throughout the remainder of this book. These three categories are: (1) civil and political rights, (2) economic, social, and cultural rights, and (3) solidarity rights. It has been typically understood that individuals and certain groups are bearers of human rights, while the state is the prime organ that can protect and/or violate human rights. The political sociology of human rights argues that historical struggles by oppressed groups have yielded a greater degree of protection for larger sets of individuals and groups whose rights have not always been guaranteed while the state itself, in attempting to construct a national identity and fortify its capacity to govern, has extended various rights protections to increasingly larger sectors of society (Foweraker and Landman 1997). The struggle for human rights and contemporary arguments about their continued promotion and protection have extended beyond exclusive attention on the legal obligations of nation states and have started focusing on how non-state actors, such as guerrilla movements, terrorist organizations, warlords, multinational corporations, and international financial institutions, may be conceived as responsible for human rights violations and how such entities may carry an obligation for their protection (see Chapter 2; also Forsythe 2000: 191–214; UN Global Compact Office and OHCHR 2004). Let us consider these different categories of human rights in turn.

Civil and political rights uphold the sanctity of the individual before the law and guarantee his or her ability to participate freely in civil, economic, and political society. *Civil rights* include such rights as the right to life, liberty, and personal security; the right to equality before the law; the right of protection from arbitrary arrest; the right to the due process of law; the right to a fair trial; and the right to religious freedom and worship. When protected, civil rights guarantee one's 'personhood' and freedom from state-sanctioned interference or violence. *Political rights* include such rights as the right to speech and expression; the rights to assembly and association; and the right to vote and political participation. Political rights thus guarantee individual rights to involvement in public affairs and the affairs of state. In many ways, both historically and theoretically, civil and political rights have been considered *fundamental* human rights which all nation states have a duty and responsibility to uphold (see Davidson 1993: 39–45; Donnelly 1998: 18–35; Forsythe 2000: 28–52). They have also been seen as so-called 'negative' rights since they merely require the absence of their violation in order to be upheld.

Social and economic rights include such rights as the right to a family; the right to education; the right to health and well being; the right to work and fair remuneration; the right to form trade unions and free associations; the right to leisure time; and the right to social security. When protected, these rights help promote individual flourishing, social and economic development, and self-esteem. *Cultural rights*, on the other hand, include such rights as the right to the benefits of culture; the right to indigenous land, rituals, and shared cultural practices; and the right to speak one's own language and 'mother tongue' education. Cultural rights are meant to maintain and promote sub-national cultural affiliations and collective identities, and protect minority communities against the incursions of national assimilationist and nation-building projects. In contrast to the first set of rights, this second set of social, economic, and cultural rights is often seen as an aspirational and programmatic set of rights that national governments ought to strive to achieve through progressive implementation. They have thus been considered less fundamental than the first set of rights and are seen as 'positive' rights whose realization depends heavily on the fiscal capacity of states (Davidson 1993; Harris 1998: 9; see also Foweraker and Landman 1997: 14–17).

Solidarity rights, which include rights to public goods such as development and the environment, seek to guarantee that all individuals and groups have the right to share in the benefits of the earth's natural resources, as well as those goods and products that are made through processes of economic growth, expansion, and innovation. Many of these rights are transnational in that they make claims against wealthy nations to redistribute wealth to poor nations, cancel or reduce international debt obligations, pay compensation for past imperial and colonial adventures, reduce environmental degradation, and help promote policies for sustainable development. Of the three sets of rights, this final set is the newest and most progressive and reflects a certain reaction against the worst effects of globalization, as well as the relative effectiveness of 'green' political ideology and social mobilization around concerns for the health of the planet.

The distinction between these sets of rights follows the historical struggle for them (Marshall 1963; Claude 1976; Barbalet 1988; Davidson 1993), the appearance of the separate international instruments that protect them, the philosophical arguments concerning their status (see the Introduction to this volume), and the methodological issues surrounding their measurement (see Chapter 5; also Claude and Jabine 1992; Foweraker and Landman 1997: 46–65; Landman 2004). But significant sections of the human rights community have challenged these traditional distinctions between 'generations' of human rights and have sought to establish the general claim that all rights are indivisible and mutually reinforcing (Boyle 1995; Donnelly 1999a). Such a challenge suggests that it is impossible to talk about certain sets of human rights in isolation, since the protection of one right may be highly contingent on the protection of other rights. For example, full protection of the right to vote is largely meaningless in societies that do not have adequate health, education, and social welfare provision, since high rates of illiteracy and poverty may mean the *de facto* disenfranchisement of large sectors of the population. Equally, those interested in combating torture need to examine possible underlying socio-economic, cultural, and organizational reasons for the practice of torture, which themselves may rely on the variable protection of other human rights (see Huggins 2000).

This human rights challenge also suggests that there is a false dichotomy between negative and positive rights (Shue 1980; Hurrell 1999: 278; Donnelly 2003: 30–33) that tends to privilege civil and political rights over economic and social rights, since the protection of the former appear less dependent on state resources than the latter (Foweraker and Landman 1997: 14–17). One response to this false dichotomy is to claim that 'all rights are positive' (Holmes and Sunstein 1999) since the full protection of all categories of human rights ultimately relies on the relative fiscal capacity of states. In this view, the protection of property rights requires a well-funded judiciary, police force, and fire service, as well as a well-developed infrastructure that can relay information, goods, and services in the event that property is under threat in some way. A similar argument can be made about guaranteeing the right to vote. Beyond prohibiting intimidation and discrimination at the polls, running a free and fair election requires a tremendous amount of financial support, technology, and infrastructure, the need for which has been illustrated dramatically by the highly contested process and result of the 2000 Presidential Election in the United States. And as above, the prevention of torture involves training and education within police and security forces, which entails the need for significant financial resources from the state.

Another response to the traditional division between positive and negative human rights is to view them as having *positive and negative* dimensions, the full delineation of which is essential for a social science of human rights (Landman 2004: 922–923). By claiming that all rights are positive, we may lose sight of significant negative characteristics of human rights. While it is clearly possible to see how civil and political rights have positive characteristics (i.e. the provision of well-funded judiciaries, training and education programmes, and well-developed infrastructure), it is equally possible to see how economic and social rights have significant negative characteristics. For example, just like torture by the state is seen as preventable if only the state refrained from torturing, discrimination in public education and healthcare is equally preventable if only the state refrained from so discriminating. In this way, it is equally possible to have a 'violations approach' (Chapman 1996) to studying the promotion and protection of economic, social, and cultural rights as it is to studying the promotion and protection of civil and political rights.

Table 1.1 shows how such a conceptualization of human rights looks if we are to include their positive and negative dimensions. The table is a 2 × 3 matrix resulting from three categories of human rights, each with corresponding positive and negative dimensions. Positive dimensions include those actions that states can take to provide resources and policies for improving the protection of human rights while negative dimensions are those actions that states do (or do not do) that deliberately violate (or protect) human rights. Certain cells in the matrix have been well covered in the theory and practice of human rights. For example, the negative dimensions of civil and political rights in Cell II are the traditional focus of human rights international standards (e.g. the 1966 International Covenant on Civil and Political Rights), systems (e.g. United Nations, European, Inter-American, and African), and mechanisms for reporting and redress (e.g. Human Rights Committee, European Court of Human Rights; Inter-American Commission and Inter-American Court of Human Rights); monitoring, advocacy, and campaigns from human rights non-governmental organizations (e.g. Amnesty International

Table 1.1 Positive and negative dimensions of human rights

		Dimensions	
		'Positive' (i.e. provision of resources and outcomes of policies)	'Negative' (i.e. practices that deliberately violate)
Categories of human rights	Civil and political	**I** Investment in judiciaries, prisons, police forces, and elections	**II** Torture, extra-judicial killings, disappearance, arbitrary detention, unfair trials, electoral intimidation, disenfranchisement
	Economic, social, and cultural	**III** Progressive realization Investment in health, education, and welfare	**IV** Ethnic, racial, gender, or linguistic discrimination in health, education, and welfare
	Solidarity	**V** Compensation for past wrongs Debt relief Overseas development and technical assistance	**VI** Environmental degradation CO_2 emissions Unfair trade

and Human Rights Watch); and much of the academic scholarship in political science (see Landman 2005a). Equally, the positive dimensions of economic, social, and cultural rights in Cell III have been the traditional focus of human rights international standards (e.g. the 1966 International Covenant on Economic, Social, and Cultural Rights), mechanisms for reporting and redress (e.g. the Committee on Economic, Social, and Cultural Rights), non-governmental organizations working on social justice and minority rights issues (e.g. Minority Rights Group International) and academic scholarship primarily in sociology, developmental economics, and anthropology (Turner 1993; Freeman 2002a, 2002b).

Outside these two areas of human rights that have received wide attention and debate, there have been varying degrees of attention paid to the positive and negative dimensions of human rights depicted in the remaining cells. For the positive dimensions of civil and political rights in Cell I, the work on 'good governance' (Weiss 2000) has sought to examine the ways in which investment in judiciaries, prisons, and police forces can improve the foundations of governance and so deliver better economic prosperity (World Bank 1992; Knack and Keefer 1995; Clague, Keefer, Knack and Olson 1996, 1997; USAID 1998a, 1998b; de Soto 2000), while those interested in the administration of justice see such positive aspects of civil and political rights as essential to addressing problems of the '(un)rule' of law (e.g. Méndez, O'Donnell and Pinheiro 1999). For the negative dimensions of economic, social, and cultural rights in Cell IV, there has been much focus on general patterns of gender, ethnic, racial, linguistic, and religious discrimination, but perhaps less attention on how these practices may constitute violations to economic, social, and cultural rights (Chapman 1996). Since the debt crisis in the 1980s, there has been an increase in social mobilization and attention (e.g. Charter 99 issued by the One World Trust) around the transnational issues of debt relief, developmental assistance and distribution of global income, and 'post-colonial' reparations for past practices made most vocally at the 2001 World Conference against Racism (Cell V). Since the 1970s, groups have been mobilizing for transnational solutions to the global environmental problems and have focused on the negative dimensions of 'offending' states such as the United States (Cell VI), but there has been less of a focus on the rights issues associated with such solutions. Finally, from a human rights perspective, the work on globalization and trade has focused on the 'violation' represented by unfair trade agreements hammered out in the World Trade Organization (e.g. Compa and Diamond 1996; Francioni 2001), which is seen to be disproportionately influenced by the United States and the European Union (Steinberg *et al.* 2005), as well as unsavoury manufacturing and production techniques used by multinational corporations.

These various examples show how a social science of human rights can benefit from such a conceptual delineation, since it disaggregates the concept of human rights into different categories across different dimensions and facilitates the process of operationalizing human rights for systematic analysis. The different dimensions and categories provide the content for events-based, standards-based, and survey-based measures of human rights for quantitative analysis and provide critical differences in meaning for qualitative analysis (see Chapter 5; also Landman 2004). But beyond these conceptual distinctions of human rights, what is the extant international law that seeks to protect them? And what are the temporal and spatial patterns of state participation in the various international human rights treaties? It is to these questions that the discussion now turns.

International human rights instruments

The United Nations system and its key documents for the promotion and protection of human rights – the 1945 UN Charter and the 1948 Universal Declaration of Human Rights – formed the basis of the international human rights legal 'regime' (Donnelly 1986, 2003: 127–154). These two documents were soon followed by two more legally binding instruments, promulgated in 1966 and entered into force in 1976: the International Covenant on Civil and Political Rights and the International Covenant on Economic, Social, and Cultural Rights (Davidson 1993: 39–45; Donnelly 1989; Donnelly 1998: 18–35; Forsythe 2000: 28–52). Further treaties addressing specific human rights concerns (racial discrimination, discrimination against women, prohibition of torture, and the rights of the child) have entered into force since 1976. Table 1.2 lists the main international human rights instruments, the dates that they were open for signature, and the number and percentage of states parties to the treaties. The Convention on the Rights of the Child has the largest number of states parties, while the Second Optional Protocol to the International Covenant on Civil and Political Rights, which prohibits the practice of the death penalty in all member states, has the lowest. In addition to these legal instruments, there are monitoring bodies attached to each treaty that examine the degree to which states are fulfilling their legal obligations under the terms of each treaty (Alston and Crawford 2000). Taken together, these human rights instruments and the monitoring bodies form an international legal regime that seeks to limit state behaviour in order to protect and promote human rights (Landman 2005b).

Table 1.2 The international human rights regime: instruments, dates, and membership

Name	Date when open for signature	States parties as of 2004 N and %
International Covenant on Civil and Political Rights (ICCPR)	1966	152 (78%)
International Covenant on Economic, Social, and Cultural Rights (ICESCR)	1966	149 (77%)
Optional Protocol to the International Covenant on Civil and Political Rights (OPT1)	1976	104 (54%)
Second Optional Protocol to the International Covenant on Civil and Political Rights (OPT2)	1989	50 (26%)
International Convention on the Elimination of all Forms of Racial Discrimination (CERD)	1966	169 (87%)
Convention on the Elimination of All Forms of Discrimination against Women (CEDAW)	1979	177 (91%)
Convention against Torture and other Cruel, Inhuman, or Degrading Treatment or Punishment (CAT)	1984	136 (70%)
Convention on the Rights of the Child (CRC)	1989	192 (99%)

Data source: UNHCR (June 2004), *Status of Ratification of the Principal International Human Rights Treaties*, www.unhchr.ch/pdf/report.pdf. Reprinted with permission from Georgetown University Press, © 2005. All rights reserved.

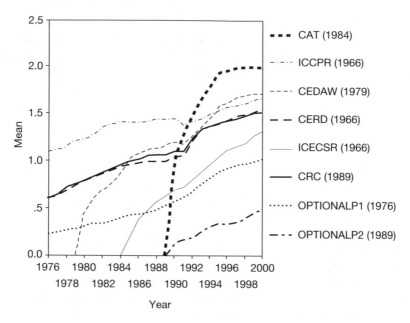

Figure 1.1 Mean ratification scores for the main human rights treaties over time, 1976–2000.

Beyond this simple tallying of current participation of states in the international regime, it is possible to examine the temporal and spatial patterns in this participation by giving a score for no signature (0), signature (1), and ratification (2), and then comparing these scores across time and space. Figure 1.1 compares the mean ratification scores for all the main international human rights treaties for the period from 1976, when the two main international covenants came into force, and 2000. The figure shows that there has been an expansion in both the breadth and the depth of the regime. On the one hand, the proliferation of human rights treaties has meant an increasingly larger set of human rights has found positive legal expression, while on the other hand a larger number of states (many of them newly independent) have ratified these main instruments. But the time-series trends also show that some of the instruments (e.g. CERD and CRC) have consistently enjoyed more support than others (CAT and the Second Optional Protocol to the ICCPR). Figure 1.2 compares the mean ratification scores for the same set of instruments by World Bank classified regions. Western Europe, Latin America, and Post-Communist Europe exhibit the highest rates of participation, while Sub-Saharan Africa, the Middle East and North Africa (MENA), South Asia, and East Asia and the Pacific exhibit lower rates of participation.

These legal documents also provide the core content of human rights that ought to be protected, where the consensus on the content for some of these rights is more widespread than the content for others. Table 1.3 lists all the rights that ought to be protected that have been compiled from various readings of the extant international law of human rights (Davidson 1993; Gibson 1996; Green 2001; Donnelly 2003). The total number of human rights found across these various instruments varies between 49 and 64 depending on different emphases and the ways in which some authors combine concepts (Green 2001:

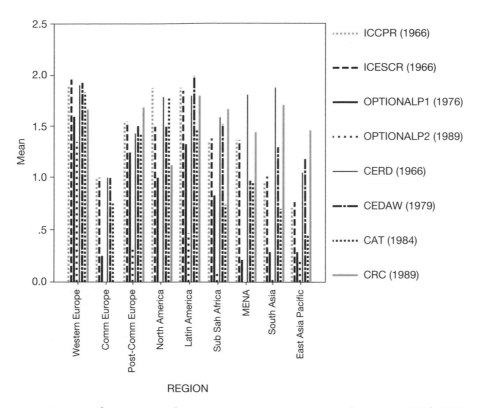

Figure 1.2 Mean ratification scores for the main human rights treaties by region, 1976–2000.
Source: Landman (2005c).

1068–1069). The list in Table 1.3 contains a total of 58 human rights found across these treaties, and it is the explanation and understanding of the variation in the promotion and protection of these rights with which a social science of human rights of the kind advocated in this present volume is primarily dedicated.

Regional human rights instruments

In addition to the international law of human rights, there are number of regional instruments and mechanisms that have developed since the 1948 UN Declaration, including the European system, the Inter-American system, and the African system. Like the international human rights treaties there are varying degrees of state participation, which can be measured through an examination of ratification behaviour. Figure 1.3 compares the mean ratification scores for the European Convention for the Protection of Human Rights and Fundamental Freedoms, the American Convention for the Protection of Human Rights, and the African Charter on Human and People's Rights. As in the case of the main international instruments, the figure shows an increasing participation of states through ratification of these various regional instruments and a general pattern of convergence in complete participation of states from each of the three regions. Indeed as of 2004, all forty-five Council of Europe states have ratified the European Convention, all

Table 1.3 List of human rights protected under international law

1. Non-discrimination	30. Trade unions
2. Life	31. Rest, leisure and paid holidays
3. Liberty and security of the person	32. Adequate standard of living
4. Protection against slavery and servitude	33. Education
5. Protection against torture	34. Participation in cultural life
6. Legal personality	35. Self-determination
7. Equal protection of the law	36. Protection of and assistance to children
8. Legal remedy	37. Freedom from hunger
9. Protection against arbitrary arrest, detention, or exile	38. Health
10. Access to independent and impartial tribunal	39. Asylum
	40. Property
11. Presumption of innocence	41. Compulsory primary education
12. Protection against *ex post facto* laws	42. Humane treatment when deprived of liberty
13. Privacy, family, home and correspondence	43. Protection against imprisonment for debt
14. Freedom of movement and residence	44. Expulsion of aliens only by law
15. Nationality	45. Prohibition of war propaganda and incitement to discrimination
16. Marry and found a family	46. Minority culture
17. Protection and assistance of families	47. No imprisonment for breach of civil obligations
18. Marriage only with free consent of spouses	48. Protection of children
19. Equal rights of men and women in marriage	49. Access to public service
20. Freedom of thought, conscience and religion	50. Democracy
21. Freedom of opinion and expression	51. Participation in cultural and scientific life
22. Freedom of the press	52. Protection of intellectual property rights
23. Freedom of assembly	53. International and social order for realizing rights
24. Freedom of association	
25. Participation in government	54. Political self-determination
26. Social security	55. Economic self-determination
27. Work	56. Women's rights
28. No compulsory or forced labour	57. Prohibition of the death penalty
29. Just and favourable conditions of work	58. Prohibition of apartheid

Sources: Davidson 1993: Appendix 1; Gibson 1996: 37–38; Green 2001: 1069; Donnelly 2003: 24.

twenty-five Organization of American States member states have ratified the American Convention, and all fifty-three African Union member states have ratified the African Charter. Of the three regional systems, the European System is arguably the strongest in terms of its overall implementation of human rights standards, followed by the Inter-American System, and the African System.

This descriptive mapping of the extant international and regional law on the protection of human rights comprises the essential universe of legal content and enumeration of human rights that ought to be protected, and which form the main 'objects of inquiry' for a social science of human rights. State participation in these instruments is still not 100 per cent, and such participation is merely an indication of the willingness of states

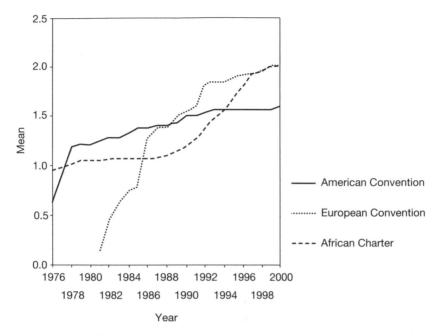

Figure 1.3 Mean ratification scores for the main regional human rights instruments, 1976–2000.

Source: Landman (2005c).

to commit to a series of legal obligations on the protection of human rights. Indeed, it is precisely the gap between the *de jure* protection of human rights represented by these formal commitments and their *de facto* realization within each state that presents a ripe area for social scientific analysis (Landman 2002; 2005b). It is safe to say that no state in the world is entirely human rights compliant and thus there is virtually an infinite supply of human rights problems to be addressed using the theories, methods, and tools of contemporary social science.

Limiting human rights?

The time-series trends and spatial patterns in the proliferation of human rights norms represented by the increasing number of instruments and increasing number of participation of states has led some commentators to argue that we are witnessing an international 'juridical revolution' (Ignatieff 2001), a process of international 'legalization' (Abbott *et al.* 2000), 'judicialization' (Stone Sweet 1999, Shapiro and Stone Sweet 2002), and 'constitutionalization' (Petersmann 2002; Alston 2002) – a process that has culminated in the Rome Statute, which established the International Criminal Court and may well represent the international 'institutionalization of criminal liability' (Falk 2000: 4). And it is precisely this norm proliferation, the ability for states to implement such norms, and the capacity for them to be adjudicated in some way that has been the 'stuff' of the discipline of law.

But are there limits to the continued expansion in the breadth and depth of human rights norms proliferation and how can a social science of human rights contribute to the work that has been carried out in the discipline of law? Clearly, the depth of 'human rights norms proliferation', as the term is employed here, would be reached once all states ratified all the extant human rights instruments, but is there a continuous need for an increasing number of instruments for new rights? And does such an attempt to expand the list of rights not undermine their value as fundamental rights that ought to be protected always and everywhere? While it is beyond the scope of this volume to provide a definitive answer to this question, it is important for a social science of human rights to examine the ways in which this particular 'basket' of extant human rights is being realized, implemented and contested across the globe. Indeed, the contribution of social science is to explain and understand the global, regional, sub-national, collective and individual variations and experiences in the enjoyment (or lack thereof) of the human rights that have been outlined in this chapter. To continue to build this notion of a social science of human rights, the next chapter examines the 'organizational field' (Di Maggio and Powell 1983) that comprises the key actors and entities that have a direct and indirect bearing on the defence and protection of human rights.

Suggestions for further reading

Bobbio, N. (1996) *The Age of Rights*, Cambridge: Polity Press.

Davidson, S. (1993) *Human Rights*, Buckingham: Open University Press.

Donnelly, J. (2003) *Universal Human Rights in Theory and Practice*, 2nd edn, Ithaca, NY: Cornell University Press.

Freeman, M. (2002) *Human Rights: An Interdisciplinary Approach*, Cambridge: Polity Press.

Holmes, S. and Sunstein, C. R. (1999) *The Cost of Rights: Why Liberty Depends on Taxes*, New York: W.W. Norton.

Ishay, M. (2004) *The History of Human Rights: From Ancient Times to the Globalization Era*, Berkeley: University of California Press.

Robertson, A. H. and Merrills, J. G. (1996) *Human Rights in the World: An Introduction to the Study of the International Protection of Human Rights*, 4th edn, Manchester: Manchester University Press.

Woodiwiss, A. (2005) *Human Rights*, London: Routledge.

2   The terrain of human rights

The previous chapter identified the current scope of human rights, which comprises civil, political, economic, social, cultural, and solidarity rights, along with their associated positive and negative dimensions. This delineation of rights categories and dimensions was followed by a brief descriptive account and portrayal of the extant international law and regional systems for the promotion and protection of human rights from which a full list of rights can be 'read' from the various articles of the various human rights instruments. In building on this general mapping of the extant scope of human rights to be protected, this chapter outlines the main actors, organizations, and institutions whose actions, structures, and behaviour may have a direct or indirect impact on human rights. Direct impact involves either (or both) the significant capacity or (and) the legal obligation to protect human rights, while indirect impact may come from those organizations and actors whose activities are not self-consciously concerned with the protection of human rights, but owing to their significance as an actor may have rights implications. Such impacts may be positive or negative, which may vary across these different actors and may vary across different periods of time. Actors that were conceived as antithetical to the protection of human rights may over time emerge as essential to their protection, while those seen as essential to rights protection may become less so. In order to understand better these different actors, organizations, institutions and the ways in which we can conceive of their having a relationship with the promotion and protection of human rights, the chapter groups them into their respective organizational fields.

Human rights organizational fields

An 'organizational field' is a set of organizations that in the aggregate 'constitute a recognized area of institutional life', which begin in any issue area as 'displaying a considerable diversity, approach and form . . . [but experience] . . . an inexorable push towards homogenization' (Di Maggio and Powell 1983: 148). There are countless such organizational fields in the world and there are many organizational fields relevant to the promotion and protection of human rights, which have experienced varying degrees of homogenization since the creation of the United Nations system. These different organizational fields can be divided across two primary dimensions: (1) level of activity and (2) the sphere of activity. The first dimension simply concerns whether the organization or actor operates primarily at the domestic or international level. Current debates in comparative political science and international relations surrounding this distinction argue that many actors inhabit both realms (see Putnam 1988, 1993; Gourevitch 2002), and the scholarship on the transmission of human rights norms is precisely concerned with those actors who transcend these two levels to bring about positive changes in the protection of human rights (see Keck and Sikkink 1998; Risse, Ropp and Sikkink 1999; Hawkins 2002, 2004; Risse 2002; Landman 2005a). Nevertheless, the distinction between the domestic and international levels is useful for social scientific analysis and mirrors the distinction made in law between international and 'municipal' levels (Malanczuk 1997: 63–74; Brownlie 2003: 31–56).

The second dimension is the distinction between the public and private, while within the private dimension there is further division between those actors and organizations that operate 'for profit' (i.e. firms) and those that operate 'not for profit' (charities, relief agencies, non-governmental organizations). As in the distinction between the international and domestic levels of activity, there are some organizations that play both a public and private role in the field of human rights. For example, many non-governmental organizations are more akin to public service delivery organizations in the absence of significant state capacity to deliver such services. They receive public funds and then redistribute them through their activities within the countries in which they operate. In this sense by performing 'statutory functions for government in a semi-independent way' they are 'quasi-autonomous non-governmental organizations' (or quangos; see Jones *et al.* 1998: 321), and they are present at the international and domestic levels within developed and developing countries alike. The further distinction between for-profit and not-for-profit private actors and organizations is useful since these different organizations may have different interests and therefore different impacts on human rights.

The combination of these different dimensions produces the 2×3 matrix depicted in Table 2.1, which shows the different levels of the activity, the different spheres of activity and the six organizational fields that result. The six cells in the table list examples found in each type of organizational field, including (1) public international organizations, (2) private not-for-profit international organizations, (3) private for-profit international organizations, (4) public domestic organizations, (5) private not-for-profit domestic organizations, and (6) private for-profit domestic organizations. Each of these different fields, their relevance to human rights, and the degree to which there has been any convergence in their activities are discussed in turn.

Public international organizations

The large proportion of human rights literature on the study of human rights has focused on the key role that has been or can potentially be played by public international organizations (Cell I). Indeed the moral outrage at the atrocities committed by Nazi Germany in part explain the founding of the United Nations system since the promotion and protection of human rights was seen as something that should come 'from above' to control the activities of unsavoury states. The organizations that make up this category are normally referred to as 'international governmental organizations' (IGOs), since they have been founded on some formal agreement between and among governments, and member states supply personnel who occupy various roles within the organizational hierarchy. The number of IGOs to which states are members has proliferated over the years, where the largest number of members in IGOs are found in Europe, followed by North America, the Middle East and North Africa, and Latin America (see Figure 2.1). But there are still relatively few IGOs that have a significant relationship to the promotion and protection of human rights. Among these there are truly international organizations with global reach (e.g. United Nations, World Bank, IMF, and WTO),

Table 2.1 The organizational fields of human rights

	Sphere of activity		
	Public	*Private*	
		Not for profit	*For profit*
International	**I** International governmental organizations (IGOs): United Nations (UN) European Union (EU) Council of Europe (CoE) Organization for Security and Cooperation in Europe (OSCE) North Atlantic Treaty Organization (NATO) Organization of American States (OAS) African Union (AU) International Criminal Court (ICC) Organization of Petroleum Exporting Countries (OPEC) Organization for Economic Cooperation and Development (OECD) International Bank for Reconstruction and Development (IBRD) International Monetary Fund (IMF) World Trade Organization (WTO)	**II** International non-governmental organizations (INGOs): Amnesty International Anti-Slavery International Article 19 Human Rights First Human Rights Watch International Federation of Human Rights Leagues International Service for Human Rights Minority Rights Group Penal Reform International World Organization Against Torture Transnational advocacy networks (TANs)	**III** Multinational corporations (MNCs): Shell Nike Reebok British Petroleum Mitsubishi Mitsui Siemens Du Pont General Motors Sumitomo Ford Motor Toyota Exxon Commercial banks and securities firms: Citicorp Merrill Lynch JP Morgan Morgan Stanley UBS Investment Bank
Domestic	**IV** Independent nation-state governments Sub-national governments (state, municipal, local) Public schools	**V** Non-governmental organizations (NGOs) Civil society organizations (CSOs) Social movement organizations (SMOs) Warlords/guerrilla movements/'uncivil' movements/death squads	**VI** Domestic business firms Commercial banks Private schools Private armies/mercenary firms

Primary levels of activity

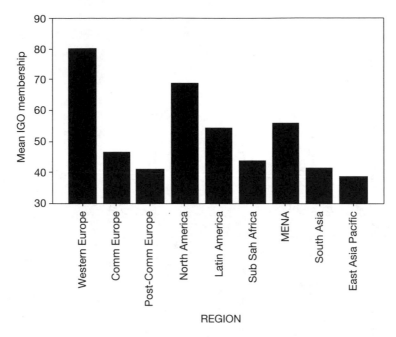

Figure 2.1 Number of IGOs in which states are a member by region, 1976–2000.

Source: Landman (2005c).

regional organizations with a global remit for many of their activities (e.g. European Union, OSCE), regional organizations with limited scope for their activities (e.g. NATO, Organization of American States, African Union), and economically defined organizations with a global scope for (or global impact of) their activities (e.g. OECD, OPEC).

While the United Nations system has been seen as the main protagonist in the struggle for the promotion and protection of human rights, many other IGOs are increasingly being seen as either having an important role in human rights or as having an obligation to uphold human rights standards in their activities. In the early years after its establishment, the human rights sections of the United Nations were dedicated to human rights while its development agencies, such as the World Bank and the IMF, pursued development objectives within strict economic parameters. These agencies initially perceived the promotion and protection of human rights as 'political' and therefore outside their domain; however, the turn towards concerns over 'good governance' and 'rights-based' approaches to development has increasingly seen human rights entering the planning and policy formation for development objectives and programmes (World Bank 1992; Lawyers Committee for Human Rights 1993; Gillies 1993; Weiss 2000; UNOHCHR 2002). This was due in part to the realization that structures of governance had an impact on development and that neo-liberal structural adjustment programmes (see below) were having an adverse effect on the poor. Such a change in focus brought law (and international lawyers) back into the field of development and economics (and economists) back into the field of human rights, where there have been attempts to mainstream human rights within the WTO and trade agreements, poverty reduction strategies, and general development and technical assistance programmes.

Thus, across the UN system there has been a certain convergence of policies with a human rights focus, and even though the different agencies perform different functions, they are increasingly guided by similar commitments to the promotion and protection of human rights. At the regional level, public international organizations have formed that in part mirror those at the global level, with accompanying hierarchies, institutions, and mechanisms for the promotion and protection of human rights. The European system has the most developed jurisprudence with respect to human rights and active institutions in the form of the European Commission of Human Rights and the European Court of Human Rights. Like the European system, the Inter-American system also has a Human Rights Commission and a Court, while both have been in active practice for a shorter period of time than their European counterparts (Harris 1998: 1–29; Forsythe 2000: 132). The African Union has a Commission for Human and People's Rights, and in January 2004 established an African Human Rights Court based on the 1998 protocol to the 1981 African Charter (Mutua 2001; Forsythe 2000: 135). The structure, function, and purpose of these human rights organizations are much like those at the global level as they seek to implement human rights norms at the regional level, while the economically defined IGOs (e.g. OECD, OPEC) have not yet mainstreamed human rights.

Private international 'not-for-profit' organizations

The second great set of protagonists and 'prime engine of growth' (Mutua 2001: 151) in the struggle for human rights has been the multitude of international non-governmental organizations (INGOs) whose primary purpose and function are to promote human rights. Currently, these organizations represent a subset of about 250 organizations (Smith, Pagnucco and Lopez 1998) from the total number of INGOs, which has grown from just over 300 in the mid-1970s to well over 700 by the turn of the century (see Figure 2.2). While INGOs in the human rights field do not have the same legal authority as the UN agencies, their activities predate the establishment of the UN and the UN Declaration (e.g. Anti-Slavery International was founded in 1839, the International Federation of Human Rights Leagues was founded in 1922, and the International League of Human Rights was founded in 1942), and have become increasingly important in the evolution of human rights protection ever since, effectively 'transforming the words of the Declaration from a standard into reality' (Korey 1998: 2). Human rights INGOs such as Amnesty International and Human Rights Watch have been instrumental in developing systems for monitoring human rights abuses throughout the world and alerting the public to such practices in an effort to stop them. In addition to monitoring and alerting, typical INGO activities include setting international standards for existing and new sets of human rights; contributing to the international human rights agenda through interaction and consultation with relevant personnel and institutions in IGOs with a mandate to protect human rights (see above); building capacity, training, and service delivery for domestic NGOs in the struggle for human rights; and conducting research, publishing findings, and issuing handbooks and manuals on specialized human rights issue areas (see Welch 2001b: 1–13; Landman and Abraham 2004).

The mandates for INGOs laying out their main aims and objectives vary from very broad aims to promote and protect all human rights found in the Universal Declaration of Human Rights (e.g. the International Federation of Human Rights Leagues), to the struggle for better protection of a discrete set of human rights, such as freedom from servitude (Anti-Slavery International) or freedom of expression and freedom

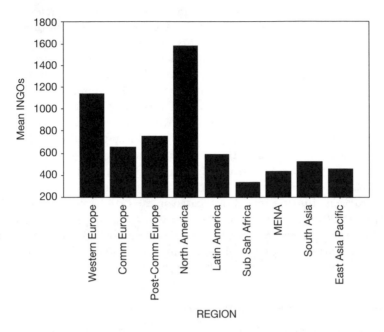

Figure 2.2 Number of INGOs with office registration in states by region, 1976–2000.
Source: Landman (2005c).

of information (e.g. Article 19). INGOs receive funding from a variety of sources, including international donor agencies (charitable trusts and research councils), foreign governments (e.g. Sweden, Denmark, Canada, and the Netherlands are prominent human rights donor governments), private contributions from members and philanthropists, and interest earned on investments. A typical INGO will have 'core' funding for the day-to-day running of long-term activities (e.g. legal clinics and publications) and for meeting particular needs in the short term (e.g. urgent appeals for victims, media appearances, etc.) and 'project' funding for specific projects that fall under the general programme activities (see Landman and Abraham 2004). They also seek to diversify their funding base to maintain their overall autonomy and reduce their dependency on one donor, and some have an official policy not to accept government funds (Mutua 2001: 154).

INGOs can vary in size from a handful of people in one office to one hundred full-time staff working in the offices of their international secretariats (usually London, New York, Washington, and Geneva), while their organizational structure can vary from highly centralized and hierarchical structures to loose federated and decentralized structures. INGOs also have different ways of managing their partnerships with other INGOs and domestic NGOs, where some organizations assume a leading role while others maintain more equal partnerships. The main INGOs listed in Table 2.1 have consultative status with the Economic and Social Council within the United Nations, which allows them to participate in key meetings of the United Nations, such as the annual meeting of the United Nations Commission for Human Rights, and UN meetings in New York.

There are many ways in which INGOs and their activities have become more homogenized since the early years of their formation and appearance on the international stage.

First, most INGOs engage in similar sets of activities across the broad spectrum of human rights issues, including monitoring, standard setting, advocacy, training, publications, and capacity building. Second, the proliferation of human rights INGOs has meant an increasingly competitive funding environment where organizations have had to become more professionalized and more accountable to their donors. They must have strategic plans, published financial accounts, measurable objectives, and 'deliverables' that can demonstrate their effectiveness to donors (Welch 2001b: 13; Landman and Abraham 2004). Third, and related to the second point, INGOs have diversified the range of human rights topics they address such that those organizations traditionally engaged in work on civil and political rights are branching out into work on economic and social rights (e.g. International Commission of Jurists, Amnesty International, and Human Rights Watch), those INGOs that were more 'developmental' are mainstreaming human rights into their work (e.g. Oxfam and Care), those that initially were primarily human rights organizations have adopted work programmes that include service delivery (e.g. Penal Reform International), and new INGOs have been established that are primarily dedicated to economic and social rights, such as the FoodFirst Information and Action Network (FIAN) (Scott 2001; Hamm 2001: 169).

Finally, networks of INGOs at the international level work with networks of NGOs at the domestic level (see below) and have formed so-called 'transnational advocacy networks' (TANs) in an effort to change the human rights practices of particularly unsavoury states (Keck and Sikkink 1998; Risse, Ropp and Sikkink 1999; Risse 2002). While the overall impact of such networks and INGOs is difficult to assess (see Chapter 8; Cingranelli and Richards 2001; Landman and Abraham 2004), a comparative political science study of human rights NGO networks in eleven countries examines the degree to which these advocacy networks alert IGOs about human rights situations, which in turn put pressure on states to change their practices (Risse, Ropp and Sikkink 1999). The study argues that INGOs are able to link monitoring and reporting activities taking place at the grassroots level to the advocacy strategies at the international level, whose institutions apply pressure on offending states to change their behaviour. This change in behaviour ranges from a minimal 'tactical' concession to the full internalization and institutionalization of a human rights culture. While this relationship between INGOs, domestic NGOs, IGOs, and individual states is examined in only eleven countries with a limited set of inferences (see Landman 2003: 209–213; 2005a), the study represents a social scientific analysis of the possible positive impact that INGOs can have on the promotion and protection of human rights.

Despite the general optimism surrounding human rights INGOs for promoting and protecting human rights, critical perspectives on their formation, bases of support, mandates, and strategies focus on their essentially Western, legal, and universalizing ideologies. The base of social and political support for the major human rights INGOs has come from the associates of their white male 'founding fathers' located in the 'private, nongovernmental, and civil society segments of the industrial democracies', including 'lawyers, academics at leading universities, the business and entertainment elite, and other professionals' (Mutua 2001: 153). And despite a new focus on economic and social rights, INGOs have traditionally focused on legal solutions to the promotion and protection of civil and political rights (Mutua 2001), while many continue to pursue pro-Western and anti-Southern policy strategies. The deep divisions between and among INGOs with respect to focus and strategy were made starkly apparent at the 2001 World Conference against Racism.

Private international 'for-profit' organizations

The group of organizations in Cell III in Table 2.1 comprise both multinational corporations (MNCs) and commercial banks and securities firms. Unlike the organizations in Cell II, neither type of organization in Cell III has been seen as a protagonist in the struggle for the promotion and protection of human rights, but their activities have had direct and indirect impacts on human rights that make them an important organizational field for this volume. Multinational corporations typically have their headquarters in one of the industrialized democracies and have a significant presence in the global South through direct investment in a variety of industries, including large-scale extractive industries for minerals and raw materials (e.g. oil, gas, gold, copper, and bauxite); end-assembly and manufacturing of consumer durables for export (e.g. CD players, stereos, cars, washing machines); textiles, clothing, and shoes; cosmetics, toiletries, soaps, and cleaning supplies (e.g. Procter and Gamble); and production and distribution of fresh produce for supermarkets in the North. MNCs thus vary greatly in the types of activities they carry out and the types of goods they produce, which makes their impact on human rights issues vary greatly.

The territorial and financial expansion of multinational corporations involved in manufacturing since the 1960s has been 'pushed' by a drive to the bottom within competitive global markets for cheaper and cheaper production processes, as well as access to raw materials, and 'pulled' by developing countries in need of foreign capital to fuel processes of industrialization. Extractive MNCs may have long-lasting relationships with host countries and may form new ones in the event that new sources of raw materials for extraction have been identified. MNCs in manufacturing seek to reduce their marginal costs by 'farming out' the final assembly of goods in countries that have a cheap and abundant labour supply and then re-importing at a tax discount the assembled goods for consumption in the North. Developing countries wanting to break their dependency on the export of primary goods have often undergone processes of import-substitution industrialization (ISI) and export-oriented industrialization (EOI) both of which require substantial inward investment partly financed by multinational capital (see Moran 1985, 1998; Brohman 1996: 35–80; Todaro 1997: 534–545), the nature of which is highly diversified across different MNCs and different business sectors.

Arguments within the development community have raged about the positive and negative impact of MNCs and direct foreign investment. Developmental economists see great benefits to direct foreign investment, including an improvement in a country's balance of payments by contributing to its savings and foreign exchange reserves and by raising government revenue in the form of taxes; enhancing management expertise through the relocation of business executives to the recipient country; increasing demand for labour through helping to fuel the process of industrialization; and transferring technology developed within the core economies to the peripheral economies. Economic arguments against the presence of MNCs include the fact that they widen income gaps in recipient countries through concentrations of income to a small proportion of the population; a decrease in domestic savings and investment through preferential treatment of particular MNCs by recipient governments; a weakening of the current account (i.e. the difference between imports and exports) as new dependencies develop for the importation of intermediate goods; less tax revenue owing to concessionary rates offered by recipient countries; and exclusive control over privileged company knowledge and the transfer of technology that is inappropriate to the skill base of the available labour supply in the recipient country (see Todaro 1997: 537–543).

In addition to these economic arguments, human rights organizations and activists have added a series of objections to the presence of MNCs in developing countries on normative grounds that are linked to the different kinds of activities and production processes carried out by different firms. Their objections include the presence of MNCs in countries responsible for gross violations of human rights (e.g. oil companies in Myanmar/Burma); their disregard for international labour standards and worker's rights (e.g. the famous cases of Nike, Reebok, and Levi Strauss); their infringement of intellectual property rights in the development of drugs and pharmaceuticals; their role in displacing indigenous communities to gain access to raw materials; their disregard for local customs in trying to develop markets for their products (e.g. the Nestlé baby formula scandals); and their negative impact on the environment. MNCs have been the subject of large 'name and shame' campaigns and boycotts of particular products, the production of which the human rights community has linked to infringements and violations of human rights.

The second set of international 'for-profit' organizations in Table 2.1 are the large commercial banks and securities firms that lend capital to developing countries in need of inward investment and/or invest in stocks, bonds, and notes (known as 'portfolio investment'), which fuels financial speculation. The private loans are a direct transfer of money to the developing countries on which there is charged some kind of interest rate (fixed or variable). After the 1973 oil crisis, European and North American commercial banks were awash in so-called 'petrodollars' invested by oil-producing countries. Commercial banks at this time were bullish about the prospects of earning profits through lending money to developing countries. The petrodollars were thus lent to developing countries at highly concessionary rates, both in terms of long maturity rates and low variable interest rates pegged at a few percentage points above the global lending rate. The subsequent oil and interest rate crisis in 1979 meant that debt servicing on the principal loaned to developing countries grew exponentially to the point that in 1982, Mexico, Brazil, Argentina, and Chile could no longer afford to pay their international debt obligations.

The 'debt crisis' ensued, as international strategies were developed to address the repercussions of sovereign countries effectively going bankrupt. One solution (see above) was for the World Bank to become a 'lender of last resort' and extend loans to cover debt servicing while imposing new conditions (structural adjustment and macro-stabilization) for reforming the recipient country's economy. Other responses included the development of a secondary debt market, where investors bought debt from those countries in crisis; 'debt-for-equity swaps' where investors traded equity in the indebted country for assets; 'debt-for-nature' swaps, where investors bought debt in exchange for protected environmental conservation sites within the indebted country; and debt reduction strategies that sought debt forgiveness on the basis that many debts would simply never be repaid. Of these different strategies, the IMF- and World Bank-inspired structural adjustment programmes (SAPs) and macro-stabilization policies have received the most attention from human rights groups who argue that their imposition has increased income disparities, increased poverty, weakened domestic demand, reduced public expenditure on the provision of healthcare, education, and welfare, and led to overall increase in societal polarization (see Brohman 1996: 132–168; see also Stiglitz 2002).

Portfolio investment is completely different from commercial lending and consists of the foreign purchase of assets and equity, which are then traded on markets for financial gain. Such investment can be beneficial to a developing country since it raises the value of domestic firms and contributes to overall economic growth. For the private firms investing in a developing country, or 'emerging market', annual returns on investment can be particularly high (as much as 40% in some countries), but these markets also tend to be highly volatile, where speculative capital can flee a country as quickly as it has entered it. For example, in 1994, Mexico experienced a collapse in the value of the peso, which was propped up through an emergency rescue package from the Clinton Administration. But while the package stabilized the Mexican economy in the short run, investors dumped their assets at a loss and took their investments elsewhere. In this way, speculative investment of this kind can be a benefit to developing countries if they have a solid economic base, but a serious liability if they do not, since investors can remove capital quickly from a vulnerable market (see Todaro 1997: 543–545).

While the activities, functions, services, and products of MNCs, banks, and securities firms are different, they are not completely separate since consortia of banks and securities firms may back an investment package and business opportunity carried out by an MNC in a developing country. Within the discrete sub-sectors of this general organizational field there has been some homogenization as similar sets of firms offer similar sets of products and services, and carry out similar sets of activities within different contexts. In addition, across many MNCs, oligopolies have formed where fewer and fewer firms dominate a particular business sector, thus reducing the number of MNCs that may have an impact on human rights in any given country. Human rights organizations have argued that the sheer size, power, and potential impact of private firms on human rights make them a legitimate focus for advocacy and change. Indeed, the annual turnover of the top twenty MNCs is much higher than the annual GDP of most countries, even those in the developed world (see Forsythe 2000: 192–193). For firms operating in countries notorious for committing gross human rights violations, human rights arguments focus on the moral obligations of these firms that are in a position to protect human rights, a position that does not necessarily affect their ability to function and earn profits (Sorell 2004). Even in countries where there are not gross violations, a human rights perspective focuses on the vulnerability and powerlessness of ordinary people to have any control over their socio-economic fortunes, and the ways in which MNC operations and policies can help alleviate the worst forms of their negative externalities.

Given the size and power of MNCs, some human rights NGOs have adopted an antagonistic approach that draws a distinct line of demarcation between their realm and that of the private firm. Such a position has led to the name-and-shame campaigns and direct-action campaigns against firms across the extractive, textile, manufacturing, and pharmaceutical sectors. Another approach has been to engage constructively with firms to explore the ways in which so-called 'corporate social responsibility' can be enhanced, a process that improves the firm's public image, while at the same time addressing important human rights concerns. Measures including 'voluntary codes of conduct', human rights 'audits', and formal commitments of firms to uphold human rights found in the Universal Declaration have all sought to mainstream human rights into the concerns of big business. Both the antagonistic and engaging approaches have sought to increase the overall accountability of firms that moves beyond the shareholders to include all the relevant stakeholders (McBarnet 2004: 63).

Public domestic organizations

The essential public domestic organization for consideration in this volume is what has been called the 'modern' or 'nation' state, which under the current international law of human rights remains the primary agent for promoting and protecting human rights. The history of the modern state argues that states emerged through the amalgamation of smaller administrative units (usually feudal) and were combined with some notion of national identity. The primary function of this early state form was to raise revenue to run and maintain a standing army, while over time state functions have become more diversified and have permeated many aspects of modern life (Bendix 1964, 1978; Mann 1993; Münkler 2005: 32–50). The sociology of the modern state holds that it is 'human community that (successfully) claims the *monopoly of the legitimate use of physical force within a given territory*' (Weber 1991: 78, emphasis in the original). The political economy of the modern state holds that such monopoly of legitimate use of force is essential for economic prosperity, since it provides a secure environment (in particular the protection of property rights) in which to carry out productive economic activities (Gray 1998; Drazen 2000; Bates 2001; Jessop 2002). But such a conception is also important for human rights since it contains a minimum requirement of *legitimacy* and rules out *other sources of violence* that may threaten its integrity, both of which have been essential for the emergence of 'old' and 'new' democracies throughout the 19th and 20th centuries (Rueschemeyer, Stephens and Stephens 1992: 63–69; Linz and Stepan 1996: 16–37). The political sociology of citizenship rights argues that rights claims develop throughout processes of state formation and nation building as new sectors of the population seek inclusion. This account includes a 'top-down' explanation for the expansion of rights protected by the state and a 'bottom-up' explanation for the expansion of rights demanded by mobilizing groups (see Marshall 1963; Barbalet 1988; Foweraker and Landman 1997). Finally, the development of international law is based on the twin assumptions of state sovereignty and non-intervention, most notably embodied in the 1648 Treaty of Westphalia, while international relations has long grounded its inquiry on the strategic interaction of states, which have been conceived in the realist tradition as 'unitary rational actors' at the global level of analysis (see Chapter 3; Morgenthau 1961; Krasner 1999; Donnelly 2000; Snidal 2002).

It is no surprise then that states and their ability to protect (and violate) human rights are at the centre of the international law of human rights and have featured in a large proportion of research, policy, and advocacy in the field of human rights. Human rights treaties are international multilateral agreements that oblige their individual states parties to uphold a common set of human rights norms. While the international 'regime' of human rights is still relatively weak (Donnelly 1986, 2003), the full implementation of human rights protections is the onus of individual states, while scholarship and advocacy focus on what states are and are not doing to achieve the full implementation of human rights. Some have claimed that the process of globalization that emerged in accelerated fashion since the expansion of multinational economic activities of the 1960s has begun to undermine the centrality of states in the global system, while the overall effects of globalization on human rights is a highly contested area of social scientific research (see e.g. Meyer 1996, 1999a, 1999b; Li and Reuveny 2003). But many academics and practitioners have argued that state authority has not diminished with globalization, and certainly since the September 11 terrorist attacks in the United States, there has been a reassertion of state authority and control over the lives of individuals (citizens and non-citizens) who are still in many ways bound to the territorially defined independent nation state in which they reside (see e.g. Booth and Dunne 2002; Gray 2002; Strawson 2002). For example, significant anti-terror legislation has been passed in many countries in the world that allows states to curb the rights of those suspected of terrorism, and that represents significant derogation from international human rights commitments that had already been undertaken.

The state thus remains the central actor in the world of human rights and it is the organization that carries the primary responsibility for protecting and defending human rights, as well as the key actor that denies rights (Foweraker and Landman 1997). While states vary in size, history, power and other features, they do perform approximately the same set of functions across the world. Thus, we may speak of a certain functional homogenization of state organization that has emerged in the modern era, but states are not monolithic organizations. Rather, they comprise different branches (executive, legislative, and judicial), separate ministries (interior, justice, treasury, defence, social security, education), and can be divided between national and sub-national level institutions, all of which have a bearing on the promotion and protection of human rights. For example, there are numerous institutional explanations for the precariousness of rights protection, such as the presence of strong executives and weak judiciaries, powerful provincial governments within federal systems, under-resourced police, justice, and prison systems, and *de facto* discrimination in health, education, and social service departments. Other social science arguments have looked at the state more holistically and have tried to determine whether its degree of 'relative autonomy' *vis-à-vis* strong social and political groupings in society is related to the promotion and protection of human rights. This has been particularly so in those areas of the world characterized by the presence of strong patron–client networks (as in Latin America), neo-patrimonialism, and 'predatory' states (as in many parts of Africa). Moreover, there is considerable attention given to so-called 'failed' states, where there is the absence (or partial absence) of legitimate monopoly over the use of force in a given territory, such as Burundi, Angola, Sudan, and Colombia. Failed states have had tragic consequences for security, development, and the protection of human rights (see e.g. Rotberg 2004).

Private 'not-for-profit' organizations

Like their counterparts at the international level, there are countless non-governmental organizations at the domestic level that work directly and indirectly for the promotion and protection of human rights. They vary in form, size, and function with regard to their connection and impact on human rights, including developmental work, legal advocacy and aid, and human rights documentation and monitoring. They vary in the degree to which they work with partner organizations at the international level (both IGOs and INGOs) and the degree to which they are willing to work with the various organs of their own domestic states. Some NGOs form larger alliances with INGOs (see above), or work with IGOs on particular projects at the grassroots level, while at the same time having different strategies for working closely with domestic states or remaining relatively autonomous from them. It has thus far been nearly impossible to document or count the number of such NGOs throughout the world, since their formation, amalgamation, and dissolution is frequent and constantly shifting. Moreover, the continued maintenance of NGOs is often a function of the availability of international funds for particular and/or fashionable issues, the state of freedom within the given country, and the relative success or failure of their activities. NGOs can form and dissolve around particular issues, can be shut down by states through repressive measures, and may disappear for having achieved their aims as much as for not having achieved their aims.

In addition to NGOs, there are a number of other not-for-profit organizations that may have an impact on human rights, including that broad set of 'civil society organizations' and social movement organizations, which are largely voluntary, pursue stated aims and objectives through recruiting and mobilizing members, and maintain various degrees of autonomy from the state and from political and economic society. Such organizations can include social clubs, guilds, popular economic organizations, church groups, charities, self-help organizations, soup kitchens, food cooperatives, women's collectives, indigenous groups and movements among many others. The vast body of social scientific research on social movements analyses the emergence, trajectory, and impact of social mobilization, which oftentimes comprise these groups, in terms of their ability to change dominant discourses, set public policy agendas, influence positive legislation within the issue area, and bring about lasting changes in the political system, whether it be a liberalizing authoritarian regime, consolidating democracy, or mature democracy (see e.g. Piven and Cloward 1977; Tarrow 1989; 1994; Dalton and Kuechler 1990; Foweraker 1995; Banaszak 1996; McAdam, McCarthy and Zald 1996; Foweraker and Landman 1997; Della Porta and Diani 1999; Landman 2000b, 2003).

Many of the individuals, groups, and movements within civil society that work in the area of human rights have become known as 'human rights defenders' (HRDs). There are several definitions of human rights defenders, which in many ways can affect the degree to which they attract attention, become targeted by groups and organizations that oppose their activities, and become part of international systems for monitoring and reporting. The 1998 Declaration on Human Rights Defenders does not define HRDs *per se*, but Article 1 stipulates that,

> Everyone has the right, individually and in association with others, to promote and to strive for the protection and realization of human rights and fundamental freedoms at the national and international levels.

This article in the declaration means that any individual or group can be a human rights defender, while the subsequent articles stipulate what rights protections ought to be in place in order for such individuals and groups to carry out work on human rights. Frontline, an Irish human rights NGO, defines a human rights defender as 'a person who works, non-violently, for any or all of the rights enshrined in the Universal Declaration of Human Rights'. The International Federation of Human Rights Leagues (FIDH) and the World Organisation Against Torture (OMCT), which jointly run the Observatory for Human Rights Defenders provide a slightly more cumbersome definition of HRDs that focuses on their victimization:

> Each person victim or risking to be a victim of reprisals, harassment or violations, due to his compromise exercised individually or in association with others, in conformity with international instruments of protection of human rights, in favour of the promotion and realization of rights recognized by the Universal Declaration of Human Rights and guaranteed by several international instruments.
>
> (FIDH-OMCT 2003: 274)

Even this more victim-centred definition leaves open the possibility of many different actors qualifying as HRDs. Nevertheless, the nascent monitoring and advocacy systems in place try to record and follow up on those actors who have suffered violations precisely because they have been outspoken in their work on behalf of human rights in particular domestic political contexts. Figure 2.3 shows the total number of abuses committed against such HRDs across over sixty countries for the 1997–2003 period, incuding arbitrary detention, threats and harassment, and summary execution. The data are from coded narrative accounts of abuse against HRDs collected by the joint FIDH-OMCT Observatory for human rights using a modified version of the 'who did what to whom' data model popular in truth commisions (see Chapter 5 and Ball, Spirer and Spirer 2000, Landman 2005d; Landmann 2006).

But not all civil society organizations and social movements are inherently 'good'. Indeed, many forms of oppressive discourses, exclusionary politics, and violent behaviour that have grave consequences for human rights emerge from organizations and groups within civil society. Such 'uncivil' movements engage in violence against other social movements and democratic governments through kidnapping, murder, destruction of property, coups, and coup attempts. They seek to eliminate competition from their adversaries, and expand political power for an exclusive sector of the population. Like 'civil' social movements, they use identity and symbolic politics and unconventional political strategies, and they straddle the divide between societal autonomy and integration by participating in the political system through existing forms of interest inter-mediation (Payne 2000: 3). Unlike civil movements, they engage in violent political action against their government or adversaries within civil society (Payne 2000: 220–221). Since they target adversaries in civil society and ultimately seek power within political institutions, such movements represent pathologies of both civil society and democracy. Unlike their civil counterparts that broadly support the idea of democracy, but seek to deepen it or transform it, uncivil movements threaten democratic stability and erode civil society, particularly in countries where both are relatively weak.

Examples of uncivil movements in Latin America include paramilitary organizations in Colombia and Argentina, the Shining Path in Peru, the Rural Democratic Union (UDR) in Brazil, the National Republican Alliance (ARENA) in El Salvador, the counter-revolutionaries (Contras) in Nicaragua, the Revolutionary Front for the Advancement and Progress of Haiti (FRAPH), and the Bolívar Revolutionary Movement (MBR-200) in Venezuela. In other parts of the world, such movements include guerrilla organizations and movements (e.g. Nepal, Sri Lanka, the Philippines, and Chechnya), warlords (e.g. Somalia), and terrorist organizations in the Middle East, all of which have had grave consequences for human rights, and in particular children's rights (see Kaldor 1999; Münkler 2005). While these and other related organizations are primarily interested in power and provoking political instability and less interested in profit *per se*, there are yet other locally based organizations responsible for human rights violations that have other motivations for their actions. For example, in Latin America communal groups and popular organizations, in a perverse form of (re)claiming their sense of citizenship and providing local security in the absence of state capacity engage in vigilantism against local criminals, practices that include public lynching and other extra-judicial killings (see Speed and Reyes 2002; Goldstein 2003, 2004). Throughout many tribal organizations and local communal groups in Africa, ritual killings are part of daily life, where women often find themselves the target of local custom, which requires sacrifices to rid the community of illness.

Total violations against HRDs (*N*)

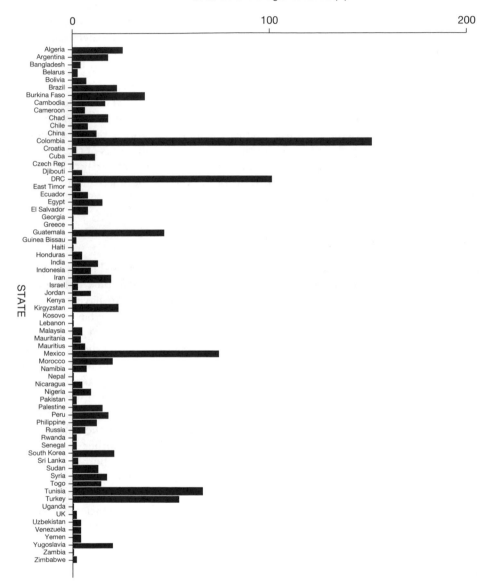

Figure 2.3 Total violations against HRDs, 1997–2000.

Source: FIDH-OMCT, 1997–2003.

Private 'for-profit' organizations

The final organizational field to be considered here is that set of private for-profit organizations, including small and large businesses, banks, and private schools. Like their international counterparts (MNCs), domestic private businesses and banks may not have an explicit relationship with human rights, but their corporate practices from human resource management down to the shop floor may have rights implications, including forms of gender, racial, and ethnic discrimination; infringement of worker's rights; and practices that may have health and welfare implications. In addition, like the public counterparts, private schools have a significant role to play in the area of human rights, although they will be less bound by rules on freedom of religion, dress codes, and discrimination. But they may want to exercise their own voluntary codes of conduct and act in ways that are consistent with domestic equal opportunities legislation and other socially responsible practices. In addition to these legal organizations, private armies and firms of mercenaries carry out violent activities for profit in many parts of the world in a trend that has seen the increasing commercialization of war, a process partly driven by the structural inequalities associated with patterns of uneven development in much of the global South (see Münkler 2005: 17–22).

The complex terrain of human rights

This overview of organizational fields at the domestic and international levels of analysis has shown that the overall *terrain* of human rights is exceedingly complex and comprises a great diversity of actors, organizations, and institutions that can have a variety of different positive and negative impacts on human rights. While there have been some homogenizing tendencies in each of the organizational fields, a good social scientist needs to understand the significant remaining differences between and among the organizations that comprise these different fields and not to homogenize them into monolithic 'us' and 'them' typologies. Indeed, it is precisely within the grey areas that a social science of human rights can begin to contribute to our understanding of the different ways in which the elements within these organizational fields are related to the promotion of human rights. Moreover, a social science of human rights also needs to examine the different ways in which elements from these different fields interact with one another and how the relative power relations between such fields affects the ways in which human rights will be protected or violated. But specifying these relationships and power balances, and the ways in which they affect human rights requires theoretical underpinnings and consideration of methodologies that are designed to provide systematic analysis and meaningful answers to significant human rights problems and puzzles. It is to these questions that the next two chapters turn.

Suggestions for further reading

Boli, J. and Thomas, G. (eds) (1999) *Constructing World Culture*, Stanford, CA: Stanford University Press.

Forsythe, D. P. (2000) *Human Rights in International Relations*, Cambridge: Cambridge University Press.

Korey, W. (1998) *NGOs and the Universal Declaration of Human Rights: A Curious Grapevine*, London: Palgrave.

Risse, T., Ropp, S. C. and Sikkink, K. (1999) *The Power of Human Rights: International Norms and Domestic Change*, Cambridge: Cambridge University Press.

Welch, S. (ed.) (2000) *NGOs and Human Rights: Promise and Performance*, Philadelphia: University of Pennsylvania Press.

3   Social theory and human rights

The previous two chapters have outlined the scope of human rights that form the main object of inquiry for the social scientific study of human rights and provided an overview of the terrain of human rights in an effort to identify the main sets of actors, organizations, and institutions that are relevant to the study of human rights. This chapter turns its attention to how social theory can be used to study human rights problems. Social scientists apply the categories and concepts of empirical theories in social science through the use of a particular method or set of methods (see Chapter 4) in an effort to *explain* and *understand* the variable promotion and protection of human rights across different political and social contexts in the world. Empirical theories differ fundamentally from normative theories since their main purpose and function is to explain and understand *why* and *how* social phenomena are the way they are, *when* they are, and *where* they are, rather than *how they ought to be*. In this way, social theory helps identify the salient factors that may account for observed social phenomena and reduce the complexity of the observed world in an effort to provide various degrees of substantive knowledge about that world. Social theory tells us what to look for in analysing human rights problems and the answers we get to our enquiries may vary from conclusions of a very general nature (i.e. empirical generalizations at high levels of abstraction) to conclusions about the meanings, choices, expectations, and practices of a very specific nature (i.e. grounded case analysis of particular groups and individuals). The variance in these answers is more a function of the research questions posed and the research designs employed than the application of social theory itself (see King, Keohane and Verba 1994; Geddes 1990, 2003; Landman 2002, 2003).

This chapter outlines groups of social theory that have developed in the social sciences that are (and have been) most applicable to the empirical analysis of human rights problems. Clearly any such attempt to provide a definitive and full account of all the different theoretical traditions across the disciplines of sociology, economics, political science, international relations, and anthropology goes well beyond the scope of this volume, but based on the extant literature from these disciplines on the study of human rights and on surveys of social scientific theories in general (see e.g. Lichbach 1997, 2003; Risse, Ropp and Sikkink 1999; Ritzer and Smart 2001; Carlsnaes, Risse and Simmons 2002; Schmitz and Sikkink 2002; Landman 2005a, 2005b), it is possible to identify three groups of social theory that serve the purposes of this volume. These are *rationalism, structuralism*, and *culturalism* (Lichbach 1997). While not mutually exclusive categories (see below), these groupings are useful devices to consider the different ways in which social scientists seek to explain and understand the social world in general, and human rights problems in particular. Each group has its own sets of sub-traditions, levels of analysis, units of analysis, assumptions, and propositions about the variations observed in the promotion and protection of human rights throughout the world. The chapter begins with a separate examination of each group at the domestic and international levels and considers the types of propositions each can make about the promotion and protection of human rights. It then discusses the significant areas of intersection and complementarity between and among these groups of theory with application to the study of human rights.

Rationalism

The first theoretical grouping to consider partly for its straightforward approach and set of simple assumptions and partly for its perceived antipathy to the idea of human rights is *rationalism*. At the domestic level, rationalist approaches include rational choice, public choice, and variants of game theory, while at the international level, they include variants of realism (offensive realism, neo-realism and structural realism) and game theory. Rationalist perspectives at the domestic level concentrate on the actions and behaviour of individuals who make reasoned and intentional choices based upon sets of preferences, or interests. Those who adhere to the rationalist perspective are 'concerned with the collective processes and outcomes that follow from intentionality, or the social consequences of individually rational action' (Lichbach 1997: 246). The notion of intentionality is central for rationalist explanation, where '"bed rock" explanations of social phenomena should build upwards from the beliefs and goals of individuals' (Ward 1995: 79). The development of the rationalist perspective followed earlier individual theories that emphasize the non-rational aspects of human behaviour such as mass theories of grievance and relative deprivation (e.g. Smelser 1962; Gurr 1968, 1970). In contrast to these earlier individual-level theories, rationalists claim that grievance alone is not enough to explain social action and that real choices at the individual level must be examined. The assumptions of orthodox rational choice are that individuals pursue their material self-interest through utility-maximizing strategies, which involve choices across all aspects of their lives from shopping to voting to joining groups and engaging in social action of any kind (see e.g. Green and Shapiro 1994). Since it combines notions of material self-interest with individual rationality, rational choice seeks to provide *microeconomic foundations* for social action. And since the individual rational actor is the primary unit of analysis for rational choice, its body of research engages in what has been called 'methodological individualism' (Przeworski 1985).

One of the key insights that flows from the material assumption of rationalist analysis is that in seeking social, economic, and political change, *lone individuals* may not be willing to join groups or engage in 'collective action' since their goals for change could be achieved whether they join the activities of a group or not. This 'logic of collective action' (Olson 1965; see also Lichbach 1995: 3–13) becomes even more acute the larger such groups become, since any difference that can be made by one individual faces a decreasing level of impact with the increasing size of the group. Ironically, in the late 1960s when the logic of collective action argued that individuals were unlikely to join groups seeking social change, numerous social protests were breaking out throughout the United States (e.g. Washington, DC 1968), Europe (e.g. Paris 1968), and parts of Latin America (e.g. Mexico City 1968). Moreover, history is replete with examples of collective action in the forms of local and national protest movements, peasant rebellions, and full-scale social revolutions (see e.g. Tilly, Tilly and Tilly 1975; Tilly 1978; Wickham-Crowley 1992; Lichbach 1994; Tarrow 1994). In light of this apparent empirical contradiction for the logic of collective action, a rationalist explanation for collective social action looks for the material benefits or 'selective incentives' that individuals might receive through joining a group and engaging in some form of social action (Lichbach 1995).

Such an insight into the motivations and constraints on the propensity for individuals to engage in collective action of some kind is crucial for studying human rights in many different ways. First, human rights discourse makes a normative claim in its appeal to mobilize those that are oppressed. But it is not obvious that 'moral outrage' (Moore 1978) or 'moral sentiments' (Franck 1990) are enough to motivate individuals to join groups that mobilize for the promotion and protection of human rights. Rationalist analysis of such mobilization would need to either (1) relax its assumptions about the maximization of material interests to include norms and therefore possibly weaken its analytical and explanatory purchase (Franck 1990), or (2) identify the material incentives that might lie behind a group's strategy in mobilizing people to struggle for their rights (see Lichbach 1994). Second, human rights violations are oftentimes highly *individuated*, which may obscure any collective sense of oppression and limit the propensity to mobilize for change. Even where collective violations occur, such as genocide and mass killing, it is still not obvious, given the fear and possible reprisals for joining a protest group, why individuals would mobilize against their oppression. Third, violations of economic and social rights do involve material interests of the victims, but it is not clear what selective and immediate gains an individual joining a group could make. The fact that individuals all over the world *do* join groups often under highly risky circumstances, however, remains a significant challenge for rationalist analysis on the struggle for human rights (see Green and Shapiro 1994).

A second major contribution of rationalist analysis at the domestic level (and as it happens at the international level) has been the application of game theory to problems that relate to the promotion and protection of human rights. Building on the assumptions of rationalist analysis, scholars using this approach examine the different ways in which rational individuals *interact* with one another as they pursue their various preferences. One way to examine this interaction is to use 'game theory', which specifies a simple set of choices available to the individuals (players) and then models their interaction given their preferences. This game can involve many players with many choices; however, in order to reduce the complexity associated with a game with many players, it is common for analysts to specify a game of two players each with two choices, yielding a 2 × 2 matrix of possible outcomes. Given the ranking of these outcomes by the two players, certain 'payoffs' or rewards can be assigned to the players. Knowing the preferences and payoff structures allows for the examination of all possible combinations of choices by the two players. In addition, the players can engage in a single interaction with one another at one point in time (a one-off game scenario), or multiple interactions with one another over a given period time (iterative games).

Probably the most famous game in game theory is that of the 'prisoner's dilemma', which formalizes an interaction of two players made popular in police and crime programmes. In this common scenario, two thieves have been arrested by the police for the same crime, are locked away in two separate cells in the county jail, and are unable to communicate to each other. Each thief has two choices, either to confess to the crime or not confess to the crime. The police use the fact that the two thieves are separated to their advantage by giving the thieves a range of options. If one thief confesses to the crime and the other does not, the thief that confesses gets a sentence of two years while the thief that did not confess gets twelve years. If both thieves confess to the crime, they get a sentence of six years. If both thieves do not confess to the crime, they both get a sentence of three years. This simple situation is depicted in Figure 3.1. For each thief, the dilemma rests with the expectation of what the other thief will choose while both know that it is rational to minimize their prison sentences. Since neither can trust the other, the rational solution to the dilemma is for both to confess, which gives them both a six-year sentence. While the sentence is not the least or the greatest number of years, it is the best outcome for both given the nature of the game.

The main task in using game theory to analyse social action is to identify the actors in the game and specify their choices as well as their preferences so as to model their strategic interaction. The most important aspect of game theory is that none of the outcomes is certain, but *contingent* upon the actions of both (or many) players. The basic form of the prisoner's dilemma (and many other types of games) has been used to model trench warfare (Axelrod 1984), as a basis for a liberal theory of society (Gautier 1986), to explain the reform of bureaucracies in Latin America (Geddes 1991), to address a series of substantive research problems in comparative politics (Tsebelis 1990; Munck 2001), as well as international relations, such as modelling the arms race between the Soviet Union and the United States and analysing the formation and effectiveness of international regimes (see below, and Keohane 1984, 2001, 2002; Hansclever, Mayer and Rittberger 1997). The domestic application of game theory to problems of democratic breakdown (Cohen 1994) and democratic transition (Przeworski 1991; Colomer 1991; Colomer and Pascual 1994; Gates and Humes 1997) has been important for the study of human rights, since human rights violations tend to *increase* after a democratic breakdown and *decrease* after a successful democratic transition (see Chapter 6 and Zanger 2000a). Thus, a formal model of both processes can be useful since understanding the forces that maintain and threaten democracy within a given context will suggest strategies for upholding democracy and thereby promoting greater protection of human rights.

In both accounts of breakdown and transition, game theory posits a spectrum of actors that have different sets of preferences. For one model of democratic breakdown (Cohen 1994), the actors are arrayed on an ideological spectrum from left to right, and include stylized actors labelled *radical left*, *moderate left*, *moderate right*, and *radical right* (see Figure 3.2). Each of these actors is motivated by the desire to maintain or enhance his or her political power. As a consequence, each of these actors has varying degrees of support for maintaining the status quo in any given moment when democracy is facing a potential crisis of governance. The radical left and the radical right on the ideological spectrum have a greater propensity to want to change the status quo in dramatic fashion in an

| | | Thief 2 | |
		Confess	Do not confess
Thief 1	Confess	Both get 6 years	Thief 1 gets 2 years Thief 2 gets 12 years
	Do not confess	Thief 1 gets 12 years Thief 2 gets 2 years	Both get 3 years

Figure 3.1 The prisoner's dilemma.

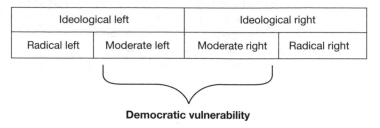

Democratic vulnerability

Figure 3.2 Actors in democratic breakdown.

attempt to enhance their power. In contrast, the moderate left and moderate right have a greater propensity to want to maintain the status quo and thus maintain the power that they already possess under the current democratic regime. The problem for game-theoretic analysis is that all the actors are operating under great uncertainty since the game is modelling a moment of democratic crisis (e.g. stagnated economic growth, balance of payments problems, social protest, and political violence). Game theory thus focuses on the democratic vulnerability represented by both types of moderates (left and right).

In applying the logic of the prisoner's dilemma, Cohen (1994: 66–68) shows how the moderates can either break or not break with their radical counterparts on the left and the right. Breaking with their counterparts is a form of cooperation, while not breaking with their counterparts is a form of defection, since cooperation refers to the two moderate factions maintaining democracy. The resulting combination of choices, outcomes, and payoffs is depicted in Figure 3.3, where the strategic interaction between the two groups of moderates is assumed to be a one-off game. The upper left cell shows that in breaking with their counterparts the two moderate factions maintain democracy and receive a reward (*R*) in the form of continued democracy, continued hold on power, and some agreement on the necessary reforms to oversee the period of crisis. If the moderate left

		Moderate right	
		Breaks from radical right (Cooperate)	Does not break from radical right (Defects)
Moderate left	Breaks from radical left (Cooperate)	*R, R* Agreement on reforms Democracy is preserved	*S, T* Left defeated Minimal reforms
	Does not break from radical left (Defects)	*T, S* Right defeated Radical reforms	*P, P* Agreement impossible Democracy breaks down

Figure 3.3 Game theory and democratic breakdown.

Note: *T* = temptation to defect, *R* = reward, *P* = punishment, *S* = sucker's payoff, these are listed in order of preference such that $T > R > P > S$.
Source: Adapted from Cohen (1994: 67–68).

breaks with its counterparts (i.e. a bid to cooperate) but the moderate right does not (i.e. a defection), then the moderate left loses significant power (i.e. gets 'the sucker's payoff', or S), the moderate right wins (i.e. gets its best reward 'the temptation to defect', or T) and is able to implement minimal reforms to oversee the crisis (upper right cell in the figure). Alternatively, if the moderate right breaks with its radical counterpart (i.e. in a bid to cooperate) and the moderate left does not break with its counterpart (i.e. defects), then the moderate right gets the sucker's payoff (S) and the moderate left gets its best outcome (T). In this case, the moderate right is defeated and radical reforms are implemented to deal with the crisis (lower left cell in the figure). Finally, if both defect (i.e. do not break with their counterparts), then no agreement on reforms is possible, both actors receive punishment (P) and democracy breaks down. The game is modelled on the assumption that all actors prefer the temptation to defect (T) to getting some reward (R) to punishment (P) to the sucker's payoff (S).

The so-called 'moderate's dilemma' (Cohen 1994: 66–68) captures the notion of a 'weak centre' in the political spectrum and if that centre collapses, there is a power vacuum that is often filled by the military, which was certainly the case in Brazil in 1964 and Chile in 1973 (see Cohen 1994: 76–124). Such a model could also be applied to other breakdowns of democracy, such as those in Uruguay in 1973, Argentina in 1966 and again in 1976, and possibly even the collapse of the Weimar Republic in Germany, which preceded the rise of the Nazi regime. In all such cases, the collapse of democracy has been followed by periods of authoritarian rule under which the protection of many human rights was either outright violated as a matter of policy, or as a *de facto* consequence of the regime operating under a 'state of emergency', where the 'reasons of state' subordinated any concern over the protection of human rights. Inferences about how and why the centre may or may not collapse is helpful for those seeking to maintain democratic forms of governance and by extension the protection of human rights.

What is intriguing about this form of rationalist analysis is that it has also been applied to the moment when such authoritarian regimes have experienced their own crises and undergone processes of democratic transition. Again, such analysis identifies a spectrum of political forces that are divided between the authoritarian regime and the opposition and include *hardliners*, *reformers*, *moderates*, and *radicals* (see Figure 3.4). (Przeworski 1991: 66–72; see also Gates and Humes 1997: 113–139). Hardliners want to maintain the authoritarian regime to stay in power and are not afraid to use repression to quell any uprising from the opposition. Reformers are concerned over the continued use of repression and its possible consequences for regime legitimacy and thus to stay in power want to liberalize the authoritarian regime. Moderates in the opposition want to bring about liberalization rather than a radical uprising and overthrow of the authoritarian regime.

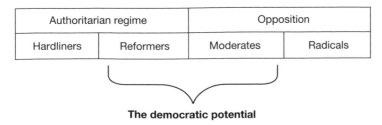

The democratic potential

Figure 3.4 Actors in democratic transition.

Radicals, as their name suggest, want to overthrow the regime, bring about a rapid political transformation, and are not afraid to use violence to do so.

Like the 'moderate's dilemma' outlined above, game-theoretic analysis of democratic transition focuses on the 'centre' of the political spectrum (i.e. the reformers within the authoritarian regime and the moderates in the opposition), and how those actors engage in a prisoner's dilemma game. The game is modelled around the choices that either the reformers or the moderates can make. Reformers can break or not break from the hard-liners in the authoritarian regime. Moderates can either break or not break from their radical counterparts in the opposition. In this sense, the game and its four possible outcomes (see Figure 3.5) is a mirror image of the moderate's dilemma outlined above. If both the reformers and the moderates break from their respective sides (i.e. from the hardliners and radicals), then democracy is established with guarantees. Such an outcome is also known as an 'elite pact' (see Higley and Gunther 1992), where both players receive a reward (*R*) by staying in power. If the reformers do not break from the hardliners and the moderates break from the radicals, then the moderates receive the sucker's payoff (*S*) and the reformers receive the temptation to defect (*T*). Alternatively, if the reformers break from the hardliners and the moderates do not break from the radicals, the reformers receive the sucker's payoff (*S*), and the moderates receive the temptation to defect (*T*). Finally, if both the reformers and the moderates do not break from the hardliners and radicals, respectively, then the authoritarian regime survives and political polarization, violence, and repression continue, where both actors receive their punishment (*P*).

Moments of democratic transition have been modelled as one-off games as well as a series of iterated games in the cases of Spain (Colomer 1991) and Poland (Colomer and Pascual 1994). Geddes (1999) has added further refinements to modelling democratic transitions (or 'authoritarian collapses' as she puts it) in taking into account the nature of the authoritarian regime itself (military, personalist, one-party) and the different types of games that may apply to the strategic interaction of key political actors (e.g. the 'battle of the sexes' for military regimes and 'staghunt' for one-party regimes). The different

	Reformers in the authoritarian regime	
	Break from authoritarian regime (Cooperate)	Do not break from authoritarian regime (Defects)
Breaks from their radicals (Cooperate)	*R, R* Democracy with guarantees, elite pact in the centre	*S, T* Authoritarian regime remains with some concessions
Do not break from their radicals (Defects)	*T, S* Democracy, but with no guarantees, always a threat from the radicals	*P, P* Authoritarian regime survives, polarization continues

Moderates in the opposition

Figure 3.5 Game theory and democratic transition.

Note: *T* = temptation to defect, *R* = reward, *P* = punishment, *S* = sucker's payoff; these are listed in order of preference such that *T* > *R* > *P* > *S*.
Source: Adapted from Przeworski (1991: 69) and Cohen (1994: 67–68).

game forms are based on identifying different sets of actors than those identified above, who necessarily have different preference orderings given the different games of transition in which they are engaged. The key insight from such rationalist analysis for human rights is that neither democratic breakdown nor democratic transition is an inevitable outcome from the strategic interaction of key actors in the system. Rather, each outcome is one of many possibilities mapped out by considering all logical combinations of 'moves' in the game. Thus, those interested in democracy promotion from a human rights perspective must recognize the *contingent* nature of any transitional outcome. As we shall see, many sub-traditions within the structuralist and culturalist theoretical groupings also emphasize the contingent nature of social phenomena.

In addition to the collapse and re-emergence of democracy, game theory has also been applied to the use of torture (Wantchekon and Healy 1999). Here, a 'signalling' game is modelled using three players: the state, the torturer, and the victim. The use of torture by the state is seen as a rational strategy for either *gaining information* or *maintaining social control*, where the former is prevalent in democratic and non-democratic countries alike and the latter more prevalent in non-democratic societies (ibid.: 597). The state balances the benefits of gaining information or establishing social control against the costs of increased international outrage over the use of torture. The state carries out its torture through the use of torturers, who are further differentiated into *sadists* (who enjoy the use of torture for personal reasons), *zealots* (who actively carry out the state's wishes and obtain results at all costs), and *professionals* (who deliberate carefully over the use of torture relative to the gains that are likely to be achieved) (ibid.: 600). Victims choose first whether to reveal information and then how much to reveal once they have chosen to do so. Victims are differentiated further into four types: 'weak and guilty' (has information and is willing to reveal it), 'strong and guilty' (has information but resists attempts to extract it), 'weak and innocent' (does not have information but is likely to make a false confession), and 'strong and innocent' (does not have information and is unlikely to make a confession) (ibid.: 600).

Each of these different sets of players faces a different set of payoffs for the choices that they make, where the state provides incentives for the torturer to carry out torture, which is further mediated by the different preference orderings of the different torturers who interact with different types of victims. There is a great deal of uncertainty among the players about one another that has to be inferred from the choices or 'signals' they send to one another. The resulting game moves through a series of stages, where the equilibrium obtained is that torture takes place with a probability of 1.00, where 'the intensity and scope of torture are much higher under the social control case than under the information extraction case' (ibid.: 599). While the use of game theory to something as morally repugnant as torture seems objectionable at first glance, and while many may object to the stylized way in which the various players have been specified, the application of formal logic to the interaction of states, torturers, and victims can yield important insights into finding the structure of incentives that may reduce state propensity to rely on torture. Such formal analysis seems all the more appropriate given the propensity for democratic and non-democratic states to employ torture, an unfortunate fact made even more salient by the abuses that have been committed by US forces in Guantánamo Bay in Cuba, Bagram Air Base in Afghanistan, and Abu Ghraib Prison in Iraq, as well as the catalogue of legal reasoning produced by the Bush Administration on the trade-offs associated between extracting information and international legal obligations to protect human rights in waging the 'war on terror' (Greenberg, Dratel and Lewis 2005).

The domestic application of rationalist analysis has thus been particularly fruitful in (1) identifying the problems of collective action and why individuals may not be automatically motivated to join groups out of some sense of grievance or moral outrage, (2) demonstrating that both democratic breakdown and democratic transition are highly contingent outcomes that result from the strategic interaction of dominant actors within the political system at given moments in time, (3) and modelling the possible interactions that occur when states choose to use torture. It is also possible to combine the insights of the work on collective action and game theory to examine the ways in which social mobilization and the struggle for human rights are related to regime transition, a convergence that is discussed in more detail below. But how do these rationalist insights and tools of analysis apply to the international level of analysis? Rationalist theories of international relations and international affairs long predate rationalist theories at the domestic level, which first started appearing in the 1950s (Green and Shapiro 1994). Indeed, from Thucydides' account of the Peloponnesian War, through Machiavelli's *The Prince*, Morgenthau's *Politics among Nations*, and Waltz's *Theory of International Politics*, theorists of international affairs have used rationalist assumptions to build empirical explanations for inter-state relations and state behaviour more generally. This body of theory is broadly classified as 'realist' since it focuses on state power and the desire for enhancing state power as a prime motivating force for state action in the international arena (see Donnelly 2000).

Such state action can be carried out unilaterally, multilaterally, through alliances, peaceful negotiations, or warfare, but realists assume that these actions are motivated by the desire to maintain or enhance political power relative to other states. Since realists use the individual nation state as the basic unit of analysis rather than individual human beings, realist research in international relations engages in what has been called 'methodological nationalism' (Zürn 2002: 248). Realists have used this set of assumptions about human nature to model and explain state behaviour in international affairs, where the system of states is described as anarchic without a single authority. Variants on realism, such as balance of power theories and hegemonic stability theory, argue that a small number of powerful states dominate world affairs, contribute to long-term patterns of stability, and may guarantee the enforcement of certain norms of international behaviour (see Viotti and Kauppi 1999; Donnelly 2000). Like rationalist analysis at the domestic level, realist analysis at the international level uses the logic of collective action and game theory to demonstrate the possible combinations of choices that states make when interacting with other states, and can help explain observable patterns in discord and cooperation (see Keohane 1984: 65–109) across a range of policy areas in the international arena, such as environmental protection, trade, and arms control.

In the field of human rights, traditional realism argues that state concessions to international human rights norms is a way for states to gain short-term benefit and raise international legitimacy while counting on weak sanctions and largely unenforceable legal obligations. Thus, a realist would argue that China stands to gain in international legitimacy for agreeing to sign and ratify the two international covenants on human rights (ICCPR and ICESCR – see Table 1.2), while being able to avoid any sanctions for continued violations of human rights. The virtual absence of real enforceability behind the extant international law of human rights (or any international law for that matter) has led many realists to claim that it is merely 'epiphenomenal' and that the structure of power between and among states as they maximize their preferences remains the key determinant of political outcomes (e.g. Kennan 1951; Morgenthau 1961; Waltz 1979; Schmitz and Sikkink 2002; Donnelly 2000).

To understand state behaviour in relation to human rights in realist terms, one needs to collect empirical information on the material and/or power incentives that lie behind any choice a state makes to defend human rights. In this perspective, a state will pursue a pro-human-rights policy if and only if that policy is in line with its other geo-strategic interests. Such a view explains the apparent human rights 'double standard' of powerful states, which have at times pursued policies consistent with the promotion of human rights (e.g. interventions in Haiti in 1994 and Kosovo 1999) and at other times pursued policies that are not consistent with human rights (e.g. the absence of intervention in Rwanda in 1994). In a variant of this perspective, Krasner (1997: 143) argues that the relative power and interests of states best explain the variation in success of human rights protection. Human rights are promoted if powerful states in the world system choose to do so. For example, he shows that the slave trade in the 19th century would not have been abolished without the naval dominance of Great Britain (Krasner 1997: 152; 1999: 105–126), while the protection of minorities in Central Europe in the late 19th and early 20th centuries was a failure since the dominant powers of the day were not 'willing to enforce the norms and rules which they had themselves initially imposed' (Krasner 1997: 166).

Structuralism

While the application of rationalism and realism to human rights problems seems at first counter-intuitive, it is clear that basing explanations on self-interested motivations provides useful insights into why individuals and states make certain choices that may or may not have an impact on human rights. But rationalist and realist analyses are based on one set of assumptions and a particular ontology of the world that uses unitary actors (individuals and states) as the basic building blocks for explanations. In contrast, structuralist analysis moves away from individuals and states as unitary actors and fundamental units of analysis and focuses on the holistic aspects of society, including the interdependent relationships among individuals, collectivities, institutions, and/or organizations. Structuralist analysis is interested in the social, political, and economic networks that form between and among individuals. Adherents to this perspective insist that structures that have become reified over time constrain or facilitate social action such that individual actors are not completely free agents capable of determining particular outcomes (Lichbach 1997: 247–248). Rather, individuals are embedded in relational structures that shape their identities, interests, and interaction. Such relational structures have evolved owing to large historical processes such as capitalist development, market rationality, nation state building, political and scientific revolutions, and technological progress (Katznelson 1997: 83). And it is these large historical processes that provide both possibilities and limits for human action. Indeed, behavioural and rationalist analyses in the social sciences have 'often obscured the enduring socio-economic and political structures that mould behaviour in distinctive ways in different national contexts' (Thelen and Steinmo 1992: 1).

So-called 'classic' structuralist analysis not only identifies key structures that constrain the choices of actors, whether they be individuals or states, but posits further that relational structures actually move through time and determine particular outcomes. For example, Marxist analysis identifies class structures and the natural contradictions between them as not only moving through time, but also creating a layer of ideological identification and culture on top (i.e. superstructures) that defines the interests and actions of individuals (see below). Historical materialism thus posits a relationship between powerful and subordinate classes (owner and slave, lord and serf, bourgeoisie and proletariat) that reaches moments of incompatibility and revolutionary change. Outside strict Marxist analysis, structural analysis of regime change identifies key structures that have determined the weakening of some state forms, the collapse of others, and the rise of successful social and political revolutions that fundamentally transform the social and political organization of whole societies. For example, Barrington Moore (1966) identifies classes that result from patterns of economic development, alignments and coalitions that form between and among these different classes, and the variable role of state power in explaining the rise of liberal democracy, fascism, and socialism. Theda Skocpol (1979) identifies class structures, class alignments and state power as key 'causal variables' that account for the positive and negative instances of social revolution. Gregory Luebbert (1991) compares different class coalitions across twelve European countries to explain differences in political outcomes (liberalism, fascism, social democracy) during the inter-war years.

While such studies focus on macro-historical domestic change, structuralists have also sought to identify global structures and posit explanations for how their movement through time explains particular outcomes. For example, in the 1960s dependency theorists identified a certain division of labour in the world between the 'core' of industrialized countries and the 'periphery' of developing countries to explain persistent patterns of underdevelopment in the world (Baran 1975; Cardoso and Faletto 1979; Lewellen 1995; Todaro 1997). Peripheral countries face unfair advantages in their terms of trade, access to foreign capital, and ability to make maximal use of their own factor endowments in ways that would promote economic growth with equity. Strong versions of dependency theory argue that core countries intentionally created conditions that would keep peripheral countries underdeveloped, while weaker versions argued that the core–periphery relationship was a natural outgrowth of global capitalist expansion. Although largely discredited by the 'neo-liberal counter-revolution' throughout the 1970s and 1980s (Todaro 1997), new research has begun to incorporate 'world position' in the global economy as an important variable that may mediate other important empirical relationships, such as that between economic development and democracy (Burkhart and Lewis-Beck 1994; Boix and Stokes 2003; Foweraker and Landman 2004). Moreover, research on the GATT/WTO continues to emphasize the structural disadvantage of developing countries in their terms of trade (Pogge 2002; Steinberg, Barton, Goldstein and Josling 2005) as those countries with large markets (i.e. the US and EU countries) continue to structure the rules of the game in their favour.

Beyond such large and arguably more intangible structures as 'class', 'class coalitions', 'state power', and the 'global division of labour', social scientists also focus their attention on institutions as structures, which also have a constraining effect on individual and state action. At the domestic level, institutions include political parties and the structure of political party systems, organs of the state (treasury, military, social security and welfare), and governmental institutions, such as the executive, legislative, and judicial branches, as well as different electoral systems. For example, actors are differently constrained under presidential systems than parliamentary systems (e.g. countries in the Americas versus countries in Europe), under proportional (e.g. the Netherlands) than plurality systems (e.g. the United States), and under unitary (e.g. the United Kingdom) than federal systems (e.g. Brazil).

Outside the formal institutions of government, there are non-governmental domestic institutions such as large trade union organizations, business organizations, church organizations and hierarchies, and family and other civil society organizations. Much of the activity of political party organizations reaches deep into society and does not necessarily involve the organs of government. As Chapter 2 in this volume made clear, there are many institutions and organizations in civil society that may have quite detrimental effects on the protection of human rights despite the general tendency to assume that such organizations are inherently good for human rights. There are also quasi-non-governmental institutions in society that transgress the divide between the state and society. For example, there are those organizations that bring peak associations of society (i.e. labour and business) together either coercively or voluntarily into the 'corporatist' organs of the state (e.g. Schmitter and Lehmbruch 1979; Hague, Harrop and Breslin 1992: 224). The experience in the advanced industrial democracies has been one of voluntary formation of such associations, sometimes referred to as 'society-led corporatism', while in developing countries, especially those in Latin America, such organizations have been organized through less voluntary means, sometime referred to as 'state-led corporatism'.

At the international level, institutions include many of the public organizations considered in Chapter 2 of this volume, such as the United Nations, the European Union, the OECD, OPEC, the Organization of American States, among many others. There are also international laws and the mechanisms for enforcement (however weak they may be) that have been the subject of institutional analysis that examines the degree to which state behaviour is constrained. Unlike rationalist and realist analyses, which employ a 'logic of consequences' to understand state choice and state behaviour, international institutional analysis concentrates more on a 'logic of appropriateness' that guides state action through reference to the expectations generated through the establishment of international institutions (March and Olsen 1998).

Structuralist analysis provides many additional factors to those found in rationalist and realist approaches that may account for the variation in human rights protection. Analysis that focuses on class structure and the structure of social relations at the domestic level examines the ways in which individual access to justice, enjoyment and exercise of rights, and realization of rights may be constrained or facilitated by an individual's social location. Human rights scholarship has long sought to demonstrate that individuals living in poverty often experience a different *de facto* realization of human rights, not only economic and social rights (almost by definition), but also civil and political rights. Those living in poverty, on balance, have less access to the kind of economic resources that are necessary for adequate healthcare, education, and welfare services, which may in turn affect the degree to which they enjoy their civil and political rights. Many criminal justice systems tend to provide differential treatment for those individuals that are poor, such that they may experience disproportionate cruel and inhuman treatment while in custody and may receive harsher sentencing once convicted.

At the international level, human rights arguments claim that countries at a structural disadvantage in the global capitalist system have difficulty in overseeing successful models of development that not only produce growth with equity, but also provide the kinds of resources necessary for the full protection of civil and political rights. Systemic approaches, such as dependency theory or theories critical towards processes of economic globalization privilege the difficult circumstances in which developing counties find themselves and that have a long-term impact on the ability of countries to bring about the kinds of changes necessary for the establishment of 'rights-protective' regimes (Donnelly 1999a). For example, in his critique of unfair trade relations, Pogge (2002: 3) argues that owing to their relative market size the advanced industrial countries (or the top quintile of wealthy countries) have manipulated the global trading system to such a degree that their total income gains from trade between the late 1980s and early 1990s grew more than twice as much as the mean of world income. The population of the high-income countries (903 million) have about 79.7 per cent of global income, while the population of the poorest economies (2.8 billion) have about 1.2 per cent of global income. The continued maldistribution of income is directly related to an increase in poverty-related deaths within the developing world that could be avoided with a minor restructuring of the global capitalist system that transfers approximately 1 per cent of GDP from the rich countries to the poor (Pogge 2002: 2; see also UNDP 1999).

Institutional approaches examine how the variety of institutional forms at the domestic and international levels may have an impact on human rights protection. For example, across a sample of democratic countries, Foweraker and Landman (2002) find that presidential regimes have worse records of democratic performance than parliamentary regimes, where the main areas of difference centre on their ability to protect civil, property, and minority rights. At the international level, regime analysis examines the relative strength of the international human rights regime to enforce human rights norms. For Donnelly, the international human rights regime has an extensive and coherent set of norms across the various categories of rights (see Chapter 1 in this volume), which form an 'interdependent and synergistically interactive system of guarantees'; however, states maintain virtual autonomy in implementing them and the regime itself has limited decision-making powers (Donnelly 1986: 607–608, 619). Thus, at best, the regime as an institution is a strong promotional one that is lacking in real capacity for international enforcement (Donnelly 1986: 614; 2003: 130–131).

Culturalism

Pure rational and structural approaches provide two extreme points of an explanatory triangle in the social sciences, where one extreme focuses on the choices that individuals and states make (rational agents without structure) and the other extreme examines social outcomes that are the product of large, historical, and embedded structures (without autonomous agents). While the division between these extremes does represent a false dichotomy (discussed further below), there is a third point to the explanatory triangle that needs to be addressed first before moving on to the ways in which these theoretical perspectives have been integrated (Lichbach 1997; Hay 2002; Landman 2005b). Cultural approaches represent this third point. Like structural analysis, cultural analysis seeks an understanding of social phenomena by focusing on the broader holistic and shared aspects of collectivities of individuals and states. But rather than look at the relational networks and institutions, they focus on the shared meanings, inter-subjective understandings, and norms that develop between and among individuals and states. In contrast to rationalist analysis, single individual interests and actions cannot be understood in isolation, but must be placed in the context of the shared understandings, inter-subjective relationships, and mutual orientations that make human communities possible (Lichbach 1997: 246–247). These shared meanings and understandings form broader cultures and communities that can be grouped together and analysed as whole units. Such cultures and communities are held together by certain social rules that are emblematic of the identities of both the individuals and the groups themselves (ibid.: 247). Identifying the boundaries of these cultural units and separate identities remains problematic for systematic social scientific research; however, scholars have tried to examine the world views, rituals, and symbols that provide 'systems of meaning and the structure and intensity of . . . identity' across different geographical regions of the world (Ross 1997: 43–44).

As in the discussion of rationalism and structuralism, there are a number of culturalist approaches in the social sciences that vary according to the degree to which universal knowledge claims about the world can be made and the degree to which comparative inferences are possible across different cultural contexts. First, one set of culturalist approaches adopts an anthropological perspective and focuses on in-depth ethnographic analysis (see Chapter 4 in this volume) of localized systems of meaning and shared understanding among particular sets of human beings. The scope of such analysis tends to be quite focused on the subject population, the context in which they live, and their understandings of their own social world. The anthropologist is always cognizant about the degree to which his or her presence in the subject community has an impact on its value orientations, norms, and belief systems, while at the same time trying to elicit evidence and information on that very set of factors within the community in order to make a contribution to the study of human populations. Research in this set of culturalist analysis tends to avoid making cross-national generalizations and focuses rather on the specific ways in which different human communities are formed and establish meanings, shared systems of belief and the construction of collective identities.

Second, some culturalists expand the scope of the subject population to conduct cross-national comparative research on attitudes, values, norms, and beliefs using mass public-survey instruments and tracking the 'culture shift' (Inglehart 1990) between and within different countries. Such an approach is radically different from the first, since it accepts that universal knowledge claims and valid cross-national comparisons are possible. For example, there is a long tradition of trying to study 'political culture' in order to understand the different ways in which citizens identify with politics in general, and democratic politics in particular. The seminal work *Civic Culture* (Almond and Verba 1963) compared the value orientation and identification of citizens towards their respective political systems in the United States, Germany, Italy, and Mexico. This research agenda and approach has been expanded to include analysis of political culture in advanced industrial democracies (Inglehart 1977, 1990) and many countries in the developing world (Inglehart 1997). Related social scientific research deploys an equivalent theoretical focus and tools of analysis to examine the causes and consequences of 'social trust' and 'social capital' (e.g. Whiteley 1999, 2000; Putnam 2002).

Third, some culturalist analysis looks at the ways in which social practices 'construct' norms and beliefs at the domestic and international levels (Wendt 1999; Green 2002), and how the analysis of 'discourse' itself as a cultural practice is a fruitful way in which to analyse social phenomena (Howarth 1995, 2000a). These forms of culturalist analysis question the degree to which independent knowledge of the world is possible and whether social science can engage in positing causal explanations for observed events and outcomes. The production of independent knowledge assumes that the observer has no influence or impact on that which he or she is observing. As noted above, many anthropologists seek to limit the connection between the observer and the subject population, but analysts adopting the kind of culturalist analysis in this third category assume that such a distancing is problematic. Rather, the perspective suggests that knowledge claims about the world are a function of the 'discursive power of the putative knower' (Fearon and Wendt 2002: 57) and therefore *relative* to the subject position of that knower. Explanations within this form of culturalist analysis tend to be constitutive rather than causal, where the focus is not on causes and effects as independent phenomena but on the 'conditions of possibility' for events, outcomes, and objects of inquiry, how they are constructed and how they are organized (Fearon and Wendt 2002: 58).

This outline of the different types of culturalist analysis is by no means exhaustive, but it gives an indication of how this form of analysis is internally differentiated as well as externally differentiated from rational and structural analysis. There has been wide application of culturalist analysis to important questions in the field of human rights and there has been a natural tension between the universal aspirations of the human rights project and the focus of most culturalist analysis on the particular ways in which knowledge of the world is organized, shared, and understood. Indeed, for much of the half-century after the 1948 Universal Declaration of Human Rights, culturalist analysis adopting an anthropological approach was either outright hostile to or deeply sceptical of the idea of universal human rights grounded in liberal and rational individualism (Messer 1993; Freeman 2002a; Wilson and Mitchell 2003). Indeed, during this period anthropological analysis has been criticized for its relative disinterest in human rights stemming from five main factors: (1) its insistence that human rights are culturally relative, (2) its advocacy of collective and indigenous rights over individual rights, (3) its commitment to action in the field to overcome certain forms of oppression, (4) the sensitivity of doing field research, and (5) its use of small-scale sociocultural analysis that moves away from questions of sovereign states and rights-based legal systems (Messer 1993: 221–222).

Against this general critique, however, anthropologists and those engaged in similar such cultural approaches have demonstrated that human rights problems have featured in a vast array of extant studies and that the discipline of anthropology can make and has made a valuable contribution to the practice of human rights. Extant studies have examined the cultural relativity of human rights through regional research (e.g. conceptions of 'people' and social relations of power in Africa, the privileging of development and the analysis of religious conceptions of duties and obligations in Asia, and the focus on indigenous rights and state brutality in Latin America); religious research on the transcendence of nationally based identities; and cross-cutting research on such topics as women's and children's rights (Messer 1993: 227–235; see also Hurrell 1999: 294–297). The main contribution today starts from the basic formulation that if human rights are culturally relative, then how can cultural approaches 'identify commonalities and structure interpretations so that essential human rights are universally respected' (Messer 1993: 227). But this contribution is set against the two main challenges of how 'to achieve unity in basic human rights practices without destroying cultural diversity' and how 'to bring about respect for an ever expanding corpus of human rights without watering down the concept' (Messer 1993: 322). Indeed, in light of the expansion of rights discourse and rights mechanisms, Wilson and Mitchell (2003: 4) argue:

> The culture concept and its accompanying discourse of relativism no longer seems appropriate to the task. Clearly, there are problems in translating a global rights language to the local level, and there are slippages between how officials use rights and how people understand them in their everyday lives, but the old relativist vision of a "clash of cultures", or the polarities of tradition vs. modernity, or western vs. non-western are too crude to generate much insight.

The second type of culturalist analysis outlined above sidesteps many of these questions by trying to capture identification with and understandings of human rights through the aggregation of individual responses to survey questions related to human rights concerns. From this perspective, progress toward a 'culture of human rights' can be studied through the different ways in which mass publics express their knowledge of human rights and their understanding about the different types of human rights. For example, the Home Office of the United Kingdom interviewed 10,000 respondents to gauge the degree to which the British public knew about the existence of the 1998 Human Rights Act, the different kinds of human rights that are meant to be protected, and the degree to which there ought to be a balance between rights and responsibilities (Home Office 2003). The *World Values Survey* project routinely asks mass publics across the world whether they identify in general with the idea of human rights. In the context of its research on democracy and support for democratic institutions, the *World Barometer* surveys have many questions on institutions of governance and the protection of liberties. Such cross-national culturalist analysis rests on the assumption that the same set of questions can be asked to different sets of respondents from different countries and that their general understanding of what is being asked remains the same.

The third type of culturalist analysis borrows heavily from linguistic theory in an effort to understand how ideas are constructed through historical and iterative practices. At the domestic level, discourse analysts examine the ways in which different identities are constructed through the discursive practices of grouping different individuals or ideas into homogeneous categories (i.e. *the logic of equivalence*) or grouping similar individuals or ideas into different categories (i.e. *the logic of difference*) (Howarth 2000a: 106–107). In the former case, the attempt to group together putatively different individuals or ideas is done to construct a greater 'whole' ($a + b + c$) that is then drawn in opposition (or antagonism) to another grouping of individuals or ideas (d). In the latter case, the attempt to deconstruct an existing grouping of individuals or ideas (breaking the chain of equivalence between a, b, and c) is done to disempower, fragment, and weaken existing antagonisms. These analytical categories have been applied to a variety of empirical examples relevant to human rights, such as the construction of Black Consciousness and non-racial democracy in South Africa (Howarth 2000b), women's struggles in Chiapas, Mexico (Harvey and Halverson 2000), Provisionalism and justice in Northern Ireland (Clohesy 2000), and New Labour's attempt to construct a human rights discourse around the enactment of the 1998 Human Rights Act in the United Kingdom (Clohesy 2005).

At the international level discursive analyses question the 'essentializing' and 'universalizing' tendencies within human rights discourse (Hurrell 1999: 298) as it seeks to construct its own form of international social, legal, and political hegemony, where rights concerns 'trump' all other claims and entitlements made by individuals and groups. The many human rights declarations start by claiming inalienable and inherent sets of rights drawn from the fact of human existence and then move on to declare that since we are all human we all have such rights, thereby negating any claim to differentiate individuals or any alternative claims that may arise from human communities. Thus, during the latter half of the 20th century there has been a 'particular construction of right and wrong in international relations' that has become increasingly articulated through an appeal to human rights (Donnelly 1999b: 100). Before the Universal Declaration, human rights were not a concern within international relations or international law since realism saw human rights as irrelevant to the national interest defined in terms of power and the legal positivists saw human rights as the pure prerogative of states (see also Freeman 2002b; Landman 2005b). But despite these limitations, states have continued to pursue moral objectives in international relations, the major form of which can be traced through the proliferation of human rights instruments, enforcement mechanisms, and monitoring procedures (Donnelly 1999b).

Areas of convergence

These three theoretical perspectives have thus far been addressed separately for ease of presentation, discussion, and comprehension, but it is clear both from a theoretical and a practical view that they should not necessarily be considered mutually exclusive, where there are significant areas of convergence between and among the perspectives at the domestic and international levels. In this sense, beyond the three points of the explanatory triangle (rationalism, structuralism, and culturalism) there are three *sides* of the triangle that depict the interaction between the various perspectives (structure–agency, structure–culture, culture–agency) and there is the *space* within the triangle that captures the interaction among the various perspectives (socially embedded acts). Moreover, the explanatory triangle has been applied to empirical problems at the domestic and international levels, as well as to the interaction between the domestic and international levels. This final section explores these areas of convergence at the various levels of analysis and how they have been and can be applied to the study of human rights.

There has been a very long debate in the social sciences about the structure vs. agency problem. On one hand, an extreme structuralist would argue that the world is comprised of 'agentless structures' and that the explanation of social phenomena necessarily rests on examining such structures in the ways outlined above. On the other hand, an extreme rationalist would argue that the world is comprised of 'structureless agents' and that explanation of social phenomena necessarily rests on examining the strategic interaction of such agents in the ways outlined above. The debate between these two extremes has moved on in many productive ways, however, such that even the most die-hard rationalists will now concede some role for the influence of structure on the choice of agents and equally the most die-hard structuralists will concede some role for agency in the face of constraining structures. Indeed, it was Karl Marx ([1851] 1978b: 595) who claimed that 'Men make their own history' (i.e. agency) . . . 'but they do not make it just as they please; they do not make it under circumstances chosen by themselves, but under circumstances directly found, given, and transmitted from the past' (i.e. the influence of structure).

Hay (2002: 89–134) provides an excellent overview of this debate, and shows that two common solutions to this problem are 'structuration theory' (Giddens 1976, 1979, 1981) and 'critical realism' (Bhaskar 1975, 1986; Archer 1995), while offering a third solution that moves beyond these two, which he calls a 'strategic relational' approach (Hay 2002: 117). In the Giddens view, structure and agency represent different sides of the same ontological coin, while remaining analytically distinct. Structures are both the product of and medium for conduct, while social relations are structured through time and space (Hay 2002: 118–121). For critical realism, structure and agency are both ontologically and analytically separate, where only theory provides the means through which to reveal a structured reality of the world that lies beneath the everyday appearances that present themselves to our senses (Hay 2002: 122–126). In both these solutions to the structure and agency debate, structure is either claimed to be mutually constitutive of agency or lying deeply beneath the more superficial observed actions of agents.

The strategic relational solution to the debate follows more in line with the former approach than the latter in specifying separate spheres for the strategic actor and the 'strategically selective context', which come together in any one strategic calculation that is made in context (Hay 2002: 131). In other words, the strategic relational approach suggests that all choices take place within certain selective contexts and that any decision is always made in relation to certain constraints. For Hay, these constraints are considered 'context', but his use of context elides structure and culture as having an impact on agency rather than keeping them as separate spheres. For example, he provides competing explanations for the rise of Fascism in Germany that use socio-economic structural factors, cultural factors, and historical factors, which he groups together under the general category of 'context'.

As this chapter has made clear, however, such an elision between structure and culture muddies the theoretical waters, where it is empirically useful to maintain a special and separate role for structure and culture, while exploring the relationship between the two. Again, Karl Marx is instructive for the relationship between structure and culture, where for him the underlying social relations of production were related to an overarching ideological superstructure that maintained certain exploitative practices through long periods of time. Culturalists have long analysed the relationship between underlying social structures (e.g. the economy and the occupational system) and expressive symbolism and system of meanings. Indeed, there has been much analysis on 'class culture' in modern industrialized societies and how (and whether) cultures and value systems shift when such societies make the transition to post-industrialism (Bell 1976; Inglehart 1990, 1997; Wilensky 2002: 186–208).

Just as it is important to maintain a separation between structure and culture, it is equally important to maintain the separation between agency and culture to make possible an exploration of the ways in which certain cultural understandings and systems of meanings are born of the choices and practices of individuals, as well as the ways in which such systems of meaning and belief constrain the types of choices that individuals make. Like the strategic-relational approach, the discourse-analytic approach outlined above sees agency and culture as mutually constitutive, where choices and the solution to problems of collective action are found in the cultural realm. For example, Griggs and Howarth (2000) show how 'not in my back yard (NIMBY)' homeowners formed alliances with radical green protestors and constructed an identity around 'vegans and Volvos' to overcome their problem of collective action to fight against the proposed airport expansion in Manchester. In this way, the traditional use of 'selective incentives' was not seen to be enough and identity politics at the cultural level provided the added impetus to forge an unlikely alliance to fight for a common cause. At the international level, social constructivists have long argued that international norms and state choices are mutually constitutive, where state behaviour may create new norms that in turn constrain the choices that states make in the future. Again, ideas, beliefs, norms, and values, it is argued, provide the added impetus for states to cooperate.

These developments suggest that there have been important processes of theoretical convergence at the domestic and international levels, which have consequences for the study of human rights. At the domestic level, Lichbach (1997: 260–267) has maintained the threefold distinction between rationalist, structuralist, and culturalist approaches, but draws on Talcott Parsons (1937) and Max Weber ([1924] 1968) to synthesize these perspectives through the idea of the 'socially embedded unit act'. At the individual level, the unit act involves an individual whose world is 'partially under his or her control', where 'desires and beliefs direct action' (Lichbach 1997: 261). At a collective level, the unit act comprises a set of individuals, where individual desires reflect and produce social norms, individual beliefs influence material conditions, and individual actions are aggregated. In taking into account both levels, 'Individuals are therefore more or less intentional agents who make history, society, conditions, and rules and yet history, society, conditions, and rules make individuals' (Lichbach 1997: 263). It is plausible to argue that a similar convergence applies at the international level, where states are more or less intentional agents who make history, international society, conditions, and international rules (law and regimes) and yet history, international society, and rules also make states. The notions of 'embedded liberalism' (Ruggie 1982) and 'progressive enmeshment' (Hurrell 1999) capture this synthesis since the spread of democracy, international commerce, and the formation of inter-governmental institutions have meant a greater constraint on state action even though such processes are the result of state action in the first place. For example, research on the 'Kantian Tripod' shows that three factors identified in Kant's perpetual peace – civic republican states, international commerce, and international organizations – have served to limit the probability of inter-state conflict (see, e.g. Russett and Oneal 2001).

This 'double convergence' (Landman 2005b) in empirical theory at the domestic and international levels is particularly useful for studying human rights. As outlined in Chapter 1 of this volume, the history of rights is rooted in groups overcoming their problems of collective action in particular contexts to press for their demands to be heard, while the advance of the legal protection of rights flows from states having granted such protection. The domestic fight for rights has been internationalized through a variety of state and non-state actors (see Chapter 2 in this volume) that have established a set of institutions, laws, and expectations about appropriate behaviour of states towards their own citizens. In this way, the embedded unit acts at both the domestic and international levels have created the international human rights system, which continues to provide the discourse and leverage for individuals and groups living in contexts where rights protections are precarious to struggle for their greater protection. The comparative studies found in *The Power of Human Rights* (Risse, Ropp and Sikkink 1999) and a further excellent study of the struggle for human rights in Chile (Hawkins 2002) show how the inter-relationships between and among rationalism, structuralism, and culturalism at the domestic and international levels provide valuable insight and explanatory power for understanding the ways in which the transmission of human rights norms can take place.

Theorizing human rights

This chapter has presented the three dominant areas of empirical theory in the social sciences at the domestic and international levels. It outlined their main assumptions, differences, contributions, points of convergence, and application to the study of human rights. Table 3.1 on pages 56 and 57 summarizes these three areas across different levels of analysis and specifies their various sub-traditions, units of analysis, assumptions, and propositions about human rights protection. While not representing an exhaustive reading of empirical theories, the areas of agreement and difference, or their full applicability to human rights problems, the discussion in this chapter has shown how the different theoretical perspectives provide important lenses through which to view human rights problems. The fact that many of these perspectives appear as hostile to the idea of human rights or counter-intuitive as tools to understand their protection actually represents their many strengths. The fact that human rights violations occur on a regular and daily basis all around the world means that we cannot explain them away as an unfortunate irrational feature of the world. Rather, we need to understand the rational, structural, and cultural basis for their continued occurrence in an effort to provide solutions that will lead to their elimination.

Suggestions for further reading

Forsythe, D. P. (2000) *Human Rights in International Relations*, Cambridge: Cambridge University Press.

Krasner, S. D. (1999) *Sovereignty: Organized Hypocrisy*, Princeton, NJ: Princeton University Press.

Lichbach, M. (2003) *Is Rational Choice Theory All of Social Science?*, Ann Arbor: University of Michigan Press.

Lichbach, M. and Zuckerman, A. (eds) (1997) *Comparative Politics: Rationality, Culture, and Structure*, Cambridge: Cambridge University Press.

Ritzer, G. and Smart, B. (eds) (2001) *Handbook of Social Theory*, Thousand Oaks, CA: Sage.

Table 3.1 Theoretical traditions in empirical social science and their relation to the protection of human rights

Theory group	Level of analysis	Sub-traditions	Unit of analysis	Assumptions	Propositions about human rights protection (positive and negative)
Rationalist	Domestic	Rational choice Public choice Game theory	Individual actors 'methodological individualism'	Instrumental rationality Material self-interest Utility maximization Collective irrationality	Problem of collective action in the struggle for human rights 'Reasons of state' subordinate rights protections internally (e.g. anti-terror)
	International	Realism Structural realism Neo-realism Game theory	Individual states 'methodological nationalism'	State as unitary rational actor States act to maintain or enhance power Strategic interaction Logic of consequences for state action	Human rights are a concern if in the geo-strategic interests of powerful states
Structuralist	Domestic	Marxism Institutionalism State theory Modernization theory	Collectivities Institutions Inter-relationships Legal constraints	Constrained individual agency (e.g. by class structures, institutions, state power) Historical 'movement' of structures	Constitutional arrangements and institutional design can protect rights Socio-economic structures can undermine or support rights
	International	Marxism Dependency theory Neo-liberal institutionalism	World systems Global power 'polarities' International legal order International institutions	Constrained state agency (e.g. by global capitalist structures, international institutions, legal orders) Mutual gain through institutions	Growth and effectiveness of the international human rights regime and international law Global economic structure maintains global injustice

Culturalist				
	Domestic	Historical institutionalism Discourse theory Post-modernism	Clusters of meaning Shared understandings Inter-subjectivity Belief systems/norms	Norms, beliefs, and ideas are socially constructed Individual identity and agency are culturally determined	Rights discourse can mobilize oppressed peoples Rights discourse may be relative
	International	Constructivism Globalization of culture Value diffusion Legal proceduralism	Clusters of meaning Shared understandings Inter-subjectivity International norms	Norms, beliefs, and ideas are socially constructed Individual identity and agency are culturally determined Logic of appropriateness for state action	International human rights norms shape state behaviour

Sources: Higgins (1994), Lichbach (1997), Krasner (1997, 1999), Donnelly (2000), Wendt (1999), Mearsheimer (2001), Hay (2002), Fearon and Wendt (2002), Snidal (2002), Adler (2002), Simmons and Martin (2002), Landman (2005b).

4 Social science methods and human rights

The primary function of method in the social sciences is to establish a direct connection between the main research question, the empirical theories used to provide possible answers to the question, the propositions they make about the social phenomena under investigation (or the observable implications of a particular theory), and the collection of evidence that may or may not support these propositions (King, Keohane and Verba 1994; Landman 2000a, 2003). In this way, methods establish the ground rules of any enquiry, specify the types of knowledge that are possible given the theoretical expectations and assumptions of the researcher, and set the parameters for how evidence is collected and analysed. There is thus no one preferred method. Rather, method is a function of the research question that is posed, the theories used to help answer the question, and the epistemological orientation of the researcher. This volume has made it clear that at a bare minimum, social scientific analysis of human rights should be able to make meaningful analytical statements about observed (and in some instances, unobserved) social phenomena that either specifically involve human rights or are related in some important way. It is committed to enhancing the types of inferences that can be drawn about the variable protection and lived experience of human rights around the world.

With these initial statements in mind, this chapter provides an overview of the methodological options available to scholars and practitioners wishing to explain and understand human rights problems from a social scientific perspective. This overview is organized across three inter-related dimensions that frame the overall analysis of human rights problems. The first dimension represents an 'epistemological continuum' ranging across methodological approaches that vary according to the types of knowledge claims they make (universal vs. particular), the type of reasoning that connects their theory and evidence (inductive vs. deductive), the balance between evidence and inference, and the scope of coverage for their evidence (from sub-national units and single countries to global comparisons). The second dimension deepens the discussion concerning the degree to which cross-national comparisons and empirical generalizations frame the analysis of human rights problems; examining the general methodological trade-off between the 'ladder of abstraction' (Sartori 1970; Mair 1996) in the concepts that are used and the scope of units that form the basis of the analysis (Landman 2000a, 2002, 2003). The third dimension concerns the relative balance or mix between quantitative and qualitative evidence used in making inferences about human rights problems. These three methodological dimensions and their implications for human rights research are considered in turn.

An epistemological continuum

In an influential essay on the divisions in the discipline of political science, Gabriel Almond (with Genco 1977: 489) argued that Karl Popper's (1972) metaphors of 'clouds' and 'clocks' to describe the continuum between indeterminacy and determinacy in physical systems equally apply to questions in political science research. On one end of the continuum, the cloud metaphor captures the irregular, disorderly, and unpredictable nature of things (e.g. swarms of gnats and flies), while on the other end of the continuum, the clock metaphor captures the regular, orderly, and predictable nature of things (e.g. pendulums, precision clocks, and motor cars). While Almond applies these metaphors and their challenges to research in political science, it is entirely possible to extend their application to the social sciences to argue that social science methods and research continue to vary a great deal across this continuum from those approaches that concentrate on the indeterminate and unpredictable cloudlike aspects of the social world to those that concentrate on its determinate and predictable clocklike aspects. The continuum has also been described as ranging from 'soft' interpretative and descriptive approaches to 'hard' rigorous and analytical approaches, but as we will see, the notion of rigour can apply to a wider range of methods and research than is typically understood (see King, Keohane and Verba 1994; Brady and Collier 2004). Table 4.1 lays out this continuum and specifies seven main categories of social science methods ranging from 'soft' hermeneutic approaches to 'hard' nomothetic approaches, which are further broken down by the type of reasoning, the balance between evidence and inference, the nature of the knowledge claims that each purports to make, and the scope of their empirical coverage. The table also includes examples from extant human rights research that fall within each of these different categories of analysis.

The hermeneutic and 'thick-description' (Geertz 1973) end of the continuum (Column I) contains those approaches that rely on descriptive and interpretative analysis of the social world, using a variety of qualitative methods such as participant observation, in-depth interviews and ethnographic methods, oral histories and narratives, archival documentation, and formal and informal discourses of individuals, as well as images, symbols, constructs, and architectures (see Devine 1995; Travers 2001; Howarth 2005: 335–343). The goal of research that adopts these methods is to *understand* the nature and meaning of the social world that is constructed by the subject population under investigation. Less emphasis is placed on *explanation* of that social world, and there is rarely an attempt to make generalizations that extend too far beyond the evidence that has been examined. In this way, these approaches make knowledge claims that are limited to the particular social phenomena under investigation rather than make knowledge claims that have universal applicability. The units of analysis in such approaches tend to be individuals and groups that share common features and identities, sub-national units and geographical spaces, and single countries. Methodological criticisms of these approaches argue that pure descriptive studies have little social scientific value, since they are 'atheoretical' and 'interpretative' (Lijphart 1971: 691), 'configurative–ideographic' (Eckstein 1975), and may simply provide 'evidence without inference' (Almond 1996: 52). But scholars who adopt these approaches (and many who do not) argue that such in-depth studies, while not seeking universal applicability, have tremendous inherent value, are full of inferences that add to our pool of knowledge about the social world, and have significant practical and policy implications (Hirschman 1970; Geertz 1973; Almond 1996; Landman 2000a, 2003; Flyvberg 2001).

Table 4.1 The epistemological/methodological continuum of the social sciences

Range	I	II	III	IV	V	VI	VII
Type of approach	Hermeneutic/thick description	Discourse analysis	Theory-driven empirical	Theory-driven empirical	Theory-driven empirical	Theory-driven empirical	Nomothetic
Reasoning	Inductive	Inductive and analytical	Inductive and analytical	Inductive and analytical	Inductive and analytical	Deductive and analytical	Deductive
Evidence vs. inference	'Evidence without inference'	Meaning and understanding from language and action	Qualitative evidence and inference	Quantitative/qualitative evidence and inference	Quantitative evidence and inference	Inference with confirmatory evidence	'Inference without evidence'
Nature of knowledge claim	Particular Context-specific	Particular Context-specific	Universal with room for exceptions	Universal with room for exceptions	Universal with room for exceptions	Universal	Universal
Scope of coverage	Single countries Sub-national analysis	Single countries Limited comparison	Comparative and single-case analysis	Comparative	Global comparative	Small-N comparative	Theoretical constructs only
Examples in human rights research	Goldstein (1996) The Spectacular City; Huggins et al. (2002) Violence Workers	Norval (1996) Deconstructing Apartheid Discourse; Roniger and Sznajder (1999) The Legacy of Human Rights Violations in the Southern Cone	Risse, Ropp and Sikkink (1999) The Power of Human Rights; Hawkins (2002) International Human Rights and Authoritarian Rule in Chile	Foweraker and Landman (1997) Citizenship Rights and Social Movements; Gómez (2003) Human Rights in Cuba, El Salvador, and Nicaragua	Poe and Carey (2004) Understanding Human Rights Violations; Landman (2005) Protecting Human Rights	Mitchell (2004) Agents of Atrocity	Wantchekon and Healy (1999) 'The "Game" of Torture'

Two examples of empirical research relevant to human rights that fit into this category of research include Huggins *et al.*'s (2002) study of police torturers and murderers in Brazil and Goldstein's (2004) study of vigilante violence in Villa Pagador in Cochabamba, Bolivia. Both studies adopted ethnographic methods, in-depth interviews, and interpretative analysis to understand why and how human rights violations have occurred in particular economic, social, and political contexts. While their analyses are grounded in the particular contexts of Brazil and Bolivia, the accounts are located in larger questions concerning the motivations for violent action, the conditions and settings in which they take place, and the larger understandings and cultural meanings of the violence that stretch beyond the confines of the subject population under investigation. In the Brazilian study, the analysis examines a sample of twenty-three former and serving police officers whose careers spanned the prolonged period of authoritarian rule (1964–1985) and who became either direct perpetrators or 'atrocity facilitators' in carrying out systematic torture and extra-judicial killings. Its methods include network analysis (see Scott 2000) of the sample of police officers, deconstruction of the categories of 'victims' and 'perpetrators', and storytelling from the violence workers themselves (Huggins, Haritos-Fatouros and Zimbardo 2002: 17–28). This combination of methods is used to weave together five significant themes that influenced the memories, perceptions, and consequences of their actions: secrecy, occupational insularity, organizational fragmentation, personal isolation and the changing nature of the Brazilian state (Huggins *et al.* 2002: 2).

In similar fashion, Goldstein uses evidence collected through participant-observation to examine the ways in which public 'spectacles' of seasonal festivals and vigilante violence represent forms of local expression of citizenship and modes of action that recapture control of individual and collective security in the face of enhanced socio-economic marginality. In making justice 'by one's own hands' the attempted and actual lynchings of thieves by the residents of Villa Pagador 'form a spectacular cultural performance, a means for people ordinarily excluded from the political, economic, and social mainstreams of Bolivian society to force themselves violently into the public eye' (Goldstein 2004: 3). By comparing these violent activities with other public spectacles such as the annual Fiesta de San Miguel, Goldstein (2004: 2–4) argues that not only do they represent 'vivid, visual displays of collective identity for barrio residents' but also 'a claim to citizenship and a demand for citizens' rights in a context of political, legal, and socio-economic exclusion'. These 'dramas of citizenship' (Holston and Appadurai 1999: 14) are part of a larger crisis in contemporary Bolivia, where poverty and social exclusion have resulted from the prolonged implementation of neo-liberal economic programmes and the violation of human rights has increased under prosecuting the 'war on drugs'.

The next category in the continuum (Column II) includes those approaches that adopt discourse-analytic techniques to problem areas in the social sciences. Such analysis is much akin to hermeneutic analysis in that it seeks to elucidate 'problematized objects of study by seeking their description, understanding, and interpretation' (Howarth 2005: 319). The goal of such analysis is to produce new interpretations about specific objects of investigation through either uncovering phenomena previously obscured and undetected by dominant social scientific theories and approaches or by 'problematizing existing accounts and articulating alternative interpretations' (Howarth 2005: 320). Such analysis relies on inductive and analytical reasoning that examines the social and political 'logics' at work in the construction of meanings, understandings, and articulatory practices. Such meanings and understandings are obtained through an analysis of language and action, which are seen as mutually constitutive phenomena. Like its hermeneutic counterpart, discourse analysis eschews making universal generalizations and tends to analyse small sub-national units and single countries, although it has begun to explore ways in which to carry out comparative analysis that is 'problem-driven', but does not sacrifice attention to historical context and concrete specificities of the cases under comparison (Howarth 2005: 332).

Two examples that fit into this category of method and analysis include Norval's (1996) study of the construction of apartheid in South Africa and Roniger and Sznajder's (1999) comparative study of the legacies of human rights violations in Argentina, Chile, and Uruguay. While Norval's (1996) study is more wedded to post-Marxist and post-structural social theory, both studies analyse the ways in which discursive practices and understandings constructed coercive systems with grave consequences for human rights that have lasted well beyond the actual periods of authoritarianism. In line with the international legal definition of apartheid as a 'crime against humanity' (see Buergenthal 1995: 67–68; Ghandhi 2002: 91–95), Norval's (1996: 2) task is to explain how and why the establishment and maintenance of such a system was made possible, who became 'interpellated' by its hegemonic discourse, how that hegemony was called into question in the 1980s, and what the legacies of apartheid are for the new democratic South Africa. Through an analysis of discourses located throughout the period extending from the 1930s and 1940s to the 1980s and 1990s, her account shows that apartheid was not an automatic outgrowth of the 'dislocatory' upheavals in the 1930s and 1940s (e.g. the capitalization of agriculture, rapid urbanization, and World War II), nor was it created in the service of particular economic interests. Rather, it competed with many other discourses of the day, instituted a new form of social division and associated modes of identification, and drew two sets of 'political frontiers' upon which it was situated (Norval 1996: 5–11). Such hegemony, however, became unravelled in the 1980s, when apartheid failed to maintain its system of social division, and had to compete with new discourses that challenged it.

In similar fashion, Roniger and Sznajder (1999: 1–2) argue that post-authoritarian processes of democratization, reconciliation, and construction of the 'truth' are not inevitable outcomes to broad structural changes, but contingent and contested discursive processes where the re-emergent civilian rulers and representatives from different sectors in society are 'caught between contrasting and sometimes polar versions of the past, between normative expectations and the constraints of contingency, and between their will to consolidate democratic rule and the impossibility to do so without grappling with the past legacy of human rights violations'. Their analysis of these processes in Argentina, Chile and Uruguay uses analytical concepts from theories of democratization, globalization and the discourse of human rights, collective memory and identity. It adopts a 'multi-level' approach through a systematic comparison of the three cases by combining a political-institutional approach, a sociological and comparative approach, and a cultural approach that focuses its attention on the discourses of key political and cultural actors (Roniger and Sznajder 1999: 2–5). They are less sceptical of comparative analysis than most discourse analysts (see Howarth 2005: 332–335) and adopt a version of the 'most similar systems design' (see discussion below, and Skocpol and Somers 1980; Faure 1994; Landman 2000a, 2003), which compares different outcomes across a set of similar countries. In this way, Argentina, Chile and Uruguay share a relatively common background and confronted similar legacies of human rights violations, but differed greatly in the institutional paths they took as well as the 'actual interpretations' of human rights issues among different social sectors (Roniger and Sznajder 1999: 2). The key discursive contribution of the study is its analysis of how cultural elites use symbols and models of social order to construct identities and draw boundaries of inclusion and exclusion during the periods of redemocratization across the three cases (Roniger and Sznajder 1999: 6).

The next three categories in the continuum (Columns III, IV, and V) share a general orientation to providing theory-driven empirical analysis that is inductive, comparative, and seeks to make broad generalizations that still leave room for some exceptions. While they differ in the degree to which they use qualitative and quantitative analysis and in the number of countries that feature in their comparisons, they are all self-conscious about research methods and the strength of the inferences that are drawn from their analyses. For example, Risse, Ropp and Sikkink (1999) and Hawkins (2002) engage in qualitative comparative and single-country analysis to examine how the transmission of human rights norms from the international level to the domestic level shapes state behaviour towards human rights over time. Gómez (2003: 83–96) uses quantitative data to set basic timelines of human rights abuse in the cases of Cuba, Nicaragua, and El Salvador and then uses comparative historical analysis across these 'most similar' cases to understand why they have had quite different patterns in human rights abuse. Foweraker and Landman (1997) use a mixture of time-series quantitative analysis and qualitative histories across the four cases of Brazil, Chile, Mexico, and Spain to examine the variable relationship between social mobilization and the protection of individual civil and political rights of citizenship. In contrast, the studies on the human rights violations in Poe and Carey (2004) and the analysis of the growth and effectiveness of the international human rights regime in Landman (2005b) use global quantitative analysis across large samples of countries ($150 \leq N \leq 194$) and over long periods of time ($16 \leq T \leq 30$).

Finally, the last two categories in the continuum (Columns VI and VII) share the same orientation toward providing universal knowledge claims and explanations for human rights violations based on deductive reasoning, while differing in their reliance on evidence. Most rationalist forms of analysis engage in a process of theorizing (see Chapter 3 this volume), where assumptions about human nature are combined with a series of 'stylized facts' and then used to derive a set of propositions about social phenomena that can be observed. Approaches in the penultimate category (Column VI) involve deriving a set of propositions deductively from starting assumptions and then testing them with limited empirical evidence, which typically consists of confirmatory case studies. In contrast, approaches in the final category (Column VII) deduce their propositions in exactly the same manner, but do not subject them to empirical testing. Rather, they present their analysis in abstract form only and have thus been criticized for providing 'inference without evidence' (Almond 1996: 52). A classic example from political science in this category is Anthony Downs's (1957) *An Economic Theory of Democracy*, which treats democracy as a market, politicians as firms with something to sell (i.e. their policies) and voters as consumers who 'spend' their votes on the candidates that best 'supply' goods that maximize their preferences.

In the field of human rights, there are two examples from the extant literature that illustrate these methods and their different uses of evidence: Mitchell's (2004) study of human rights atrocities during civil wars and Wantchekon and Healy's (1999) analysis of torture using game theory (see Chapter 3 this volume). Mitchell (2004) develops a quasi-rationalist account using analytical concepts of 'principals' and 'agents' drawn from the fields of organizational behaviour, management studies, and economics. Principals task agents with certain functions that they carry out with limited degrees of accountability to the principal (e.g. presidents and vice-presidents, generals and foot soldiers, leaders and security personnel). Using the great historical figures of Machiavelli, Dostoevsky's Grand Inquisitor, and Count Tilly, Mitchell (2004: 29–56) argues that principals may be motivated by the desire for political power and/or the pursuit of an ideal, which helps explain their relative propensity to tolerate human rights violations as a means to a greater end, while agents may be motivated further out of pure self-interested greed and sadism.

The analysis of different combinations of differently motivated actors serves to 'restore the focus to choice and to responsibility in the use of violence' (Mitchell 2004: 6). This simple yet powerful model is then tested across three civil wars – the English Civil War (1642–1651), the Russian Civil War (1917–1921) and the Arab–Israeli conflict (over the period 1948–2002) – in an effort to demonstrate its logic and extend its inferences to other cases. The analysis of torture using game theory outlined in Chapter 3 also restores focus to the role for individual choice, while the stylized specification of 'the state' and 'the torturer' as actors is in line with Mitchell's (2004) use of principal and agent. In contrast, however, Wantchekon and Healy (1999) make little reference to the empirical world and do not test their model using evidence. Rather, they derive an equilibrium solution and draw their implications based on the formal analysis of the strategic inter-action between the torturer and the victim. Thus, in both examples deductive logic provides a parsimonious framework for analysing human rights problems, which in the former study are examined through comparative cases, while in the latter example they remain inferences defended through formal analysis only.

This section considered a broad range of methodological approaches to studying human rights. It delineated the different methods according to a general epistemological con-tinuum ranging from 'cloudlike' to 'clocklike' extremes, the type of reasoning (inductive versus deductive), the balance between pure evidence and pure inference, the nature of the knowledge claims, and the scope of geographical coverage in the collection and analysis of evidence on human rights problems. It is clear that extant and new studies located along this continuum ask different research questions or examine similar sets of questions differently, such that the universe of human rights issues and topics for research can be confronted by a plurality of methodological approaches. But to recognize such a plurality is not to adopt an 'anything goes' position with respect to social science research methods (see Feyerabend 1993). Rather, it is to adopt the position that a number of significant, valid, and recognized research traditions characterize the social sciences and that each of these traditions asks particular questions of its research material and applies different methods to its objects of inquiry. Using the discussion of this continuum as a backdrop, the next section examines in greater detail the various trade-offs associated with different comparative methods, whose aim is to provide generalizations about human rights problems based on the comparative analysis of countries.

Cross-national generalizations and comparative methods

At a fundamental level, comparative methods provide ways in which to compare similarities and differences across countries to arrive at a series of generalizations about particular human rights problems. There are three general comparative methods available to social scientists of human rights: global comparisons, few-country comparisons, and single-case studies. The trade-offs associated with these methods involve the degree to which each can make broad-ranging empirical generalizations at different levels of theoretical and conceptual abstraction (Mair 1996; Landman 2000a, 2002, 2003, 2005b). Global comparisons tend to make broad-ranging empirical generalizations using concepts and constructs at a fairly high level of abstraction. Few-country comparisons tend to limit their generalizations and lower the level of abstraction in analysing human rights problems across a selection of countries. Single-case analysis tends to limit further its empirical generalizations and concentrates on the contextual particularities of the single case under investigation, but can be constructed in such a way as to contribute to larger theoretical and empirical problems. These three comparative methods and their associated strengths and weaknesses are considered in turn.

Global comparative analysis

Global comparative analysis typically involves the use of large and complex data sets comprising variables that have been operationalized quantitatively (see below) and have been specified in such a way that they can be measured over time and across space (see Chapter 5). Rarely do such studies carry out their analysis using qualitative methods, which focus more in-depth on particular features within countries and is therefore not possible with sample sizes that often exceed 100 countries (see Chapter 6). With such a large number of observations (typical time and space combinations exceed 4,000 such observations), global comparisons make empirical generalizations about relationships between and among variables that have associated degrees of statistical significance. For this reason, such studies are known as 'variable-oriented' since their focus is on 'general dimensions of macro-social variation' and the relationship between variables at a global level of analysis (Ragin 1994: 300). The main strengths of this kind of analysis include statistical control to rule out rival explanations, extensive coverage of cases, the ability to make strong inferences, and the identification of 'deviant' cases or 'outliers'. For example, one typical finding from the extant global comparative literature on human rights suggests that 'personal integrity rights' violations are lower in countries that have high levels of economic wealth and democracy (see Chapter 6). The fact that there are numerous wealthy countries and/or democracies that continue to violate human rights does not undermine this general finding. Rather, such countries become significant outliers to the general relationship that are in need of further analysis to explain why their practices appear anomalous. For example, Saudi Arabia is a classic outlier that is wealthy and has significant problems with human rights violations, while Brazil and India are seen as consolidated democracies with exceptionally high levels of torture (Landman 2005b).

Global analysis also has a number of weaknesses, including data availability, validity and reliability of rights and other measures, and its limited application to human rights problems. First, until very recently, there had been a dearth of cross-national data on human rights practices. As the next chapter shows, there are still only five major sources of human rights measures available for global comparative analysis, all of which are limited ordinal 'standards-based' scales of human rights practices (see also Landman 2004). The 'political terror scale' (Mitchell, Stohl, Carleton and Lopez 1986; Poe and Tate 1994; Gibney and Dalton 1996; Gibney and Stohl 1998), the Freedom House civil and political liberties scales (Gastil 1978, 1980, 1988, 1990; <www.freedomhouse.org>), and the torture scale (Hathaway 2002) measure a narrowly defined set of civil and political rights, while the Cingranelli and Richards human rights data set (<www.humanrights data.com>) includes measures of civil, political and some economic rights. Second, there are serious questions remaining about the validity and reliability of these rights measures, which code qualitative information typically found in Amnesty International and/or US State Department human rights country reports into quantitative scales. Third, global comparative analysis cannot address a whole range of important research questions in the human rights field, since many such topics are not susceptible to quantitative methods. Even if they are, global quantitative analysis provides generalizations that need greater specification and in-depth research that can only be carried out on smaller samples of countries (Landman 2005a).

Few-country comparisons

It is precisely because of the limitations and weaknesses of global comparative analysis that many human rights scholars carry out their analyses on a smaller selection of countries. Variously called the 'comparative method', the 'comparable cases strategy' (Lijphart 1975), or 'focused comparison' (Hague, Harrop and Breslin 1992), comparing few countries achieves control through the careful selection of cases that are analysed using a middle level of conceptual abstraction. Studies using this method are more *intensive* and *less extensive* since they encompass more of the nuances specific to each case. The outcomes that feature in this type of comparison are often seen to be 'configurative', i.e. the product of multiple causal factors acting together. In contrast to global comparative analysis, this type of comparison is referred to as 'case-oriented' (Ragin 1994), since the case is often the unit of analysis and the focus tends to be on the similarities and differences among cases rather than the analytical relationships between variables. Such comparisons tend to make generalizations that are less broad using concepts and constructs that have been analysed in greater depth across the countries that have been selected for analysis.

In order to make these generalizations, the comparison of the similarities and differences across a small number of countries is meant to uncover the empirical relationship between the presence of key explanatory factors ($X_1, X_2, \ldots, X_n$) and the presence of an observed outcome (Y). The isolation of these explanatory factors and the determination of their relationship to the observed outcome can be achieved through adopting two distinct types of research design: 'most similar systems design' and 'most different systems design' (Przeworski and Teune 1970; Skocpol and Somers 1980; Faure 1994; Landman 2000a, 2002, 2003). Drawing on J. S. Mill's (1843) 'method of difference', most similar systems design (MSSD) compares different outcomes across similar countries. Comparing countries that share a host of common features allows for the isolation of those factors that may account for an outcome. Typically, regional and area studies analysis compares countries that share similar history, language, religion, politics, and culture and then isolates the remaining factors that vary across the cases to see if that variation is related to the variation in the outcome that is to be explained. In this way, the common features are 'controlled', while the analysis focuses on the relationship between the explanatory factors and the outcome. As noted above, Roniger and Sznajder (1999) compare the different institutional paths and interpretations of human rights issues across the most similar cases of Argentina, Chile, and Uruguay, while Gómez (2003) adopted the same research design to analyse the differences in human rights abuse across the most similar cases of Cuba, El Salvador, and Nicaragua.

In contrast to MSSD, most different systems design (MDSD) compares similar outcomes across different countries. Drawing on Mill's (1843) logic of agreement, MDSD compares countries that share very few features and then focuses on those factors common across the countries that may account for an outcome. In this way, selecting countries with the same outcome and matching that outcome to the presence of key explanatory factors allows the researcher to establish their empirical relationship. Comparative studies that focus on large historical events such as revolutions, military coups, transitions to democracy, or 'economic miracles' in newly industrialized countries (Geddes 1990: 134–141) adopt this basic research design, where these types of outcomes are matched to the presence of key explanatory factor(s). In *Peasant Wars of the Twentieth century*, Wolf (1969) compares instances of revolutionary movements that had significant peasant participation in Mexico, Russia, China, North Vietnam, Algeria, and Cuba. Though these countries share few features that are the same, Wolf argues that the penetration of capitalist agriculture is the key explanatory factor (X) common to each that accounts for the appearance of the revolutionary movements and their broad base of peasant support (Y). In the human rights field, Hayner (1994, 2002) compares the outcomes and impact of similar instances of truth commissions across countries in Latin America and Africa. Her comparisons reveal that ethnic, religious, and group conflict in Africa explains why reconciliation is less likely than in Latin America, where conflict was born of an ideological struggle between forces on the political left and right. Thus the nature of conflict (X) is a key explanatory factor that accounts for the differences in impact of truth commissions (Y).

Thus, both MSSD and MDSD seek to identify a relationship between explanatory factors and outcomes by comparing different outcomes across similar countries or similar outcomes across different countries. Of the two research designs, MSSD is slightly more robust, since it allows for the presence of different outcomes across the countries under investigation. In social scientific terms, this means that the dependent variable (i.e. the outcome) is allowed to vary. In contrast, MDSD does not allow for the presence of different outcomes, and thus has no variance in the dependent variable. Thus, MDSD at best establishes a concomitance of explanatory factors and outcomes since it does not allow for 'negative' instances of the outcomes being examined (see Mahoney and Goertz 2004). In the Wolf (1969) example above, the analysis would have been strengthened through a test of whether there was (a) the presence of significant peasant support for revolution in the absence of the capitalization of agriculture or (b) the absence of significant peasant support in the presence of the capitalization of agriculture. As it stands, his analysis does not include such alternative cases.

Despite the main strengths of few-country comparisons in allowing for greater attention to the detail and specificity of country cases, such analysis suffers from two major methodological weaknesses. First, such studies may identify a large number of explanatory variables whose full variation far exceeds the number of countries under investigation. This problem is commonly labelled 'too many variables, not enough countries' (Dogan and Pelassy 1990; Collier 1991; Hague, Harrop and Breslin 1992), or 'too many inferences and not enough observations' (King, Keohane and Verba 1994). For example, a study that specifies three explanatory variables each with several categories (e.g. low, medium, and high) and outcome variable with as few as two categories (e.g. improvement in rights protection or not), and then analyses these variables across only three countries will never really be able to establish a relationship between the explanatory variables and the outcome. Solutions to this particular problem include raising the number of observations (include time, sub-national units, or more countries); resort to MSSD, which controls for the common features; or reduce the number of explanatory variables through adopting MDSD or through better theoretical specification (Landman 2003: 40–41).

Second, the *intentional* selection of cases rather than a *random* selection can seriously undermine the types of inferences that can be drawn. This problem is known as 'selection bias', and occurs in comparative politics through the non-random choice of countries for comparison, or the deliberate selection by the comparativist (Collier 1995: 462). Though selection of countries lies at the heart of comparison, selection without reflection may lead to serious problems of inference. The most blatant form of selection occurs when a study includes only those cases that support the theory. More subtle forms of selection bias, however, occur when the choice of countries relies on values of the dependent variable (Geddes 1990; King, Keohane and Verba 1994; Mahoney and Goertz 2004) and for qualitative studies, the use of certain historical sources that (un)wittingly support the theoretical perspective of the researcher (Lustick 1996). As outlined above, MDSD suffers from selection bias relating to values of the dependent variable, where only those countries with the outcome of interest (e.g. democratic transition, military coup, revolution) have been selected. Relatedly, it is possible to construct a few-country comparison that contains an indeterminate research design by comparing different outcomes across different countries. For example, in *The Power of Human Rights*, Risse, Ropp and Sikkink (1999) present five 'paired comparisons' (Kenya–Uganda, Tunisia–Morocco, Indonesia–Philippines, Chile–Guatemala, and Poland–Czechoslovakia) and one single-country analysis of South Africa to examine the transmission of international human rights norms. But the analysis reveals different outcomes across these different cases, thereby limiting the types of inferences that are drawn (Landman 2003, 2005a).

Single-country studies

The field of human rights research is full of single-country studies. By definition, they focus on countries with particularly problematic human rights records and include official reports from international governmental and non-governmental organizations, domestic commissions and NGOs, journalistic and descriptive accounts, and research monographs. The *Nunca Más* (CONADEP 1984) report from Argentina and the *Nunca Mais* (Dassin 1986) report from Brazil are classic examples of such descriptive accounts of human rights abuse under conditions of authoritarianism, and as discussed above, truth commissions often publish their findings for the general public, such as the South African Truth and Reconciliation Commission and the *Comisión de Verdad y Reconciliación* in Peru (Truth and Reconciliation Commission, CVR) (see Chapter 7). On balance, however, these descriptive accounts are not grounded in any one discipline, and they rarely make larger inferences from the intensive examination of the individual case. The descriptive accounts do, however, serve as the foundation for research monographs, which are grounded in one or more disciplines and tend to locate the country study in a broader set of theoretical and empirical questions relevant to the study of human rights.

As noted above, there have been significant criticisms made about the usefulness of single-country studies for social scientific analysis. But this volume takes the view that single-country studies can make significant and valuable contributions to the study of human rights, and that when properly carried out, they can provide a number of important functions in developing our understanding of human rights problems. First, they provide important contextual description upon which other studies build their analyses. Second, they develop new classifications of events and outcomes not yet observed in other parts of the world. Third, they can be used to generate hypotheses that can be tested in other countries. Fourth, they can be used to confirm or infirm existing theories by providing 'crucial' tests, and by extension provide explanations for anomalous outcomes or 'deviant' cases identified through global comparative analysis (Eckstein 1975).

Of these important functions, their role in new classifications, the generation of hypotheses and their use as 'crucial cases' are the most germane to the discussion here. There are several examples where the development of new classifications has advanced scholarship in describing, understanding, and explaining patterns of human rights abuse. In describing the Franco regime in Spain, Juan Linz (1964) identified a new form of authoritarianism that was different from personalistic dictatorships and totalitarian states. The Franco regime institutionalized representation of the military, the Catholic Church, and the Falange, as well as the Franco loyalists, monarchists, and technocrats. Unlike totalitarian states, the regime relied on passive mass acceptance rather than popular support (Linz 1964). Guillermo O'Donnell (1973) built on Linz's (1964) work in Spain and established the concept of the 'bureaucratic–authoritarian state' in his examination of Argentine politics and the regime's prosecution of the 'dirty war', a concept of state organization that would be applied not only to other authoritarian regimes in Latin America (see Collier 1979) but also to those in Southeast Asia (see Geddes 1990). In another example, patron–client relations and their permeation of state organization identified in Latin America have been developed into models of neo-patrimonialism and predatory states in Africa (Clapham 1982; Bratton and van der Walle 1997; Haynes 2002). In other examples, Kaldor (1999), Gilbert (2003), and Münkler (2005) have specified new forms of warfare that move beyond more traditional under-standings of conflict and that have grave consequences for human rights, and Payne (2000) has developed the concept of 'uncivil' movements that can 'travel' for subsequent comparative studies.

Single-country studies are also useful for generating hypotheses for theories that have yet to be specified fully. As 'plausibility probes' (Eckstein 1975: 108), single-country studies explicitly (or implicitly) suggest that the generated hypothesis ought to be tested in a larger selection of countries (Lijphart 1971: 692). For example, in their analysis of the effectiveness of international human rights pressure on the Argentine military regime, Weissbrodt and Bartolomei (1991: 1034) conclude by arguing 'the lessons of this case study must be tested in cases involving other countries and time periods to determine whether more general lessons can be drawn from this single case'. In similar fashion, in his study of the relationship between international human rights pressure and the transformation of the Pinochet regime, Hawkins (2002) tests the hypotheses generated in the Chilean case in the additional cases of Cuba and South Africa. His analysis of Chile shows that certain 'rule-oriented' factions within the Chilean military became influenced by outside human rights pressure, which ultimately led to gradual concessions by the regime and the transition to democracy. The further testing of his central hypothesis shows that a similar process took place in South Africa but not in Cuba, since there are not significant fissures in the ruling elite that would be susceptible to the influence of international human rights pressure.

Finally, single-country studies are useful if they act as 'crucial' cases drawn from theoretical expectations and propositions about the world. Such crucial case studies can confirm or infirm existing theories and are therefore conducted within the confines of extant generalizations (Lijphart 1971: 692). There are two types of crucial case studies: 'most likely' and 'least likely' (Eckstein 1975: 118). Least likely case studies select a country where theory suggests an outcome is not likely to occur. If the outcome is observed, then the theory is infirmed, since it suggested such an outcome should not be obtained in that particular country. For example, in their analysis of democratic transition in South Africa, Howarth and Norval (1998) argue that the South African case is the best example of a least likely case study since the longevity and strength of the apartheid regime suggested that a democratic transition was highly unlikely. The fact that there was such a transition invites deeper analysis of the case itself and greater reflection on theories of democratization. Other 'least likely' candidates in this area of research include North Korea and Burma/Myanmar, which over the next coming years may undergo similar unexpected processes of democratic transition.

In contrast, most likely case studies apply a reverse logic to least likely studies by selecting countries where theory suggests the outcome is definitely meant to occur. If the outcome is not observed, then the theory is infirmed. For example, Brazil and the United States are seen to be most likely case studies that have confounded particular social theories that link socio-economic change to political outcomes. For the Brazilian case, many varieties of social theories suggest that Brazil has had all the objective economic conditions necessary for a social revolution and yet no attempt to organize a mass-based revolutionary force has ever been made. In similar fashion, despite its rapid pace of industrialization, expansion of its labour force, and constitutional protection for the rights to assembly and association, the United States has never had a strong socialist party. The task of the analyst is thus to explain these so-called 'non-events' in these particular cases through identifying those factors that have inhibited the development of a fully fledged revolutionary movement in Brazil or a strong socialist party in the United States. In this way, Brazil and the United States represent 'deviant' cases since they fail to fall in line with theoretical expectations. Thus, most likely case analysis provides the means to explain the presence of such deviant cases. Additional candidates for most likely case analysis include Cuba and China, which have failed to undergo processes of democratic transition despite the 'velvet revolutions' and the collapse of Communism in the former Soviet Union.

Single-country studies thus serve larger comparative purposes if they lead to new classifications of social phenomena, generate new hypotheses about important empirical relationships, and provide critical tests of extant theories. Human rights abuses take place across a huge range of different social, economic, and political contexts, and single-country studies provide the richness of contextual description and the analysis of new institutional, cultural, and behavioural phenomena. Such studies should not be seen as 'merely precursory moments' (Howarth 2005: 332) in the larger quest for social scientific explanation, but as also having value in and of themselves. As we have seen, however, in making these new classifications and analyses, single-country studies can generate important hypotheses to be tested in other countries and contexts. Moreover, crucial case studies, whether 'most likely' or 'least likely' do not definitively prove or disprove a theory in line with Popper's (1959) notion of scientific falsification, but they do help *confirm* or *infirm* the applicability of social theories to all cases (Eckstein 1975; Landman 1999). They are thus particularly useful in testing the robustness of theories and research programmes in the social sciences that make universal knowledge claims, such as those outlined in the first section of this chapter.

Quantitative and qualitative evidence

The final methodological dimension in need of explicit attention is the difference between quantitative and qualitative evidence and its use in studying human rights problems.

Quantitative methods seek to show differences in number between certain objects of analysis and qualitative methods seek to show differences in kind. Quantitative analysis answers the simple question, 'How many of them are there?' (Miller 1995: 154), where the 'them' represents any object of comparison that can either be counted or assigned a numerical value. Quantitative data can be official aggregate data published by governments on growth rates, revenues and expenditures, levels of agricultural and industrial production, crime rates and prison populations, or the number of hectares of land devoted to agrarian reform. Quantitative data can also be individual, such as that found in the numerous market research surveys and public opinion polls. In the field of human rights, it is possible to count human rights violations, convert subjective accounts of human rights practices into standardized scales, or to collect survey data on human rights practices from random samples of the population. Such measures of human rights (see Chapter 5 this volume) can then be used for statistical analysis that describes and explains the nature, extent, pattern, and causes of human rights violations.

Quantitative methods are based on the distributions these data exhibit and the relationships that can be established between numeric variables using simple and advanced statistical methods. The common tools for estimating simple bivariate measures of association are correlation and cross-tabulation, where statistics help establish the magnitude, direction, and significance of the association between two variables. For example, at the individual level, there is a strong, positive, and significant bivariate relationship between years of formal education and income. At the global level of analysis, there is a strong, positive, and significant relationship between per capita income and the level of democracy (e.g. Rueschemeyer, Stephens and Stephens 1992; Przeworski, Alvarez, Cheibub and Limongi 2000; Foweraker and Landman 2004). Both of these relationships are represented by significant and positive correlation coefficients or other measures of statistical association. The common tool for estimating more complex and 'multivariate' relationships is some form of regression analysis, which determines the magnitude, direction, and significance of the independent relationships between the two or more explanatory variables and the outcome that is to be explained (see, e.g. Lewis-Beck 1980; Bohrnstedt and Knoke 1988; Fox 1997). For example, the basic relationship between education and income may want to add age of the individual to the analysis, while the relationship between development and democracy may want to add the world position of the countries in the sample (e.g. Burkhart and Lewis-Beck 1994).

In either example, multivariate analysis controls for these other factors to determine whether the original relationship is upheld. The results of this kind of analysis provide measures of association between all the explanatory variables and the outcome variable, which allows the analyst to determine their relative strength, magnitude, and statistical significance. If the original explanatory variable of interest maintains its significant relationship with the outcome variable in the presence of other explanatory variables, then it is possible to conclude that the original relationship has been upheld. The other explanatory variables are considered 'controls'. Thus for the education–income example or the development–democracy example above, age and world position serve as controls. If the relationship between education and income remains significant even after including age, then the original relationship is said to be upheld after controlling for the effects of age. In similar fashion, if the relationship between development and democracy remains even after including world position, the original relationship is upheld. These basic insights are present in all multivariate analyses of human rights violations, where typical control variables include population, regional position, British colonial influence, among others (see Poe and Tate 1994; Poe and Carey 2004; Landman 2005a, 2005b).

Qualitative methods seek to identify and understand the attributes, characteristics, and traits of the objects of enquiry, as well as the meanings, processes, and context (Devine 1995: 139; Devine and Heath 1999). The nature of the method necessarily requires a focus on a small number of units of analysis, whether they be individuals, groups, sub-national regions, countries, or supra-national regions. As discussed across many of the examples above, qualitative methods include macro-historical comparison (Skocpol and Somers 1980; Ragin, Berg-Scholsser and de Meur 1996; Mahoney and Rueschemeyer 2003); in-depth interviews and participant observation (Devine 1995); interpretivism, hermeneutics, and 'thick description' (Geertz 1973; Fay 1975); and varieties of discourse analysis (Howarth 2000a; Travers 2001). In none of these types of method is there an attempt to give numerical expression to the objects of enquiry, and in all of them the goal is to provide well-rounded and complete discursive accounts. These more complete accounts are often referred to as 'ideographic' or 'configurative', since they seek to identify all the elements important in accounting for an outcome.

There has traditionally been a deep division in the social sciences between those who use quantitative methods and those who use qualitative methods; however, it seems that this division is a false one for several reasons. First, the strict separation between quantitative and qualitative methods is minimized if both methods adhere to the goal of making inferences from available evidence (Foweraker and Landman 1997: 48–49; Travers 2001: 6–9). The same logic of inference ought to apply equally to quantitative and to those qualitative methods that seek to move beyond pure description (see King, Keohane and Verba 1994; Brady and Collier 2004). Second, the qualitative distinction made between and among categories in any attempt to classify social phenomena necessarily precedes the process of quantification (Sartori 1970, 1994). In this sense, social science needs to know 'what kind' of object to count before counting it, and this qualitative step as vitally important in the quantification of human rights (see Chapter 5). Third, and related to the first two points, there have been important and significant methodological developments in combining the strengths of qualitative and quantitative techniques by recognizing that both methods are founded on the same logic of inference and linking qualitative distinctions to quantitative representation. These developments include 'qualitative comparative analysis' (Ragin 1987, 1994) and the use of Boolean algebraic techniques to identify necessary and sufficient conditions for outcomes; text and content analysis, which codes words into numbers (Franzosi 2004); and the quantitative deconstruction of victim testimonies to truth commissions (Ball, Spirer and Spirer 2000; see also Wilson 1997, 2001).

Qualitative comparative analysis combines the strengths of both the 'case-oriented' approaches and 'variable-oriented' approaches, while maintaining the scientific rigour of comparative studies that employ quantitative methods (Ragin 1994: 304). The analytical framework considers cases holistically as the configuration of conditions rather than relationships between scores on variables (Ragin, Berg-Schlosser and de Meur 1996). It is the combination of variables rather than their independent relationships that is privileged in this form of analysis. In its simpler form, it constructs a matrix, or 'truth table' of 'causal factors' that are dichotomized according to their presence or absence within each case. These factors are then listed alongside a dichotomized form of the outcome that is to be explained. By examining the presence or absence of the causal factors and their various combinations, the analysis can find a reduced form of a combination of factors that is associated with the outcome (see Mahoney and Goertz 2004: 658–660). This kind of analysis has been used to study the necessary and sufficient conditions for social revolution in Latin America (Wickham-Crowley 1992), the division of working-class movements in the process of nation building in Western Europe (Ragin 1987: 126–133); the degree of ethnic mobilization among sub-national groups in Western Europe (Ragin 1987: 133–149); the relationship through time between social mobilization and the protection of individual citizenship rights (Foweraker and Landman 1997); and the conditions for democracy in inter-war Europe (de Meur and Berg-Schlosser 1994). More advanced forms of this analysis move beyond dichotomous variables to those with multichotomous categories (Ragin, Berg-Schlosser and de Meur 1996: 758), and the technique is very promising for carrying out human rights impact assessments (see Chapter 8 this volume).

The development in the quantification of texts draws on a long tradition in behavioural social science, which sought to break down reality into its smallest countable units (i.e. words) and then aggregate these units into larger systems of meaning and understanding (Eulau 1996). For example, in the 1940s in the United States the Experimental Division for the Study of War Time Communications at the Library of Congress analysed newspaper and newswire stories quantitatively to uncover patterns in perception of the Allied and Axis powers among significant third countries (Eulau 1996: 58–59). In drawing on this tradition, succeeding generations of behaviouralists have used newspaper sources to code events such as riots, strikes, protest, assassinations, repression, and general social mobilization across the world (see, e.g. Taylor and Hudson 1972; Taylor and Jodice 1983; Tarrow 1989; Banks 1994; Kriesi, Koopmans, Dyvendak and Giugni 1995), while other analyses have relied on multiple newswire sources to reduce bias and expand coverage (Lichbach 1984; Gerner, Schrodt, Francisco and Weddle 1994). In practical terms a coding vocabulary is applied to the raw text, which converts the text into quantitative information that recorded instances of events and outcomes of interest to the researcher. In this way, the grammar of a story or narrative is converted into a series of countable units (see Franzosi 2004).

There have been similar developments in the use of such coding techniques in the human rights field, particularly in relation to the work of truth commissions. Here, narrative accounts of human rights violations that have taken place during times of civil conflict, authoritarian rule, or foreign occupation are collected by truth commissions and then coded using human rights violation vocabularies. These coded statements are then organized into large relational databases where individual violations serve as the basic unit of analysis. Oftentimes, the official databases of the truth commissions are complemented further with additional data that have been collected by non-governmental organizations. The resulting data analysis estimates the total number of violations that have taken place (with a margin of error), and then disaggregates the pattern of violations across time, space, and characteristics of the victims and the perpetrators (see Ball, Spirer and Spirer 2000; Ball, Asher, Sulmont and Manrique 2003; Landman 2004). Truth commissions in El Salvador, Guatemala, Haiti, South Africa, Peru, Sierra Leone and East Timor have carried out data projects, which have fed into their final reports and have had significant implications for processes of reparation and reconciliation (see Chapter 7).

Methods matter

In its analysis and discussion of the different methodological traditions and options in the social sciences, this chapter shows how and why method matters for the social scientific analysis of human rights problems. Methods link theory and evidence, provide the basic rules of enquiry, and provide the tools that maximize the kind of inferences that are drawn. The chapter argued that there is not one preferred method, since method is a function of the epistemological orientations of the researcher, the theoretical perspective that is adopted, the nature of the research question, as well as the available time and material resources with which to carry out any research project. It is clear that methods vary across the epistemological continuum from 'clouds' to 'clocks', the full range of comparative analysis from global comparative to single-country studies, and the degree to which qualitative, quantitative, or hybrid methods are adopted. Nevertheless, method is a central feature of all systematic social research and is not separate from the substance of the research that is being carried out. Rather, it is the substance since it sets the parameters over what can be said about the research problem and makes possible the types of knowledge claims that can be safely advanced given the evidence that has been considered (see King, Keohane and Verba 1994: 9). Good human rights scholarship and good human rights arguments need strong methodological foundations that specify the ways in which human rights problems will be addressed, how human rights evidence will be collected and analysed, and how human rights conclusions will be drawn. Analysing human rights problems with bad methods will lead to erroneous conclusions, bad policy advice, and failure to improve human rights conditions on the ground.

Suggestions for further reading

Brady, H. E. and Collier, D. (2004) *Rethinking Social Inquiry: Diverse Tools, Shared Standards*, Lanham, MD: Rowman and Littlefield.

Flyvberg, B. (2001) *Making Social Science Matter: Why Social Inquiry Fails and How It Can Succeed Again*, Cambridge: Cambridge University Press.

King, G., Keohane, R. O. and Verba, S. (1994) *Designing Social Inquiry: Scientific Inference in Qualitative Research*, Princeton, NJ: Princeton University Press.

Landman, T. (2002) 'Comparative Politics and Human Rights', *Human Rights Quarterly*, 24 (4): 890–923.

Landman, T. (2003) *Issues and Methods in Comparative Politics: An Introduction*, 2nd edn, London: Routledge.

5 Measuring human rights

Social scientific analysis of human rights problems often depends on the use of valid, meaningful, and reliable measures of human rights across the different categories and different dimensions outlined in Chapter 1.[1] There is now a large literature on human rights measurement that has developed through contributions from the academic disciplines of political science, sociology, economics, and law, as well as from governmental and non-governmental organizations (e.g. Claude and Jabine 1992; Green 2001; Landman and Häusermann 2003; Landman 2004). Long seen as the purview of development and economic analysis, the use of indicators has increasingly been brought into mainstream analysis of human rights in the social sciences and in the work of the United Nations and the World Bank. For example, since the late 1970s and early 1980s, political scientists have been using quantitative measures in global comparative analyses of human rights protection (see Chapter 6 in this volume). The 2000 Human Development Report dedicated an entire chapter on why human rights indicators are important and how they could be incorporated into its own work (UNDP 2000: 89–111). The Office of the High Commissioner for Human Rights has been exploring the ways in which human rights indicators could be used by the treaty monitoring bodies to assist in their assessments of state compliance with the different international human rights instruments. In his annual reports to the UN General Assembly, the Special Rapporteur on the Right to Health has advocated the use of indicators to gauge different aspects of the progressive realization of the right to health (A/58/427/2003; A/59/422/2004). Finally, the World Bank has incorporated measures of human rights in its work on good governance and its relationship with development (see Kaufmann *et al.* 1999a, 1999b, 2002, 2003; www. worldbank.org).

There is thus a groundswell of support and increasing level of interest in the development and use of human rights measures. Such measures serve a variety of important and inter-related functions across the academic and non-academic sectors of the human rights community. First, they allow for *contextual description and documentation*, which provide the raw information upon which measures of human rights are based. Second, they help efforts at *classification*, which differentiates rights violations across their different categories and dimensions. Third, they can be used for *monitoring* the degree to which states respect, protect and fulfil the various rights set out in the different treaties to which they may be a party. Fourth, they can be used for *mapping and pattern recognition*, which provide time-series and spatial information on the broad patterns of violations within and across different countries. Fifth, they are essential for *secondary analysis*, including hypothesis-testing, prediction and impact assessment, the inferences from which can be fed into the policy making process. Finally, they can serve as *important advocacy tools* at the domestic and international levels by showing the improvement or deterioration in rights practices around the world. The accumulation of information on human rights protection in the world and the results of systematic analysis can serve as the basis for the continued development of human rights policy, advocacy, and education (Rubin and Newberg 1980: 268; Claude and Jabine 1992: 5–34). Moreover, 'to forswear the use of available, although imperfect, data does not advance scholarship' (Strouse and Claude 1976: 52), nor does it allow for the kind of continued human rights activism that seeks to eliminate the worst forms of human behaviour.

This increasing demand for human rights measures and the various functions that they perform across a wide spectrum of scholars and practitioners suggests that they will continue to be a central feature of systematic human rights research and applied work in the field. In order to demonstrate how to measure human rights and to examine the many remaining challenges human rights measurement faces, this chapter is divided into three sections. The first section explains how social scientific measurement moves through four different levels ranging from general background concepts to specific scores on specific human rights across specific units of analysis (e.g. a high score on civil rights $CR\uparrow$ in country X in year T). The second section discusses extant measures of human rights, including those that measure rights 'in principle' (i.e. *de jure* state commitment), 'in practice' (i.e. *de facto* realization), and as a government 'policy' (i.e. inputs, outputs, and outcomes). The third section identifies areas in need of better and more appropriate measures to fill important lacunae that remain.

From concepts to indicators

Chapter 1 showed how the scope of human rights includes different categories (civil, political, economic, social, cultural, and solidarity) *and* different dimensions (positive and negative), the combination of which produces six main conceptual 'boxes' (see Table 1.1) that need to be operationalized. The different dimensions and categories provide the content for developing 'events-based', 'standards-based', 'survey-based' and other measures of human rights (see the next section). But what are the operational steps that allow us to move from these conceptual distinctions of human rights to the provision of valid, meaningful, and reliable measures? At an abstract methodological level, the process of measurement converts well-defined and well-specified concepts into meaningful quantitative measures or qualitative categories, and has four main steps (Adcock and Collier 2001; also Zeller and Carmines 1980). The first level concerns the *background concept* that is to be measured, which is the broad constellation of meanings and under-standings associated with the concept. The scope of human rights outlined in Chapter 1 summarizes what comprises such a broad constellation of meanings and understandings in the field of human rights. The second level develops the *systematized concept*, which specifies further the concept that is to be measured, such as a specific right (e.g. the right not to be tortured) or a group of rights (e.g. civil rights). The third level *operationalizes the systematized concept* into meaningful, valid, and reliable indicators, where decisions are taken as to the type of measure that is to be used and how it captures the positive and negative dimensions of the rights it measures. The final level provides *scores on indicators* for the units of analysis being used (e.g. individuals, groups, countries, regions, etc.). Figure 5.1 depicts these four levels graphically.

Consider a concrete example. The *background concept* to be measured is human rights, the scope of which has been *systematized*. The international community of human rights

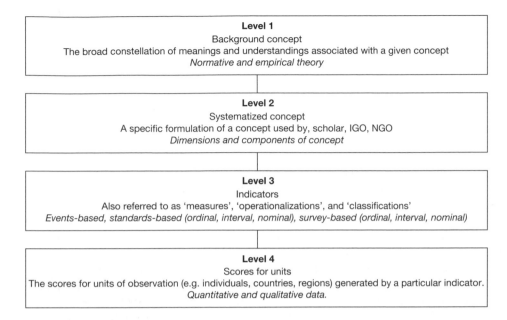

Figure 5.1 Levels of measurement.

Sources: Zeller and Carmines 1980; Adcock and Collier 2001.

scholars and practitioners have spent the years before and since the 1948 Universal Declaration of Human Rights 'constructing' (Donnelly 1999b) and 'justifying' (Sorell and Landman 2005) human rights in conceptual and legal terms. While there have not been agreed philosophical foundations for the existence of human rights (Mendus 1995; Landman 2004, 2005a), the extant international law of human rights provides a general consensus on the core content of those human rights that ought to be protected (Landman and Häusermann 2003), a consensus that found its most forceful and comprehensive expression in the 1993 Vienna Declaration and Programme for Action (Boyle 1995; Donnelly 1999a; Freeman 2002b). Such a core content represents the steps taken from the background concept to the systematized concept within the four levels of measurement depicted in Figure 5.1.

The intersection between the categories and dimensions of human rights is a systematic way of organizing the first step to measurement. Consider the right not to be tortured, which is a systematized concept of human rights that has been identified most notably in the Universal Declaration of Human Rights (UDHR), the International Covenant on Civil and Political Rights (ICCPR), and the Convention Against Torture (CAT). The systematized concept is susceptible to operationalization at Level 3. But given the two dimensions of human rights, the right not to be tortured can be measured at Level 3 both *positively* (i.e. resources a state is investing in procedures, policies, reforms, and training for the prevention of torture) and *negatively* (formal commitment to international standards on torture and actual incidence of torture). At Level 4, the right not to be tortured is measured for a unit (e.g. Brazil) at a particular time (e.g. 1985), across its positive dimension (e.g. % GDP spent on torture reform, number of police in receipt of torture training, cases of reprimand for torture) and its negative dimension (e.g. incidence of torture revealed through events counting, a scale of torture, or survey estimations on popular experiences of torture). In this way, the right not to be tortured *may have several indicators that measure its core content across its two dimensions*.

Extant measures

In many ways, the proliferation of human rights norms and the promulgation of international human rights treaties since the Universal Declaration have effectively (with minor exceptions) completed the move from background concepts (Level 1) to systematized concepts (Level 2), while the move from providing indicators (Level 3) to score on units (Level 4) comprises the continuing work of scholars and practitioners working on human rights measurement today. There is thus not yet a full set of indicators available that measures all human rights across their different categories and dimensions. Rather, those that are available measure certain categories of human rights across one or another of their dimensions. Extant approaches have measured human rights *in principle* (i.e. as they are laid out in national and international legal documents), *in practice* (i.e. as they are enjoyed by individuals and groups in nation states), and as outcomes of government *policy* that has a direct bearing on human rights protection. Measurement of human rights has taken the form of coding country participation in regional and international human rights regimes, coding national constitutions according to their rights provisions, qualitative reporting of rights violations, survey data on perceptions of rights conditions and experiences, quantitative summaries of rights violations, abstract scales of rights protection based on normative standards, and individual and aggregate measures that map the outcomes of government policies that have consequences for the enjoyment of rights.

Rights in principle

International and domestic law enshrines norms and principles of human rights, which can be coded using protocols that reward a country for having certain rights provisions in place at the domestic level and for having made such rights commitments at the international level through the ratification of international human rights treaties. Such a coding represents a negative dimension of state practice towards human rights since making constitutional provisions at the domestic level and signing and ratifying treaties at the international level carries with it only nominal cost in terms of actual fiscal capacity of the states. It is therefore a formal commitment *in principle* that can be counted. In an important precedent for measuring rights in principle at the domestic level, van Maarseveen and van der Tang (1978) coded constitutions for 157 countries across a multitude of institutions and rights for the period 1788–1975. Their study compares the degree to which national constitutions contain those rights mentioned in the UN Declaration for Human Rights by examining their frequency distributions across different historical epochs before and after 1948 (see Figures 5.2 and 5.3). Their study is broadly descriptive in nature, but their data allow for global patterns and processes of change in the formal protection of rights at the domestic level to be mapped, while secondary and more advanced statistical analysis could be conducted on the patterns within the data while exploring possible relationships with other indicators. In the spirit of this precedent, Foweraker and Landman (1997: 51–52) use an 'institutional procedural index' to code rights in principle using the various national constitutions, constitutional amendments, and executive decree laws during the years of political liberalization and

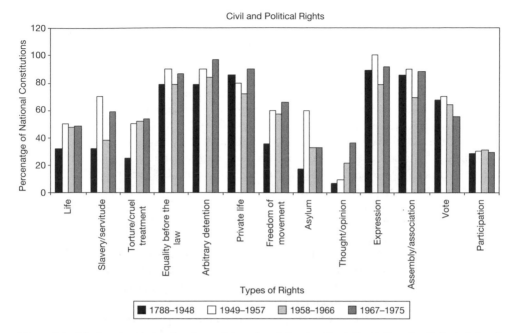

Figure 5.2 National constitutional provisions for rights in principle: civil and political rights.*

Source: van Maarseveen and van der Tang (1978: 189–211).

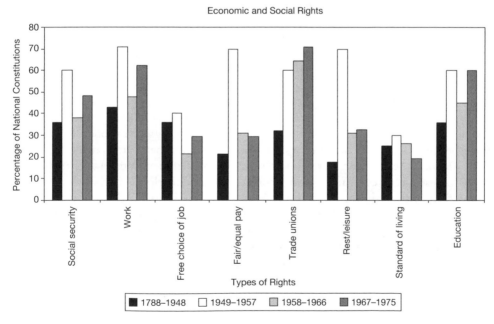

Figure 5.3 National constitutional provisions for rights in principle: economic and social rights.*

Source: van Maarseveen and van der Tang (1978: 189–211).

*Figures 5.2 and 5.3 are reprinted with permission from *Human Rights Quarterly*, © 2004 Johns Hopkins University Press. All rights reserved.

democratic transition in Brazil, Chile, Mexico, and Spain. In similar fashion, Keith (2004) codes national constitutions and their exceptional clauses to measure the ability of countries to suspend rights protection during states of emergency.

Coding rights in principle is important since it translates qualitative legal information into quantitative information that can be used to track the formal commitment of countries to rights protection against which their actual practices can be compared. Thus, Foweraker and Landman (1997: 62–65) use regression techniques to gauge the relative 'gap' between rights in principle and rights in practice in Brazil, Chile, Mexico, and Spain (see also Duvall and Shamir 1980: 162–163; Arat 1991). Their analysis demonstrates that during the process of political liberalization, authoritarian states can deny rights that they proclaim are protected (a negative gap), protect rights they proclaim are protected (a zero gap), or protect rights that they proclaim are not protected (a positive gap). Keith (2004) uses the state of emergency variable to examine the relationship between rights in principle and rights in practice, while controlling for the independent effects of democracy, wealth, warfare, and other variables.

This development of coding schemes at the domestic level has been replicated at the international level by scoring countries for signing and ratifying major regional and international human rights instruments (see Keith 1999; Landman 2001, 2005b; Hathaway 2002). Rather than code individual rights provisions, the coding schemes measure the degree to which countries are parties to human rights treaties over time. Keith (1999) and Hathaway (2002) used a simple dichotomous measure of ratification (0, 1), while Landman (2005b) combines a three-point coding scheme for treaty ratification (0, 1, 2) with a four-point coding scheme that rewards and punishes countries for the degree to which they make reservations upon ratification, where a 4 denotes a country that ratifies with no reservations and a 1 denotes a country that has made significant reservations that undermine the object and purpose of the treaty. Combining the ratification variable with the reservation variable produces a weighted ratification variable that ranges from 0 to 8.

The time-series analysis of regime participation shows an expansion in the number of countries that are now formally participating in the international regime (see Figure 1.1 in Chapter 1 this volume); that 'late ratifiers' tend to ratify more treaties with fewer reservations than 'early ratifiers'; and that democracies have a greater propensity to ratify treaties, even though 'old' democracies (i.e. those countries that were democratic before the 1970s) ratify fewer treaties with more reservations than new democracies (Landman 2005b). These measures of treaty ratification are also used in global analysis to show that regimes frequently make formal commitments to human rights treaties, but continue to violate human rights. This difference is captured by weak positive or even negative correlation and regression coefficients between ratification and rights variables (Keith 1999; Landman 2001; Hathaway 2002; see also Krasner 1999: 122). Moreover, Landman's (2005b) analysis shows that the significant relationship between treaty ratification and rights protection weakens when taking reservations into account. Carrying out such analyses, however, requires measurement of rights in practice and it is to this that the discussion now turns.

Rights in practice

Rights in practice are those rights actually enjoyed and exercised by groups and individuals regardless of the formal commitment made by a government. While there ought to be a correspondence between formal rights commitments found in national constitutions and international human rights instruments and those enjoyed on the ground, it is often the case that individuals and groups do not enjoy the full protection of their rights (a negative gap in the terminology used above). Ideally, there ought to be in place a legal appeals procedure, mechanisms for seeking domestic and international remedies, and a subsequent 'correction' in national practices to uphold the rights to which regimes have made formal commitments. In the absence of such systems or in the face of weak systems, the role of many human rights practitioners is to provide meaningful and accurate information on the degree to which human rights are being violated. Indeed, greater concerns over humans rights since World War II have led to an explosion in the number of domestic and international human rights NGOs collecting information on violations (see Chapter 2 this volume). Such NGOs have been given greater status in international governmental organizations, and their activities include setting standards, providing information, lobbying, and giving direct assistance to those suffering abuse of their rights (Forsythe 2000: 163–190; Welch 2001a: 1–6; Landman and Abraham 2004).

The increase in the salience of human rights as an issue combined with organizations dedicated to documenting human rights violations means that there is greater availability of comprehensive information on actual practices of states and the conditions under which individuals live. But this information is necessarily lumpy and incomplete, since reporting of human rights violations is fraught with difficulties, including fear within victims, power of the offenders, comprehensive evidence, quality of communications technology, among others. In recognizing this problem, Bollen (1992: 198) argues that there are six levels of information on human rights violations: (1) an *ideal* level with *all* characteristics of *all* violations (either reported or unreported), followed by (2) recorded violations, (3) known and accessible violations, (4) locally reported violations (nation state), (5) internationally reported violations, and (6) the most biased coverage of violations, which may include only those reported in US sources.

Work in this area seeks to obtain lower levels of information in much greater detail. For example, the *Torture Reporting Handbook* (Giffard 2002) and *Reporting Killings as Human Rights Violations* (Thompson and Giffard 2002) are manuals that define specific rights, outline the legal protections against their violation, and provide ways in which testimony and evidence from victims can be collected. The Human Rights Information and Documentation System (HURIDOCS), founded in 1982, provides standards for human rights violations reporting, and now represents a vast network of human rights groups (Dueck 1992: 127). While such increased information at all levels is helpful for systematic human rights research, there remains a trade-off or tension between micro levels of information gathering and the ability to make systematic comparative inferences about human rights (see Chapter 4 this volume). In order for equivalent measures to 'travel' for comparative analysis, there will necessarily be some loss of information, while the comparability of measures allows for stronger generalizations about human rights violations to be drawn.

These issues about levels of information and the commensurability for cross-national analysis delineate the three types of data available for measuring human rights in practice: (1) *events-based*, (2) *standards-based*, and (3) *survey-based*. Events-based data chart the reported acts of violation committed against groups and individuals. Events-based data answer the important questions of what happened, when it happened, and who was involved, and then report descriptive and numerical summaries of the events. Counting such events and violations involves identifying the various acts of commission and omission that constitute or lead to human rights violations, such as extra-judicial killings, arbitrary arrest or torture. Such data tend to be disaggregated to the level of the violation itself, which may have related data units such as the perpetrator, the victim, and the witness (Ball, Spirer and Spirer 2000; and see Chapter 7 this volume). Standards-based data establish how often and to what degree violations occur, and then translate such judgements into quantitative scales that are designed to achieve commensurability. Such measures are thus one level removed from event counting and violation reporting, and merely apply an ordinal scale to qualitative information. Finally, survey-based data use random samples of country populations to ask a series of standard questions on the perception of rights protection. Such measures track individual-level perceptions of rights violations and may even capture direct or indirect individual experiences of rights violations, particularly in countries that have suffered from prolonged periods of civil conflict, authoritarian rule, or foreign occupation (see Chapter 7).

There are by now many examples of each of these kinds of data that measure the negative dimensions of human rights. Events-based data analysis has a long tradition, where one of the first applications of statistics to the study of violence analysed the distribution of more than 15,000 'quasi-judicial' executions carried out during the height of the Reign of Terror (March 1793 to August 1794) after the French Revolution. Using the archived documents of the tribunals that sentenced people to death, Greer (1966) analyses the patterns of sentencing and executions over time, space, and by social class (nobles, upper middle class, lower middle class, clergy, working class, and peasants). Figure 5.4 shows the time-series pattern in executions by social class, while Figure 5.5 shows the number of executions across space (*départements*). The peasants and working classes suffered the largest number of executions, where the majority of the executions (52%) took place in the West, followed by the Southeast (19%) and Paris (16%). In this analysis, the individual victim serves as the basic unit of analysis, which allows for the kind of secondary analysis shown in the figures and the further testing of hypotheses about the causes of the violations, such as those based on class, political, economic, and/or religious variables (Greer 1966: 4).

Ball and Asher (2002) conducted a similar style of statistical analysis on the patterns of killings and refugee migration of Albanians in Kosovo between 24 March and 22 June 1999. The analysis tests whether the violence and migration during this period were due to the activities of the Kosovo Liberation Army (KLA), the NATO air attacks, or a systematic campaign by Yugoslav forces. Using detailed border records of the refugee population that left Kosovo combined with UNHCR refugee data and four sources (American Bar Association, ICTY exhumation data, Human Rights Watch, and the OSCE) of data on the killings that took place during the period, allowed the refugee migration and killings to be plotted over time (see Figure 5.6). The more advanced statistical analysis of these patterns that controlled for region, KLA activities, and NATO bombing, determined that neither the KLA nor NATO could be held responsible for the killings, while KLA activities were associated with increased refugee flows in the Northern and Eastern regions of Kosovo (Ball and Asher 2002: 22). In the absence of detailed data on Yugoslav troop movements, the analysis could neither support nor reject the hypothesis that those forces were responsible for the migration and killings. However, it was able to reject the two hypotheses about the KLA and NATO, a finding that when presented to the ICTY undermined significantly any attempt by the defence team to shift blame away from the Yugoslav forces (Ball and Asher 2002: 24).

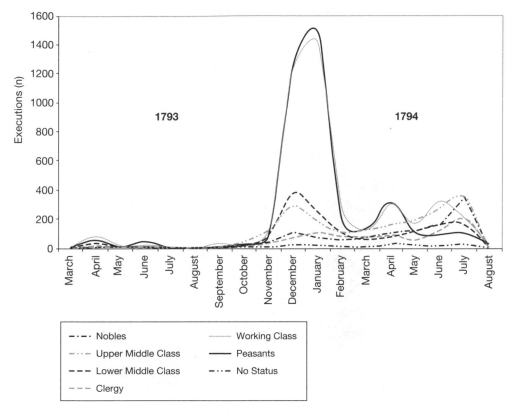

Figure 5.4 Number of executions during the Reign of Terror by social class.
Source: Greer (1966: 135–166).

This discussion of events-based data illustrates that highly disaggregated data from particular historical contexts provide an important means for explaining what happened and how, as well as ruling out rival explanations (i.e. how such events could not have happened). Events-based analysis has been used to chart the progression of the Rwanda genocide (www.genodynamics.com), to estimate civilian mortality rates before and after the invasion of Iraq in March 2003 (Roberts, Lafta, Garfield, Khudhairi and Burnham 2004), and to estimate the total number of civilian deaths as a result of the war in Iraq (www.iraqbodycount.net). It has also become a central feature of many truth commissions (see Chapter 7), such that limited time-series events data have been collected, most notably in Argentina, Chile, Guatemala, El Salvador (still under UN seal), Haiti (not yet published), South Africa, Peru, Sierra Leone, and East Timor.

In contrast to events-based data, standards-based scales provide much more aggregated forms of information that have been collected and coded across a large number of countries. The most dominant examples of extant standards-based scales of human rights include the Freedom House scales of civil and political liberties (Gastil 1978, 1980, 1988, 1990; www.freedomhouse.org), the 'political terror scale' (Mitchell, Stohl, Carleton and Lopez 1986; Poe and Tate 1994; Gibney and Stohl 1996), a scale of torture (Hathaway 2002), and a series of seventeen different rights measures collected by Cingranelli and Richards (www.humanrightsdata.com). Freedom House has a standard checklist it uses

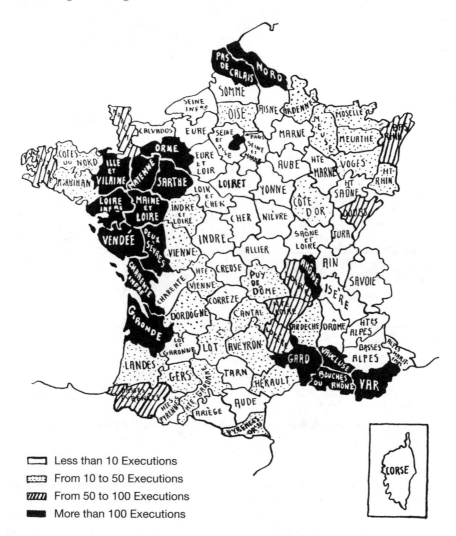

Less than 10 Executions
From 10 to 50 Executions
From 50 to 100 Executions
More than 100 Executions

Figure 5.5 Number of executions during the Reign of Terror by *département*.

to code civil and political rights based on press reports and country sources about state practices and then derives two separate scales for each category of rights on a scale that ranges from 1 (full protection) to 7 (full violation). The political terror scale ranges from 1 (full protection) to 5 (full violation) for state practice that include torture, political imprisonment, unlawful killing, and disappearance. Information for these scales comes from the US State Department and Amnesty International country reports. In similar fashion, Hathaway (2002) measures torture on a 1 to 5 scale using information from the US State Department. The Cingranelli and Richards human rights data code similar sets of rights on scales from 0 to 2, and 0 to 3, with some combined indices ranging from 0 to 8, where higher scores denote better rights protections. In addition to a series of civil and political rights, Cingranelli and Richards also provide measures for such rights as women's economic, social, and political rights, worker rights, and religious rights.

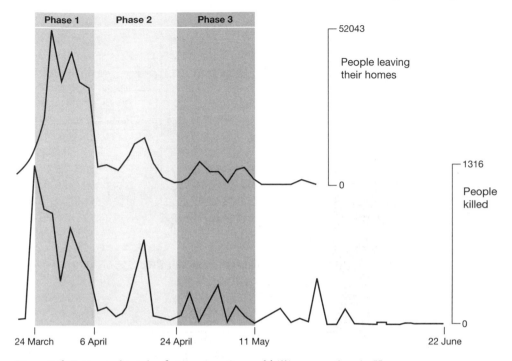

Figure 5.6 Estimated total refugee migration and killing over time in Kosovo.

Figures 5.7 and 5.8 show the Freedom House, political terror and torture scores over time and space for the period 1976 to 2000 (standardized to a common 1–5 scale). Figures 5.9 and 5.10 show the Cingranelli and Richards data for women's economic, political, and social rights on a 0–3 scale over time and space for the period 1981 to 2003.

Survey data have been less used in social scientific research on human rights than either events-based or standards-based measures. They have usually featured more often in research on the support for democracy (e.g. Kaase and Newton 1995), trust and social capital (e.g. Whiteley 1999, 2000), patterns of corruption (www.transparency.com), or as components of larger indices of 'post-material' values (see Inglehart 1997). But increasingly, household surveys have been used to provide measures for popular attitudes about rights and to uncover direct and indirect experiences of human rights violations. Some of the most notable work has been carried out by the NGO Physicians for Human Rights, who conduct surveys of 'at risk' populations (e.g. internally displaced people or women in conflict) to determine the nature and degree of human rights violations. Figure 5.11 shows the results of one of their surveys on war-related sexual violence in Sierra Leone based on 991 women (Physicians for Human Rights 2002b: 47–48; see also Amowitz *et al.* 2002).

While these examples of human rights measures focus on civil and political rights, Chapter 1 in this volume argued that it is possible to extend the methodological discussion to include these kinds of measurement for economic, social, and cultural rights, as Cingranelli and Richards have begun to do. Indeed, if the denial of economic, social, and cultural rights is the product of particular government practices, then it seems

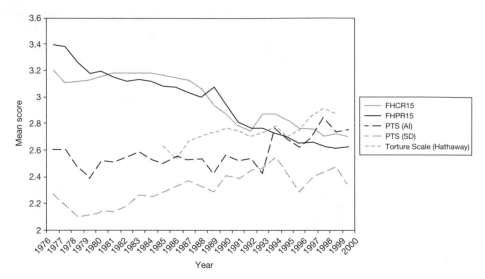

Figure 5.7 Standards-based scales of human rights protection over time, 1976–2000.*

Note: High score = high violations, low score = low violations.
Sources: Landman (2005b, 2005c).

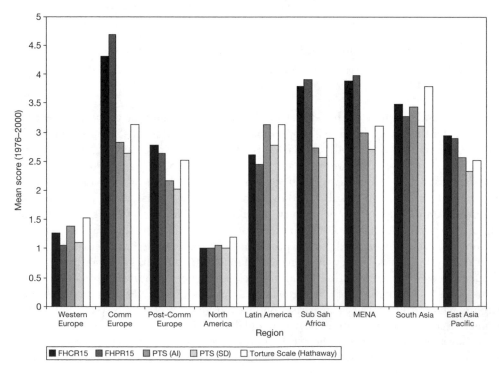

Figure 5.8 Standards-based scales of human rights protection by region, 1976–2000.*

Note: High score = high violations, low score = low violations.
Sources: Landman (2005b, 2005c).

*Both Figures 5.7 and 5.8 are reprinted with permission from Georgetown University Press, © 2005. All rights reserved.

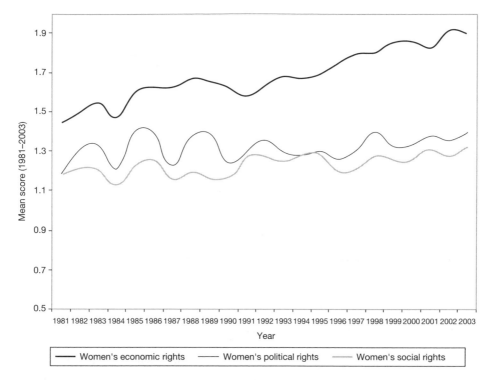

Figure 5.9 Women's rights over time, 1981–2003.

Note: High = high protection, low score = low protection.
Source: Cingranelli and Richards data set (CIRI) (www.humanrightsdata.com).

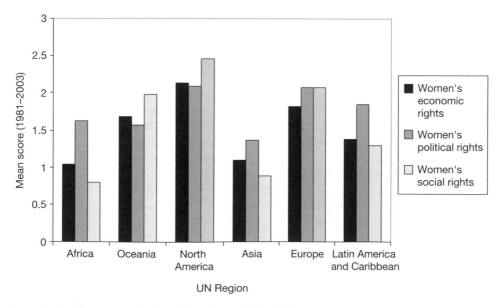

Figure 5.10 Women's rights by UN region, 1981–2003.

Note: High = high protection, low score = low protection.
Source: Cingranelli and Richards data set (CIRI) (www.humanrightsdata.com).

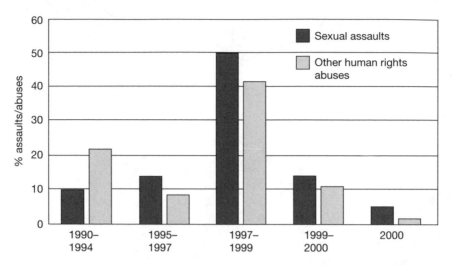

Figure 5.11 War-related sexual violence in Sierra Leone, 1990–2000 (*n* = 1,157).

Source: Physicians for Human Rights (2002b: 48). Reprinted with permission.

equally possible to use qualitative information to summarize such practices into ordinal scales like those used for civil and political rights violations. Overt, institutionalized, or implicit discrimination against individuals or groups that prevents their access to education or adequate healthcare constitutes a practice that violates a right. In theory, such a violation can be reported and coded using events-based, standards-based, and/or survey-based data. Cingranelli and Richards are coding practices that violate women's rights using an ordinal scale, while the minorities at risk project codes the degree to which 224 different minority and communal groups experience discrimination also using an ordinal scale (see Gurr 1993, and also Foweraker and Krznaric 2001). These important precedents demonstrate how the negative dimensions of economic, social, and cultural rights can be measured.

Despite their development and increasingly wider use, these three types of data are fraught with methodological problems. Events-based data are prone to either under-reporting of events that did occur or over-reporting of events that did not occur, creating problems of selection bias and misrepresentative data. It is impossible to document every last human rights violation and those organizations collecting such information tend to concentrate on conflict-stricken societies during discrete periods of time and thus cross-country comparisons using such measures is problematic. Sophisticated statistical techniques have been developed to overcome some of the limitations associated with estimation of violations (see Chapter 7), but extant data projects of this nature necessarily concentrate on limited time periods in particular cases, and it may be that some episodes of violence are simply too complex to analyse using these techniques. In contrast, standards-based data establish comparability by raising the level of abstraction, but have a tendency to truncate the variation of human rights protection across different countries. In other words, their use of a simple limited scale may group together certain countries that actually show a great difference in their protection of human rights. While these scales present a general picture of the human rights situation and are useful for drawing comparative inferences, they necessarily sacrifice the kind of specificity for pursuing direct legal action against perpetrators. Finally, survey data, especially those used across different political contexts are prone to cultural biases, where the meaning of standardized questions on rights protection are differently understood in different countries. In this way, the debate about the universality of human rights affects the method of measuring rights through surveys, since it is not obvious that human rights are understood to mean the same thing across the world. It is important therefore that those measuring human rights in practice *recognize the limits of their data*.

Government policies and outcomes

In addition to rights in principle and rights in practice, it is possible to provide more indirect measures of human rights using aggregate statistics on the outcomes of government policies. Parr (2002) makes the useful distinction between human rights conduct and developmental outcomes that may have a bearing on human rights. She stresses the fact that certain dimensions of conduct and outcomes are simply not prone to quantifiable measurement (see Radstaake and Bronkhurst 2002: 31–32). In the language of this volume, her distinction fits well with the difference between rights in *practice* (conduct) and government *policy* (outcomes). But it appears that practices and outcomes are more readily quantifiable than Parr (2002) assumes. Traditionally, development studies and development economics have often relied on quantitative indicators of the outcomes of government policies, including gross domestic product, gross domestic product per capita, income inequality, expenditure on health, education, and welfare, among many others (e.g. see www.worldbank.org). Indeed, the UNDP's human development index (HDI) combines per capita income (standard of living) with literacy rates (knowledge), and life expectancy at birth (longevity) (UNDP 1999: 127–137). While not providing a direct measure of rights protection *per se*, such measures can elucidate the degree to which governments support activities that have an impact on human rights.

One solution is to combine the HDI with standards-based measures of human rights to get a more holistic picture that captures the interaction between levels of human development and the protection of human rights. Figure 5.12 is a scatter plot between the HDI and a 'factor score' created through principal component extraction from the two versions of the Political Terror Scale, the two Freedom House scales, and the torture measure outlined above. The assumption behind using factor analysis is that each of the five measures is measuring common human rights phenomena. The curvilinear cubic functional form in the figure provides the best overall fit for the relationship between human development and human rights (i.e. has the highest R^2), but using the UNDP's cut-off points for low, medium, and high human development also shows the areas of the world most in need of attention. For example, those countries with low human development and high violations of human rights depicted in the upper left section of the figure form the main 'constituency' for attention by the international community (see Sorell and Landman 2005). Such a combination of measures goes some way in depicting the inter-relatedness of different categories of rights, and shows how aggregate development indicators can be combined with standards-based measures.

A second solution is to employ development indicators as proxy measures for the *progressive realization* of economic, social and cultural rights. Article 2 of the International Covenant on Economic, Social and Cultural Rights requires states to take steps, to the maximum of their available resources, towards the progressive realization of these rights: steps in which states set goals, targets and timeframes for national plans to implement

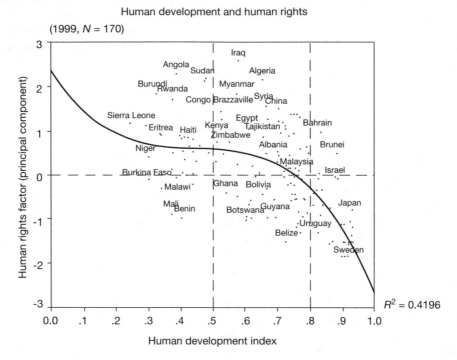

Figure 5.12 Scatter plot for civil and political rights and the human development index, 1999.
Sources: Landman (2005c), UNDP (1999: 134–137).

these rights. Development indicators are thus seen as suitable proxy measures to capture the degree to which states are implementing these obligations. For example, literacy rates and gender breakdown of educational attainment are seen as proxy measures of the right to education; daily per capita supply of calories and other nutritional rates are seen as proxy measures of the right to food; and under-five mortality rates and the numbers of doctors per capita are seen as proxy measures of the right to health (OHCHR 2002). Similar such measures can be used as indicators for the right to adequate food and housing.

   To date, such development indicators have primarily been applied to economic and social rights, but aggregate statistics can equally be used to measure the positive dimensions of civil and political rights. Following the work of the United States Agency for International Development (USAID 1998a, 1998b), new efforts propose the use of development indicators as potential proxy measures for civil and political rights (e.g. investment in prison and police reform, the processing of cases, the funding of judiciaries, the provision of legal aid and advice to suspects, the amount of time suspects spend on remand, and the proportion of cases taken up by independent reporting and investigating bodies). The extension of such indicators for measuring cultural rights is also possible. The social and spatial mobility of ethnic and cultural minority populations, as well as spending on bilingual education can approximate the degree to which countries are adopting policies to uphold their cultural rights obligations. In short, aggregate measures of provision and outcomes can depict the degree to which governments are committed to putting in place the kinds of resources needed to have a 'rights-protective regime' (Donnelly 1999a).

Lacunae

This chapter has demonstrated how the different categories and dimensions of human rights can be converted, or operationalized into meaningful, valid, and reliable measures. The background concept of human rights has been systematized by the international legal and human rights community such that there is now a known core content of human rights susceptible to social scientific operationalization using a variety of indicators across their different categories and dimensions. These include the positive and negative dimensions of civil, political, economic, social, cultural, and solidarity rights. Efforts to operationalize these different dimensions and categories of human rights have included measures of rights in principle, rights in practice, and proxy measures of government policies and outcomes. To date, most efforts have concentrated on measuring rights in practice and include events-based, standards-based, and survey-based forms of measurement.

It seems clear, however, that we still know more about *what* to measure conceptually and legally than *how* to measure it. Tremendous progress in human rights measurement has been achieved but there are serious and significant lacunae in the field that need to be addressed that include both the *content of rights that remain unmeasured* and an *over-reliance on certain forms of measurement*. With respect to content that remains unmeasured, efforts in measurement have predominantly concentrated on the *negative* dimensions of civil, political and some cultural rights (e.g. minority rights discrimination) and the *positive* dimensions of economic and social rights. There is thus a dearth of measures for the positive dimensions of civil and political rights and the negative dimensions of economic and social rights. The human rights community thus still needs to develop measures for the provision of resources that support the protection of civil and political rights and measures for the violation of economic and social rights (see Chapman 1996). In this regard, the Cingranelli and Richards data set is the first attempt to measure systematically the negative dimensions of some social and economic rights. Moreover, there is less agreement on the content of solidarity rights and at best there have been some proxy measures offered for them, such as the distribution of global income, trade dependency, and trade openness.

Finally, there has been over-reliance on standards-based ordinal measures of human rights with an emphasis on aggregation into single indices. Such measures maintain a reasonably high level of abstraction suitable for large cross-national comparisons and in part have been driven by that particular research community, but they have problems of validity, reliability, variance truncation, and in many cases follow no obvious aggregation rule. Such measures need to be improved by a greater attention to primary sources in an effort to increase their validity, and greater disaggregation into separate measures of particular human rights. If standards-based ordinal scales are to be used and greater use is made of primary source material then such measures should provide more gradation in their ordinal categories in order to reduce the worst forms of variance truncation. It seems paramount, however, that such an effort needs to be complemented by other forms of data, including events-based and survey-based, and indicators of government policies and outcomes.

Suggestions for further reading

Adcock, R. and Collier, D. (2001) 'Measurement Validity: A Shared Standard for Qualitative and Quantitative Research', *American Political Science Review*, 95 (3): 529–546.

Cingranelli, D. (1988) *Human Rights: Theory and Measurement*, Basingstoke: Macmillan.

Green, M. (2001) 'What We Talk about When We Talk about Indicators: Current Approaches to Human Rights Measurement', *Human Rights Quarterly*, 23: 1062–1097.

Jabine, T. B. and Claude, R. P. (eds) (1992) *Human Rights and Statistics: Getting the Record Straight*, Philadelphia: University of Pennsylvania Press

Landman, T. (2004) 'Measuring Human Rights: Principle, Practice, and Policy', *Human Rights Quarterly*, 26 (November): 906–931.

Online resources

Cingranelli and Richards Human Rights Data (CIRI)
www.humanrightsdata.com

Freedom House
www.freedomhouse.org

Landman Human Rights Treaty and Reservations Data
www.data-archive.ac.uk

Penn World Tables
pwt.econ.upenn.edu

Political Terror Scale
www.unca.edu/politicalscience/faculty-staff/gibney.html

Polity IV Democracy
www.cidcm.umd.edu/inscr/polity

World Bank World Development Indicators
www.worldbank.org

6 Global comparative studies

Chapter 4 showed that comparative methods for analysing human rights problems include global comparisons with a large number of observations, few-country comparisons, and single-country case studies. This chapter considers the contribution that has been made by the global comparative analysis of human rights problems,[1] including a set of studies that identified the 'determinants' of human rights protection and a set of studies that have examined the relationship between human rights protection and an additional set of factors, including foreign aid, the presence of multinational corporations, and international human rights law. Despite the different foci of these two generations of studies, they all share three main features. First, they all adopt the same research design, which constructs a large and complex data set comprised of quantitative indicators of human rights protection and other variables collected on all (or almost all) of the countries in the world for selected years. Second, they all use bivariate and multivariate quantitative techniques to test a series of hypotheses about the likely explanation for variation in human rights protection, or in the case of foreign aid, the likely impact of human rights practices on aid allocation. Third, they all tend to concentrate on a narrow conception of human rights that includes more salient violations such as torture, extra-judicial killings, political imprisonment, and disappearances.

In order to see how this method of analysis has been used to address significant human problems, the chapter is divided into three sections. The first section discusses the basic research design and assumptions of this kind of analysis and then demonstrates how different bivariate and multivariate quantitative techniques can be used to identify important explanatory factors. The second section discusses the main findings of both sets of studies. The third section concludes the chapter with an examination of important areas that remain to be examined and discusses the limitations of global comparative analysis for investigating certain human rights problems.

Research design and basic quantitative techniques

Global comparisons of human rights protection draw on the longer tradition of comparative research in political science on the 'pre-requisites' (Karl 1990) of modern democracy, which measures democracy and finds its socio-economic 'correlates' (Lipset 1959; Rueschemeyer, Stephens and Stephens 1992; Burkhart and Lewis-Beck 1994; Helliwell 1994; Przeworski, Alvarez, Cheibub and Limongi 2000; Landman 2003: 70–75). With the exception of one set of studies considered in this chapter (see below), *human rights protection* rather than democracy becomes the dependent variable (or outcome) for which a series of explanatory variables are specified. The goal of global comparison is to use quantitative analysis to test a series of hypotheses to identify which factors have significant relationships with human rights protection and which factors do not. The large number of observations across countries and time provides the necessary variation for all the variables in the analysis, and allows for statistical controls and tests to be introduced in order to avoid drawing false inferences about particular relationships.

The research design to all these studies is roughly the same and all of them employ a few standard quantitative techniques to analyse relationships between and among the different variables in the data set. Although a full discussion of quantitative analysis is a separate field in the social sciences itself and is well beyond the scope of this present volume, it is possible to provide some basic insights into how such analysis is conducted using extant data on development, democracy, and human rights. Table 6.1 has summary statistics for four variables collected on countries from around the world in 1995: (1) the political terror scale ranging from 1 (high rights protection) to 5 (low rights protection) that has been coded using Amnesty International's *Annual Reports*, (2) the Polity IV measure of democracy, which ranges from −10 (full autocracy) to +10 (full democracy) (see Jaggers and Gurr 1995), (3) gross domestic product per capita measured in 1995 US dollars (www.worldbank.org), and (4) the natural log of gross domestic product per capita, which is a standard transformation of this variable when used for global comparative analysis since the distribution of per capita GDP by country is highly skewed. The table shows the number of countries for which the data exist, the minimum and maximum values of each variable, the mean or average value of each variable, and their standard deviation, which is a statistical measure of the spread, dispersion, or variability of the different variables. Finally, the 'valid *N*' listed in the table is the number of countries for which there are data for all four variables (i.e. 115 countries).

Using these data for the 115 countries, it is possible to show how empirical relationships can be established using a variety of statistics. Figure 6.1 has two 'scatter plots' between the two measures of income (raw GDP per capita and the natural log of GDP per capita) and the political terror scale with a selected set of countries labelled. Both graphs show that there is a negative relationship between high levels of economic development on the one hand and high levels of human rights violations on the other. In other words, wealthy countries (e.g. Japan and Switzerland) have lower violations of human rights (i.e. political terror scores between 1 and 2) and poor countries (e.g. Liberia, Burundi, and Sierra Leone) have higher violations of human rights (i.e. political terror

Table 6.1 Four variables on development, democracy, and human rights, 1995

	Number of countries	Minimum value	Maximum value	Mean value	Standard deviation
Political terror scale (Amnesty)	137	1.00	5.00	2.69	1.19
DEMOC4	150	−10.00	10.00	2.82	6.99
Per capita GDP (1995 USD)	171	49.32	44176.48	5607.41	9274.31
LNPCGDP	171	3.90	10.70	7.45	1.58
Valid *N*	115				

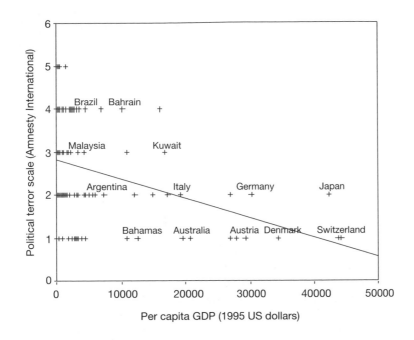

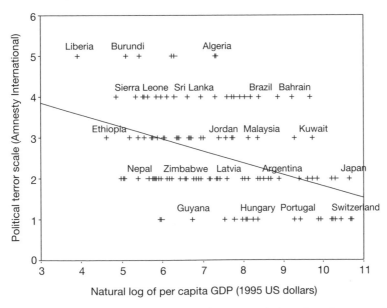

Figure 6.1 Scatter plots between the level of wealth and the political terror scale.

scores between 4 and 5). The relationship between levels of wealth and human rights protection is statistically significant at the 99% level of confidence, where for the raw level of per capita GDP the correlation co-efficient is −.37 and for the natural log of per capita GDP it is −.39. This means that if we compared a similar selection of countries at a different time, the overall general relationship would still hold even though the scores on specific countries may have changed. As we shall see in the next section, levels of wealth alone do not explain the total variation in human rights protection, as it would appear from the figure that civil war may well be an important third factor that explains the high number of violations of human rights across many of the poor countries in the sample.

Figure 6.2 is a 'scatter plot' between democracy and human rights. The Polity IV measure of democracy is narrowly focused on the procedural dimensions of democracy, the most important component of which is its measure of constraint on the abuse of executive power (see Jaggers and Gurr 1995; Foweraker and Krznaric 2001; Munck and Verkuilen 2002). Like the relationship between wealth and human rights, the figure shows that there is a negative relationship between high levels of democracy and high levels of human rights violations. In other words, high levels of democracy are associated with better human rights protection, and the correlation co-efficient, significant at the 99% level of confidence is −.38. The fact that there is a statistically significant relationship between democracy and human rights protection is not surprising given that there is a natural affinity between the two concepts (see Beetham 1999) and that a certain basic set of civil and political rights protections ought to be in place for democracy to be able to function (see Dahl 1971). The relatively 'thin' procedural measure of democracy used in the figure avoids tautology, but what is more surprising is that the correlation between democracy and human rights is not higher, suggesting that many countries have been able to secure the procedural dimensions of democracy without the same security of civil and political rights. This low but significant correlation between the procedural dimensions of democracy and rights protection provides some evidence for the existence of so-called 'illiberal' democracy (Diamond 1999; Zakaria 2003; Foweraker and Krznaric 2001; Foweraker and Landman 2002; Landman 2005b, 2005c), while there has been some

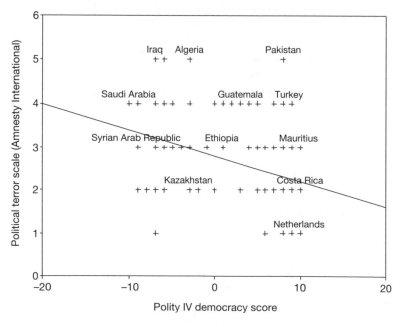

Figure 6.2 Scatter plot between the Polity IV democracy score and the political terror scale.

research exploring why human rights should necessarily be seen as a linear function of democracy (see Davenport and Armstrong 2004).

Figures 6.1 and 6.2 also have straight lines fitted to the scatter of points, which is an elementary way of defining a relationship between two variables. The most common statistical technique used to capture and represent such a relationship is linear regression, which fits a straight line to the scatter of points that represent the intersection of the two variables. Before seeing how this works, we need to review basic linear algebra using the data examples in Figure 6.1 and 6.2. If we label the horizontal axis in the figures x and the vertical axis y, we can then use the following equation for a straight line to depict the linear relationship between x and y:

$$y = mx + b \tag{1}$$

where y = the observed values of the y variable (i.e. human rights protection), x = the observed values of the x variable (i.e. wealth or democracy), b = the point where the line crosses the y-axis (i.e. the level of human rights protection in the absence of wealth or democracy), and m = the slope or 'rise over run' between x and y. For perfect linear relationships, using the values of x and y for two different points in the scatter plot, it is possible to calculate m and b, and then express the whole relationship as an equation. The following two formulas are used to calculate m and b:

$$m = \frac{(Y_2 - Y_1)}{(X_2 - X_1)} \tag{2}$$

$$b = Y_1 - mX_1 \tag{3}$$

Using the x and y values of two different data points in the scatter, m is simply the ratio of the differences between the y values and x values. Once m is known, it can be used in equation 3 to solve for b. But in the social sciences, there are no perfect linear relationships, so regression analysis estimates the degree to which a straight line fits the scatter of points and thereby acknowledges a degree of uncertainty. The standard equation for the line used in regression analysis takes the following form:

$$\hat{Y} = \alpha + \beta X + \mu \tag{4}$$

where $\hat{Y}$ = the 'predicted' values of the dependent variable (i.e. human rights protection), X = the observed values of wealth or democracy, α = the point where the line crosses the y-axis (i.e. the level of human rights protection in the absence of wealth or democracy), b = the slope or 'rise over run' between X and Y, and μ = error since not all the points in the figure fall precisely on the line.

Since many of the data points do not fall precisely on the line we need to use modified formulas to calculate α and β. The line is fitted to minimize the distance between the observed values and the predicted values. The most common mathematical solution for fitting the line to the data points is called the 'least sum of squares' or 'ordinary least squares' (OLS) regression technique, which relies on the following two formulas:

$$\beta = \frac{\sum(X_1 - \overline{X})(Y_1 - \overline{Y})}{\sum(X_1 - \overline{X})^2} \tag{5}$$

$$\alpha = \overline{Y} - \beta\overline{X} \tag{6}$$

Here, the formulas calculate the difference between actual values of X and Y on the one hand, and the means of those values on the other. The products of these differences are summed and then divided by the sum of the squared differences between actual X values and the mean of X. Once β is known, α can be calculated using equation 6. Indeed it is entirely possible to calculate α and β using a simple spreadsheet with separate columns for each component of equation 5 in parentheses to calculate β, and then substituting the results into equation 6 to calculate α. Using the data from Table 6.1 produces the following two regression equations depicting the relationship between wealth (logged per capita GDP) and human rights protection, and democracy and human rights protection:

human rights protection = 4.70 − .29 × (logged per capita GDP)   (7)

human rights protection = 2.80 −.06 × (level of democracy)   (8)

These statistical results can be interpreted literally. For the relationship in equation 7, human rights protection starts at a political terror level of 4.7 (high violations), but reduces by .29 for every logged increase in per capita GDP. For the relationship in equation 8, human rights protection starts at a political terror level of 2.8 and is reduced by .06 for every point increase in the level of democracy. In less literal terms, the analysis shows that wealth and democracy are related to lower levels of human rights violations.

But how confident in statistical terms are we with these results? In addition to calculating α and β, regression analysis also calculates their relative significance and the degree of fit achieved by the straight line. The relative significance calculation shows how confident we are in the fact that the mean values of α and β are significantly different from 0. In other words, if there were no relationship between x and y, β would not be significantly different from 0. The calculation of this significance is a function of the mean of the value itself and its standard error (see Lewis-Beck 1980: 30–37). As a general rule of thumb, if the mean of β divided by its standard error is less than 2, β is unlikely to be significant at the standard level of statistical confidence, 95% (ibid.). Including the standard error values for our results in equations 7 and 8, produces the following two new equations (with standard errors in parentheses):

human rights protection = 4.70 (.45) − .29 (.06) × (logged per capita GDP)   (9)

human rights protection = 2.80 (.10) −.06 (.01) × (level of democracy)   (10)

In applying the general rule of thumb, dividing any of the α or β values above by their standard errors yields a figure larger than 2, so our results are statistically significant at the 95% level of confidence. This means that if we used the same variables for a similar selection of countries at a different point in time, we would have very similar results.

Finally, the degree of fit calculation examines how much of the variation in y is explained by the variation in x. The statistical value for the degree of fit is called R^2, which represents a ratio of explained variance to unexplained variance and ranges from 0 to 1. For example, an R^2 value of .43 means that 43% of the variation in y is explained by the variation in x. In our two examples above, the R^2 value for wealth and human rights and the R^2 value for democracy and human rights are coincidentally the same at .14, which suggests that either wealth or democracy alone explains 14% of the variation in human rights protection.

These separate illustrations of simple relationships are examples of *bi-variate statistical analysis*, since they examine the co-variation of two variables only and do not control for any other factors. But linear regression techniques can be applied to any number of factors, providing that there are enough observations in the sample of data that is being analysed. The same basic linear equation is used in this *multivariate statistical analysis* but across *all* the variables included in the analysis. Thus, using the data from Table 6.1, we can estimate the following general equation, which depicts human rights protection as a function of wealth and democracy:

$$\text{human rights protection} = \alpha + \beta_1 \times (\text{wealth}) + \beta_2 \times (\text{democracy}) + \mu \qquad (11)$$

Here, the regression analysis will hold one variable constant while estimating the relationship for the other variable and then vice versa, thereby producing estimates for α, β_1, and β_2, their standard errors, and an overall R^2 value for the whole equation. The output, with standard errors in parentheses, is as follows:

$$\text{human rights protection} = 3.8 \, (.49) - .04 \, (.02) \times (\text{democracy}) \qquad (12)$$
$$- .15 \, (.07) \times (\text{wealth})$$
$$R^2 = .14$$

For this sample of 115 countries in 1995, the political terror scale starts with a mean value of 3.8 and reduces by .04 for every point increase in democracy and reduces a further .15 for every increase in logged per capita GDP. We can thus conclude that wealth and democracy are related to better human rights protection, since both have a significant negative relationship with the political terror scale. Both variables taken together account for 14% of the variation in human rights protection, while the remaining 85% of variation in human rights protection remains *unexplained*. The variance in human rights protection that remains unexplained suggests that there are many other variables that have yet to be specified that may explain human rights violations, including regional and cultural differences, involvement in warfare and domestic conflict, among others. Both this kind of analysis and interpretation of the statistical results are dominant features of the extant global comparisons on human rights to which the discussion now turns.

Extant global comparative studies

Using the insights from the general excursus on basic quantitative analytic techniques, it is now possible to examine the contribution of global comparisons of human rights problems. The first set of studies considered here constructed cross-national data sets of the kind outlined above and compared countries at one point in time (synchronic comparison) or over a period of years (diachronic comparison), and they tended to focus on a similar set of variables posited to account for the global variation observed in human rights protection. Using simple bi-variate and more complex multivariate analysis of the kind outlined above, their analyses examine the relative magnitude, direction, and statistical significance of the relationship between certain variables and the protection of human rights. The inclusion of time in many of the studies increases the number of observations in any one data set, which allows for more secure inferences to be drawn about empirical relationships and for time-dependent processes to be tested.

But these advantages bring with them additional problems for statistical analysis, since such cross-national time-series data sets violate some of the underlying assumptions of the linear regression techniques outlined above (see Stimson 1985; Beck and Katz 1995). Global studies using this basic time and space data format thus have to add important statistical controls in order to avoid making false inferences about the kinds of empirical relationships they are testing. The second set of studies have maintained this basic data format and set of key explanatory variables and then added new variables to test a series of policy-relevant empirical relationships, such as those between foreign aid and human rights, direct foreign investment and human rights, and international law and human rights. For the studies on foreign aid, the relationship is flipped around to examine the degree to which variation in human rights protection forms the basis for aid allocation. In this way, aid becomes the dependent variable and human rights the independent variable.

The search for determinants

The first set of global comparative studies, much like the related research on the emergence and maintenance of democracy, identify the key determinants of human rights violations in an effort to establish broad empirical generalizations and build general theories of human rights protection. To this end, they construct their data sets using standards-based scales of human rights (typically the political terror scale) and then specify key explanatory variables to account for the variation in these scales across space, and/or space and time. These explanatory variables include socio-economic factors such as wealth, the pace of development, and population size, and political factors such as the form of government (democracy, autocracy, transitional, leftist, or military), previous levels of repression, and involvement in international or domestic conflict. These variables are operationalized using continuous measures for such things as the level of economic development and size of the population; percentage measures for rates of change in economic growth and population growth; ordinal measures for changing political regimes, such as the Polity IV democracy scale outlined above; dichotomous or dummy variables for static political regimes, cultural variables, and conflict, such as leftist governments, military regimes, British colonial influence, and engagement in international and domestic warfare. Finally, a 'lagged' value of human rights protection is used as a further control for those studies that adopt a cross-national time-series data format.

Both the synchronic studies (e.g. Strouse and Claude 1976; Mitchell and McCormick 1988; Henderson 1993) and diachronic studies (e.g. Poe and Tate 1994; Poe, Tate and Keith 1999; Zanger 2000a) obtain similar statistical results using multivariate regression analysis of the kind outlined above. Their results demonstrate that, on the one hand, democracies (or those countries moving towards more democratic forms), wealthy countries, and those that have become developed are less likely to violate human rights. On the other hand, those countries involved in international and civil warfare, countries with a large population, the presence of an authoritarian regime, previous levels of repression, and those that have undergone a transition to either 'anocracy'[2] (Jaggers and Gurr 1995; Zanger 2000a) or autocracy are more likely to violate human rights. One study shows that the benefits of democracy with respect to the protection of 'personal integrity rights' (i.e. those rights specifically measured by the political terror scale) come into effect within the first year of a democratic transition (Zanger 2000a), while another study finds less political violence and fewer 'state sanctions' against civilians among democracies than non-democracies (Davenport 1999). Finally, there are mixed effects for leftist governments that depend on whether the political terror scale is coded using the US State Department reports or the Amnesty reports, a difference that may uncover possible biases against leftist regimes by the US State Department (see Poe and Tate 1994; Innes 1992).

Foreign aid, multinational capital, and international law

In moving beyond the search for determinants, another series of studies identify additional sets of economic and legal-institutional variables that may be related to human rights protection. The additional economic variables include direct foreign investment as a measure of the presence of multinational corporations (Meyer 1996; Smith, Bolyard and Ippolito 1999, Meyer 1998, 1999a), and overseas aid from the United States, the United Kingdom, the European Union, and the World Bank and International Monetary Fund (Poe 1990, 1992; Zanger 2000b; Abouharb and Cingranelli 2004; Barratt 2004). The additional legal-institutional variables include various measures of state participation in the international regime for the protection of human rights (Keith 1999; Hathaway 2002; Landman 2005b). The analysis of direct foreign investment examines whether such investment helps or hurts the protection of human rights; the analysis of foreign aid examines whether human practices form the basis for aid allocation; and the analysis of international law examines whether state ratification of international human rights treaties makes a difference for human rights protection. In this way, human rights protection is specified as the dependent variable for the examination of the impact of direct foreign investment and international law, while serving as an independent variable for the examination of foreign aid allocation. Thus apart from human rights being specified in these different ways, all of the studies use the same basic research design and similar measures of human rights as in the previous set of studies.

To date, the results for all these analyses are mixed. Using one set of measures for the presence of multinational corporations, the statistical analysis shows a strong positive association between direct foreign investment and the protection of civil, political, economic, and social rights (Meyer 1996, 1998, 1999a), while studies using another set of measures show that such results cannot be upheld (Smith, Bolyard and Ippolito 1999). For foreign aid, a large number of studies show no significant relationship between US foreign aid and human rights protection across different samples of recipient and non-recipient countries, while one study finds a positive relationship and another finds mixed results (Poe 1990). The study on European Union aid finds no relationship between foreign aid and human rights protection (Zanger 2000b), while the study on the United Kingdom shows that aid to rights-abusive countries is reduced only for those states that do not have significant economic value (Barratt 2004). For structural adjustment lending, it appears that in addition to using economic criteria for awarding loans to needy countries, both the World Bank and the IMF exercise some political judgement and do not lend disproportionately to rights-abusive governments, while the IMF does not discriminate against democracies (Abouharb and Cingranelli 2004). It thus seems that there is a mismatch between the rhetoric of governments and international financial institutions in claiming an importance for good governance, the rule of law, and human rights protection in their aid allocation decisions and the available evidence provided in these studies. Interestingly, Barratt's (2004) study provides a realist explanation for this apparent contradiction, since her analysis shows that aid allocation as a function of human rights practices interacts with the relative economic value of the recipient country.

Finally, for the Keith (1999) and Hathaway (2002) studies on the importance of international law, bivariate analysis shows a positive and significant relationship between treaty ratification and rights protection, while for their multivariate analyses that control for the other independent effects of democracy, wealth, conflict, population, among other variables, the relationship drops out. In contrast, Landman (2005b) replicates the bivariate findings, but specifies a non-recursive, or 'two-way' model that sees both treaty ratification and rights protection primarily as functions of democracy, development, and interdependence. His results show that there is a significant but limited effect of human rights law on human rights practices, while the timing of democratization accounts for differences in treaty ratification and rights protection, such that late democratizing states tend to ratify more treaties with fewer reservations but such states are less able to protect human rights. Thus all three studies find support for the bi-variate relationship between international law and human rights, but when they control for additional explanatory factors, Keith (1999) and Hathaway (2002) do not find support for the importance of international law, while Landman (2005b) does. This apparent discrepancy in results is explained by differences in model specification in the multivariate analysis and the underlying theory of state behaviour that each study adopts.

By extending the analysis of the first set of studies on the determinants of human rights protection, these additional studies by and large maintain the original research design, but include additional variables and in the case of foreign aid allocation, specify human rights protection as an independent variable. Foreign aid, the penetration of multinational capital, and the proliferation of human rights norms sit squarely in contemporary debates about policy measures that may be useful for the promotion and protection of human rights. The mixed results that are obtained in these additional studies are the product of different measures of the key variables (e.g. those used to measure the presence of multinational corporations), different samples of countries (e.g. different sets of recipient and donor states in the studies on foreign aid), and different model specifications (e.g. recursive versus non-recursive in the studies on the impact of international law), which flow from the ways in which empirical relationships between and among the variables have been theorized and estimated. It is clear that additional studies that test these different measures and models against one another would make a valuable contribution to moving this particular research agenda forward.

Figure 6.3 summarizes the results of these global comparative studies graphically, where the more robust results are shown on the left side of the figure and the mixed results are shown on the right side of the figure. While there have been both positive and non-significant findings for multinational capital, foreign aid, and international law, there is little disagreement that democracy (level and transition) and economic development (level and recent) have a positive impact on rights protection, while international and domestic conflict, prolonged periods of authoritarianism (and unstable anocracies), and population density (not change) have a negative impact on rights protection. This consensus is based on the fact that across the two sets of studies, there is robust statistical support for these relationships, which have been replicated for slightly different selections of countries and

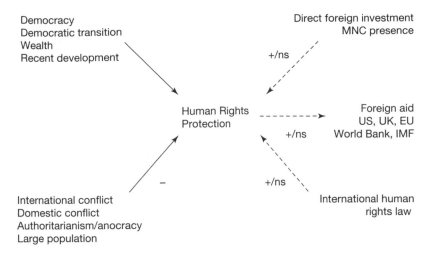

Figure 6.3 Results from extant global comparative studies.

Sources: Adapted from Landman (2003: 208; 2005a: 566).

Note: +/ns = some results show positive effects, while others find no significant effects.

years but which have achieved similar magnitude, direction, and significance in their estimations. It is important to note that these conclusions are empirical generalizations that hold more often than not across the sample of countries and time used in each study. As the discussion in Chapter 4 made clear, there will always be exceptions to these general findings, but on balance, they have been upheld at the global level of analysis.

Limitations to global comparative analysis

This chapter has shown that there has been considerable time and effort dedicated to the careful construction of large-scale global data sets that have been subjected to increasingly sophisticated statistical analysis in an effort to provide 'fair tests' of propositions drawn from the theory and practice of human rights. The goal of such analyses has been to construct data sets in which the key variables of interest actually vary across space and time, while the analysis determines whether the co-variation between and among these variables is both statistically significant and consistent with the expectations of the researchers. The results over which there is greater consensus suggest that patterns of development and democratization have had tangible benefits for the protection of human rights, echoing the more normative language found in such documents as the 1993 Vienna Declaration and Programme of Action. It is also clear that conflict resolution or even the resolution of political differences before they escalate can have a direct bearing on protecting human rights. Indeed, Poe and Tate (1994: 867) argue that the magnitude of conflict alone is so great on the protection of human rights, that beyond the promotion of democracy and economic development, 'rights can be enhanced by actors who would encourage countries to solve their political conflicts short of war, and use whatever means are at their disposal to assist them in doing so'. For the areas of research over which there is less consensus, clear policy prescriptions cannot yet be obtained and the scholarly debates surrounding them centre more on methodological issues concerning measurement, sampling strategies, and model specifications than on substantive results.

But beyond these policy-relevant conclusions, there are four important criticisms that can be made about this form of analysis and clear limitations to its applicability, including (1) the omission of variables from either side of the analysis and the absence of possible interaction effects, (2) the 'ahistorical' nature of the basic research design that is employed, (3) limited theoretical reflection in the specification of models that are tested, and (4) issue areas that may not be suitable for this kind of analysis. First, important variables have either been omitted or have not yet been operationalized sufficiently to be included in such analyses. For example, on the 'left hand' side of the regression analysis, there have been few studies that subject measures of economic and social rights to the same kinds of statistical analysis as civil and political rights. Would the same generalizations hold for these sets of rights? Are wealthy democracies better at protecting these rights? Does international human rights law matter for the protection of these rights? On the 'right hand' side of the regression analysis, there have not been studies that include poverty, income distribution, land distribution, human development as independent variables, and they have not included possible interaction effects between some of these variables and other variables. Are the tangible benefits for human rights from higher levels of wealth the same even if that wealth is differently distributed? What is the relationship between the distribution of land and human rights violations? Is there a significant interaction effect between development and democracy that will have an impact on human rights protection? Finally, are countries with persistent problems in upholding social and economic rights more or less likely to receive foreign aid?

Second, the basic research design includes data on countries from the 1970s until 2000, which is a particular period in which Cold War, decolonization, and post-Cold War events shaped and structured world history. These data contain a large selection of wealthy, democratic, and 'rights-protective' countries (Donnelly 1999a), the inclusion of which may lead to some of the significant results obtained in these analyses. While some of these studies include regional dummy variables (Landman 2005b) to capture some of these differences, more work needs to be done on longer periods of history dating back to the mid 19th century when the domestic struggles for citizenship rights coincided with the 'first wave' of democratization (Marshall 1963; Huntington 1991; Foweraker and Landman 1997; Boix and Stokes 2003; Landman 2005d). The presence of such wealthy and democratic countries in the sample also ignores the structural position of semi-peripheral and peripheral states and their relative power relations with the core countries. Studies on economic development and democracy that controlled for the historical and structural 'location' of countries in the world economy (see Boix 2003; Burkhart and Lewis-Beck 1994; Foweraker and Landman 2004) have shown that economic development is indeed a prerequisite for democracy, but that the overall relationship between levels of economic development and democracy is different over time and space such that 'early' democratizers required a lower threshold of development to secure sustainable democracy, while those countries on the semi-periphery and periphery of the world system accrue less democratic benefit from patterns of economic development. But does the same hold for the protection of human rights? Is it the case that improvements in the protection of human rights follow the same general patterns? Is it possible to use this kind of analysis to map and explain the different 'generations' of human rights?

Third, there needs to be greater reflection on the traditions and approaches in social theory outlined in Chapter 3. With a few minor exceptions (e.g. Meyer 1996; Hathaway 2002; Landman 2005b; Poe 2004; Barratt 2004), there has been little theoretical reflection about why certain variables have been selected for inclusion in these global analyses. In general, the variables that have been chosen reflect an orientation to economic structures and political institutions, with certain references to culture (e.g. British colonial experience). But to date there has been a dearth of integrated theoretical accounts from which a series of testable propositions have been derived of the kind found in the small-*N* comparative and single-country studies outlined in Chapter 4. This is in part due to the fact that it is difficult to operationalize variables for 'agential' accounts of human rights violations. Even those studies that focus on structural explanations have tended not to look at *why* processes and dynamics of economic development would necessarily be related to human rights protection despite the statistical significance of such relationships. For example, is it simply a matter of greater overall resource? Is it a matter of buying off opposition and reducing the kind of political conflict that invites state repression?

Finally, there are a series of issue areas and research questions for which global comparative analysis may not be suitable. For example, while the studies on multinational capital test for the overall presence of multinationals in a country in terms of direct foreign investment, they do not examine the specific *practices* of MNCs nor do they capture the diverse forms of MNCs that operate in countries (see Chapter 2), which may have different kinds of impact on human rights. Global comparative analysis cannot capture the intricacies of mobilization from human rights NGOs or other civil society organizations. While the number of INGOs with registered offices in countries has featured in Landman's (2005b) analysis of the relationship between human rights norms and practices, such a variable will only ever be a proxy measure for the freedom of association in civil society and/or the penetration of international civil society. Indeed, it was precisely the inability of such global studies to capture the transmission of norms through the advocacy, shaming, and lobbying strategies adopted by domestic and international NGOs that led Risse, Ropp and Sikkink (1999) to adopt a different research design. In similar fashion, Mitchell (2004) salutes the achievements of the global studies in establishing the broad parameters for understanding patterns in human rights violations, but in order to test the observable implications of his 'principal–agent' model, he adopts a small-*N* comparative research design. Finally, such analyses are limited in their ability to map inter-subjective meanings and different cultural understandings of human rights, which may or may not have an effect on human rights practices. Thus, well-chosen and systematically analysed single-country studies are a necessary feature of a social science of human rights.

Having made these criticisms and outlined these limitations, it is important to note that global comparative human rights analysis adds value to the study of human rights by providing in the first instance parsimonious models that can be tested, replicated, shared, and improved in an effort to build knowledge about the world. But that knowledge, it should be recognized, is a certain kind that stresses the importance of drawing broad empirical generalizations about the variation in human rights protection across time and space. Inclusion of new and better operationalized variables; longer periods of time that stretch well before the 1948 Universal Declaration; controls for the effects of world history and the structure of global capitalism; different model specifications; and the turn to new research topics will mean that this particular way of 'knowing the world' will continue to make its contribution to understanding and explaining the protection of human rights.

Suggestions for further reading

Carey, S. and Poe, S. (2004) *Understanding Human Rights Violations: New Systematic Studies*, Aldershot: Ashgate.

Hathaway, O. (2002) 'Do Treaties Make a Difference? Human Rights Treaties and the Problem of Compliance', *Yale Law Journal*, 111: 1932–2042.

Landman, T. (2005a) 'Review Article: the Political Science of Human Rights', *British Journal of Political Science*, 35 (3): 549–572.

Landman, T. (2005b) *Protecting Human Rights: A Comparative Study*, Washington DC: Georgetown University Press.

Poe, S. (1990) 'Human Rights and Foreign Aid: A Review of Quantitative Studies and Suggestions for Future Research', *Human Rights Quarterly*, 12: 499–509.

Poe, S. and Tate, C. N. (1994) 'Repression of Human Rights to Personal Integrity in the 1980s: A Global Analysis', *American Political Science Review*, 88: 853–872.

Poe, S. C., Tate, C. N. and Keith, L. C. (1999) 'Repression of the Human Right to Personal Integrity Revisited: A Global Cross-National Study Covering the Years 1976–1993', *International Studies Quarterly*, 43: 291–313.

7   The social science of truth commissions

One key feature characterizing post-conflict, transitional, and democratizing societies has been the establishment of some formal body that investigates past wrongs, patterns of gross human rights violations, atrocities, and/or crimes against humanity.[1] These formal bodies have included international tribunals like those used in Nuremberg after World War II, the International Criminal Tribunal for the Former Yugoslavia (ICTY) in the Hague and the International Criminal Tribunal for Rwanda (ICTR) in Arusha; and they have included domestically based (although in some cases internationally run) truth commissions, commissions for historical clarification, truth and reconciliation commissions, and community-based justice programmes (e.g. the *gacaca* system in Rwanda). They also include larger projects on historical memory and lustration processes for former agents of the authoritarian state apparatus. In each case, the establishment of such a formal body fundamentally puts down a marker to acknowledge that past wrongs must be addressed in some way and to recognize that ignoring such past wrongs is to leave open the possibility of their happening again.

These formal bodies range in the degree to which they establish criminal liability, accountability, legal justice, financial compensation, public acknowledgement, and reconciliation (Hayner 2002: 24–31). Truth commissions have been by far the dominant type of investigative body that has been used across a wide range of such transitional societies. For post-conflict situations, truth commissions represent a formal institutional mechanism for establishing a public record of violent events and gross violations of human rights, such as those that have been held in Guatemala, El Salvador, Haiti, Peru, and Sierra Leone. For those societies undergoing democratic transition, truth commissions are a product of accommodation between dominant political forces that have taken part in the transition and often involve a careful negotiation over the different roles for truth, justice, amnesty, and impunity (Skaar 1999; Skaar, Gloppen and Suhrke 2005). Such commissions include those used in Argentina after the military regime (1976–1982), Chile after the Pinochet regime (1973–1990), and in South Africa after the apartheid regime (1960–1994). In other countries, truth commissions have been set up to provide a record of human rights abuses for multiple periods of authoritarian government (e.g. in Ghana 1966–1969, 1972–1979, 1981–1993; South Korea, and Panama), while others have been set up to investigate human rights abuses during prolonged periods of foreign occupation, as in the case of East Timor (1974–1999).

To date, there have been more than thirty such commissions that have spanned the regions of Central and South America, the Caribbean, Africa, Europe, and Southeast Asia and the Pacific (see Table 7.1 for a list of the most notable ones). While these commissions have been established for different purposes with different legal mandates and under the

Table 7.1 Truth commissions around the world

Country	Date of commission	Dates covered
Uganda	1974	January 25, 1971–1974
Bolivia	1982–1984	1967–1982
Argentina	1983–1984	1976–1983
Uruguay	1985	1973–1982
Zimbabwe	1985	1983
Uganda	1986–1995	December 1962–1986
Nepal	1990–1991	1961–1990
Chile	1990–1991	September 11, 1973 – March 11, 1990
Chad	1991–1992	1982–1990
South Africa	1992	1979–1991
Germany	1992–1994	1949–1989
El Salvador	1992–1993	January 1980 – July 1991
South Africa	1993	1979–1991
Sri Lanka	November 1994 – September 1997	January 1, 1988 – November 13, 1994
Haiti	April 1995 – February 1996	September 29, 1991 – October 15, 1994
Burundi	September 1995 – July 1996	October 21, 1993 – August 28, 1995
South Africa	December 1995 – 2000	March 1, 1960 – May 10, 1994
Ecuador	September 1996 – February 1997	1979–1996
Guatemala	August 1997 – February 1999	1962–1996
Nigeria	1999–2000	1966 – May 28, 1999
South Korea	October 2000 – 2003	'past authoritarian regimes'
Panama	January 18, 2001 – April 2002	1968–1988
Peru	June 2001 – August 2003	1980–2000
Ghana	January 2002 –	March 6, 1957 – January 6, 1993
Sierra Leone	2000–2001; 2002–2005	1991–1999
East Timor	July 2001 – July 2005	April 25, 1974 – October 25, 1999

Sources: Hayner (1994); Skaar (1999); Hayner (2002: 305–311); United States Institute of Peace (www.usip.org); Gloppen (2005: 29–32).

auspices of different authorities, they share a number of common features: (1) they focus on the past, (2) they do not focus on specific events, but seek to discover a broader picture, (3) they are temporary, (4) they have the authority to access all areas to obtain information (see Hayner 1994: 604; 2002: 14), and (5) they have a legal mandate to 'clarify', 'establish the complete picture', 'investigate serious acts of violence', 'establish the truth', and 'create an impartial historical record'. The proliferation of truth commissions and the similarity in their basic features, purpose, and work has led to a burgeoning social science literature that examines their establishment, impact, and the 'essentially contested' (Gallie 1956) nature of the truth that they uncover (see e.g. Hayner 1994, 2002; Kritz 1995; Minow 1998; Popkin and Bhuta 1999; Skaar 1999; Villa-Vicencio and Verwoerd 2000; James and van de Vijver 2000; Avruch and Vejarano 2001; De Brito, Gonzaléz-Enríquez and Aguilar 2001; Wilson 2001; Skaar, Gloppen and Suhrke 2005).

In contrast to almost all of the extant social scientific studies on truth commissions, this chapter approaches the main work of a truth commission as a classic problem of social scientific analysis. The main problem facing all truth commissions is that there is an *elusive* but *circumscribed* population of total human rights violations that have occurred during the time period defined by the legal mandate of each commission. It is *circumscribed* since there have been a finite number of violations. It is *elusive* since the truth commission does not know *a priori* how many violations there have been, where they have been committed, by whom, and for what reasons. The first task for a truth commission is to estimate the total number of violations that have been committed in order to capture and represent as accurately as possible the history of the period under investigation. Such an estimation provides the public recognition of the events having occurred in the first place, and specifies the many different dimensions that characterize the patterns of violations. Public recognition and acknowledgement of this 'truth' serves a larger purpose since many victims and their families have often lived in silence, fear, and isolation about the particular set of violations that they have personally experienced (see REMHI 1999: xxxi). Estimating the total population of violations as best as possible shows to the victims that they have been part of a larger set of violations in which others like them have suffered.

The second task is to provide an acceptable explanation for how and why such a set of violations occurred. This task provides a deeper understanding of the possible causes lying behind the patterns of violations and moves beyond mere recognition of the 'truth' and seeks to explain it. Such explanation has many dimensions, including broad socio-economic forces, cultural understandings and deep antagonisms, and the exercise of political power of certain dominant groups. In this way, the estimated number and dimensions of the human rights violations become an important *dependent variable* for social scientific analysis, where theories and hypotheses can be tested and the inferences that are drawn from the analysis of the patterns of violations can inform the findings and recommendations of truth commissions. Thus, the two tasks of estimating and explaining the total population of violations are mutually reinforcing, since the explanation cannot take place without the estimation and the estimation is informed by possible explanations of the violence.

While estimation and explanation are classic functions of social scientific analysis, the work of truth commissions presents a particular problem of estimation that can be solved using data collection and analytical techniques. The day-to-day work of truth commissions involves taking statements from victims and their families, witnesses and bystanders, as well as the perpetrators themselves. But this sample of people is not random and is therefore *unrepresentative of the population* as a whole. In social scientific terms, it is considered a non-random, selective, or 'convenience' sample (Tashakkori and Teddlie 1998: 76), since the individuals that form the sample are self-selecting and voluntarily come to the truth commission to make a statement about human rights violations. Reliance on one such sample only can produce limited and/or misleading inferences about the pattern of violations that have taken place. In social scientific terms, the use of these kinds of samples can lead to under-estimating the number of violations that did occur (i.e. a Type I error) or over-estimating the number of violations that did not occur (i.e. a Type II error) (see, e.g. Vogt 1999: 297; Przeworski, Alvarez, Cheibub and Limongi 2000: 23).

The convenience samples are biased for many important reasons related to the conditions under which truth commissions take the statements. First, not all victims or witnesses come forward to make a statement; there may be geographical obstacles for victims and witnesses to come forward; and deponents may have died before the establishment of the truth commissions thereby leading to an under-representation of past events. Second, truth commissions work under limited time and financial constraints, so never hear and record every last testimony about violations; ideological differences and differences in the degree to which individuals identify with the truth commission may skew the distribution of people giving testimony; and by extension, deponents may actually provide false information about violations for personal, cultural, or political purposes. Different combinations of any of these factors will contribute to the fact that a truth commission never has all the facts about any period it is charged with investigating.

Thus the social scientific and statistical problem becomes: how from a biased and selective sample of testimonies can a truth commission estimate the total number of violations that have taken place, explain the patterns that are observed, and provide as complete a picture as possible? The purpose of this chapter is to show how social scientific and statistical methods have been used to answer this fundamental problem facing all truth commissions. Since committing either a Type I or Type II error in estimating the total population of violations that has taken place limits the overall strength of the inferences that are drawn about any period under investigation, this chapter shows how careful attention to the sampling procedure, the data-gathering phase and the analytical techniques applied to the data that have been collected can enhance the types of estimations and explanations that are ultimately offered by a truth commission. To do so, the chapter illustrates how the complexity of a human rights event can be captured, how the information within a statement is represented and coded, and how the use of multiple sources of information and multiple systems estimation (MSE) has provided a solution to the difficulty of making statistical estimations from inherently biased samples of information. The discussion of all these elements of data collection and analysis are illustrated with examples from truth commissions that have taken place.

Capturing the complexity of a human rights event

The predominant model for collecting and analysing human rights data that has been adopted by truth commissions is the 'who did what to whom' model developed at the American Association for the Advancement of Science in Washington DC (see Ball, Spirer, and Spirer 2000).[2] It has been used in the truth commissions for El Salvador, Haiti, South Africa, Guatemala, Peru, Sierra Leone, and East Timor (see Table 7.2). It is a model that produces the most disaggregated form of 'events-based' human rights data available (see Chapter 5) and is organized using the violation as the basic unit of analysis. By applying a 'controlled vocabulary' of human rights violations, the model deconstructs the narrative statement that deponents provide to the truth commission and codes each separate violation that makes up the more complex human rights 'event'. Figure 7.1 shows the complex structure of a human rights event that is revealed from a single narrative statement collected by a truth commission. The figure shows that any single statement contains information about victims, violations, and perpetrators. One or many victims have definitive characteristics, may have suffered one or many different violations, committed by one or many perpetrators. There is thus a series of complex inter-relationships between and among violations, victims, and perpetrators. As Chapter 4 in this volume outlined, such a coding of the 'grammar' of human action (i.e. who did what to whom) has its roots in behavioural social science and has been used for research on protest, social mobilization, political violence, and inter-state relations (Lasswell 1941; McClelland 1983; Goldstein

Table 7.2 Truth commissions that adopted the 'who did what to whom' data model

Truth commission	Period covered	Number of sources	MSE[a]	Number of statements taken	Examples of estimations of violations
El Salvador (1992–1993)	1980–1991	Truth commission 2 NGOs	No	7,000 by truth commission; 22,000 in total with 3,000 duplicated	60% of statements concern extra-judicial killings, 35% forced disappearance, 20% torture
Haiti (1995–1996)	1991–1994	Truth commission Morgue survey	No	7,000 by truth commission	8,667 victims suffered 18,629 violations
South Africa (1995–1998)	1960–1994	Truth commission Human rights documentation project	No	21,296 by truth commission	46,696 reported violations 36,935 reported gross violations 28,750 reported victims
Guatemala (1997–1999)	1962–1996	Truth commission 2 NGOs	Yes	7,517 by truth commission 5,465 by REMHI[b] 5,000 by CIIDH[c]	Between 119,300 and 145,000 dead, with the most likely estimate being 132,000; REMHI reports 52,427 victims
Peru (2001–2003)	1980–2000	Truth commission 5 NGOs	Yes	16,917 by truth commission	23,969 reported dead 18,397 fully identified dead 61,007 to 77,552 dead with most likely estimate being 69,280
Sierra Leone (2000–2005)	1991–1999	Truth commission	No	7,000 by truth commission	40,242 total violations reported 7,983 forced displacements reported 5,968 abductions reported 4,835 arbitrary abductions reported 4,514 killings reported
East Timor (2001–2005)	1974–1999	Truth commission Household survey Graveyard records	Yes	8,000 by truth commission 1,396 households 250,000 graveyard records	Pending final report

Sources: Kritz (1995); Ball, Kobrak and Spirer (1999); Ball, Spirer and Spirer (2000); Hayner (2002); Ball, Asher, Sulmont and Manrique (2003); Final Report of the South African Truth and Reconciliation Commission (1998); Final Report for the Truth and Reconciliation Commission for Peru (2003); Final Report of the Truth and Reconciliation Commission for Sierra Leone (2004).

Notes: [a] Multiple systems estimation; [b] Recovery of Historical Memory Project, Guatemala; [c] International Centre for Investigating Human Rights, Guatemala.

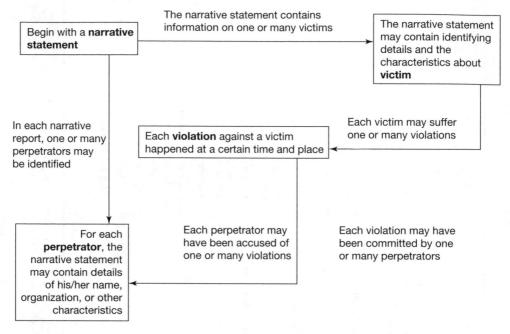

Figure 7.1 The complex structure of a human rights violation testimony.

Source: Adapted from Ball, Spirer and Spirer (2000b: 29).

Table 7.3 The 'who did what to whom' representation of human rights information

Who	*What*	*Whom*	*When*	*Where*
Perpetrator	*Violation(s)*	*Victim*	*Time*	*Space*
Individuals	Detention	Individuals	Hour	Urban
Groups	Torture	Groups	Day	Rural
Institutions	Extra-judicial killing	Institutions	Week	Administrative or political unit
Organizations	Disappearance	Organizations	Month	
	Economic crime(s)		Year(s)	
	Other violations			

1992; Franzosi 1990, 2004), and is most appropriate for the analysis of human rights violations by truth commissions. Table 7.3 shows the different dimensions of a human rights violation event, which draws on the schematic representation of such events depicted in Figure 7.1.

It is clear from the table that individuals have different *identities* (peasant, worker, man, woman, indigenous, rich, poor) and *roles* (perpetrators and victims), each of which can be contained in a testimony. Victims and perpetrators can be individuals, groups, or organizations. Violations can include a whole range of human rights abuses, which emerge *inductively* from the testimonies that are provided and *deductively* through application of a controlled vocabulary to the set of violation acts that are reported in the testimony. Like perpetrators, victims can be individuals, groups, institutions, or organizations. There are also important temporal and spatial dimensions to a human rights event that can be analysed using this model.

Organizing the database with any other unit of analysis than the violation itself leads to significant loss of information and the possibility of committing Type I and Type II errors (i.e. over- or under-counting violations). Such errors can occur if the individual is the unit of analysis and/or the analysis focuses on the most severe violations of human rights (a category that often appears in the legal mandate of truth commissions). To illustrate these points, Table 7.4 presents a hypothetical representation of information collected on human rights violations across the months of March and April. The data are organized with the individual as the unit of analysis, and column 4 codes the most severe violations for each month. Note that each individual may have suffered detention (D), torture (T), and/or assassination (A), and that the project coded the most severe violations. If the truth commission asks, 'what has been the pattern in torture over the last two months?' the project analyst using the data in column 4 of the table would wrongly conclude that torture has declined between the months of March and April (see Figure 7.2). If all violations had been coded, the answer to the same question would be that the use of torture has remained constant between the months of March and April (see Figure 7.3), and that in comparing torture to assassination, torture has remained constant while assassination has increased (see Figure 7.4). Moreover, it is clear from the table that each individual suffered multiple violations of human rights, an important fact that can be missed if the truth commission only codes the most serious violations.

While the example above is only hypothetical, in practice such a miscounting occurred in the Recovery of Historical Memory Project (REMHI) in Guatemala, in which the category of 'massacre' was used to code events that were too 'messy' to disentangle. The initial results of the analysis under-reported the number of human rights violations, which had been obscured by lumping together many different violations that occurred during a massacre. Many people in the massacres had been raped, tortured, and disappeared, but were not coded as having suffered those violations. Thus when the massacre and non-massacre data were combined, there was an under-representation of the true nature of the human rights violations that had occurred (Mazariegos 2000b: 156).

Table 7.4 Hypothetical collection of human rights violation data

Month	Individual	Types of violation	Most severe coded
March	1	D, T	T
March	2	D, T	T
March	3	D, T	T
March	4	D, T, A	A
April	5	D, T, A	A
April	6	D, T, A	A
April	7	D, T, A	A
April	8	D, T, A	A

Note: D = Detention, T = Torture, and A = Assassination.

Figure 7.2 Miscounting the incidence of torture.

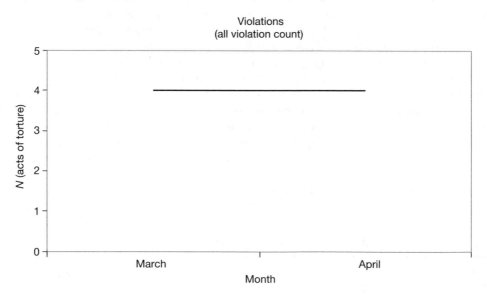

Figure 7.3 Actual incidence of torture has remained constant.

A similar problem occurred as part of the work carried out by the United Nations Mission for the Verification of Human Rights in Guatemala (MINUGUA). It initially coded 'primary' violations suffered by victims (i.e. those that were most serious) and therefore grossly under-represented the 'victimization' of the individual and created a 'false view of the events and distortion of trends' (Ward 2000: 138). Using the violation as the basic unit of analysis can thus alleviate some of these problems of misrepresentation of the true nature and pattern of human rights violations.

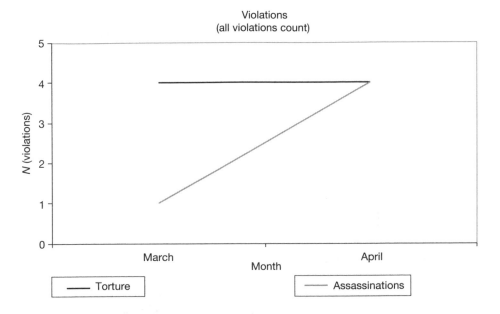

Figure 7.4 Actual incidence of torture and assassination.

A 'who did what to whom' database is constructed by coding the raw information gathered by the truth commission, known as the 'source layer' through application of the controlled vocabulary, while the matching of accounts between statements is called the 'judgement layer'. Figure 7.5 shows that it is entirely possible to have two statements for the same violation (i.e. two different people witness the same event). Statement 1 revealed three different violations (A, B, C), while Statement 2 offers a separate additional account of violation A. Using the idea of source and judgement layers means that there are 'reporting densities' associated with each violation. In this case, the reporting density for violation A is 2, and for violations B and C is 1. There are probability distributions associated with reporting densities that assist in drawing inferences about the number of violations that have been reported to the truth commission by overcoming the problem of 'double counting' associated with multiple accounts of the same set of violations.

While an initial list of violations may emerge *inductively* from the testimonies, the use of controlled vocabularies reduces the complexity of the information *deductively* to a certain degree by providing the core content of violations that are to be analysed, boundary conditions to distinguish between violations, and counting rules to provide continuity over time and across space. The general dimensions of such a vocabulary and set of boundary conditions are agreed upon by the truth commission in advance, while leaving some room for adjustment as the information from statements begins to be processed. The core content of violations can come from international human rights law, human rights violation documentation organizations (e.g. HURIDOCS), or can emerge as a consensus among the commissioners in interpreting the legal mandate of the truth commission (for problems with such interpretation in Sierra Leone, see Schabas 2005: 134–140). In this way, the data model remains a relatively flexible instrument that can be used by different truth commissions investigating human rights abuses that have taken place under very different circumstances.

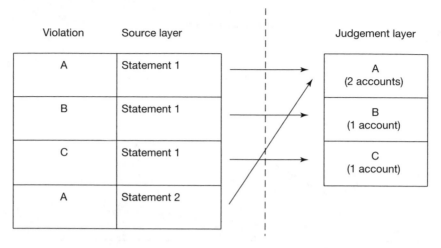

Figure 7.5 Source and judgement layers.

This model for capturing the true nature and extent of human rights violations that have been committed effectively takes a set of narrative accounts, breaks them down into their constituent parts, quantifies the violations according to victims, perpetrators, and acts, and then reconstitutes the information through the production of summary and descriptive statistics (see also Wilson 2001: 40–41). The resulting data allow for a series of inferential and analytical statements that take the following generic form:

1. There are N instances of detention reported to the truth commission;
2. There are N instances of torture reported to the truth commission;
3. There are N instances of assassination reported to the truth commission;
4. There have been a total of N violations reported to the truth commission;
5. It has been reported to the truth commission that perpetrator P1 has committed N total violations;
6. $N\%$ of deponents are victims and $N\%$ are perpetrators.

These types of statements remain as close as possible to the true record of violations reported to a truth commission, but it is impossible to use that record to make any secure inferences to the true population of all violations that have taken place, since the sample of testimonies is significantly biased. Thus, truth commissions that have relied on such single-source non-random samples confine their findings to the sample itself. For example, the truth commissions in South Africa and Sierra Leone relied on single non-random samples for drawing their conclusions, while those in El Salvador and Haiti had multiple sources of information whose full analytical potential for drawing inferences were not harnessed. Across all of these truth commissions, the reported findings make analytical statements that are relative to the sample itself (see the last column in Table 7.2).

Multiplying sources and statistical estimation

The limitations associated with single-source non-random samples have been overcome by including information that has been collected by organizations outside the truth commission (as in Guatemala and Peru), or by the truth commission collecting information form alternative sources itself (as in East Timor). Before discussing how truth commissions collect and use these different sources of information to complement the information gathered through statement taking, it is first necessary to understand why using multiple sources of information significantly enhances the capacity for truth commissions to draw inferences that are much closer to the true population of violations that have actually taken place. The use of multiple samples of information controls for more of the systematic sources of bias and allows for inferences to be generated about the true population of violations through the use of multiple systems estimation (MSE).

MSE is a statistical technique originally used to estimate fish populations from 'captured, tagged, and recaptured' samples of fish from which inferences to the total population are made possible (see Peterson 1896; Bishop, Fienberg and Holland 1975). The technique has been used to estimate a variety of unknown or 'closed' populations, such as the number of children with a certain congenital anomaly in Massachusetts, feral dogs in Baltimore, and drug addicts in the United States (Bishop, Feinberg and Holland 1975: 230–231), and it is particularly suited for the problem of estimation confronting truth commissions. The basic principle behind MSE is that 'the chance of an individual appearing on two lists is equal to the product of their chances of appearing on each list separately' (Knight 2003: 6). MSE provides a point estimate with an associated margin of error (or standard error, SE), which reflects the statistical confidence with which the estimate has been made, a level of confidence that increases in proportion to the number of samples of information that are used (see Bishop, Feinberg and Holland 1975: 229– 256). It is thus in the interest of the truth commission to identify as many alternative sources of information as possible if it wishes to capture the true nature and extent of all the violations that have taken place.

In order to explain how multiple samples and MSE help strengthen the types of inferences that are drawn about the true population of human rights violations, consider the following hypothetical example. Two organizations have collected information on human rights violations for a given period of time in the same country. Let N represent the total number of violations and let A and B represent the number of violations that have been reported to the two different organizations. Some violations will have been reported only in A, some have been reported only in B, some have been reported in both A and B, and some have not been reported at all. Let M represent the number of violations that have been reported in both A and B. Figure 7.6 depicts these different numbers of violations (N, A, B, and M). The figure also shows that there are different probability statements associated with violations that end up being reported and that there is a relationship between the number of violations that have been reported (A, B, and M) to the total number of violations that have occurred (N).[3]

The probability that violations will be reported in A is A/N; the probability that violations will be reported in B is B/N; and the probability that violations will be reported in both A and B (i.e. M) is M/N. Following on from these separate probabilities, there is a ratio between those violations that have been reported and the total number of violations (N). The ratio of the number of violations reported in both A and B (M) to the number of violations reported in A is proportional to the ratio of the number of violations reported

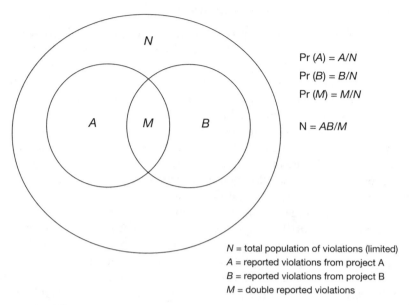

$$Pr\,(A) = A/N$$
$$Pr\,(B) = B/N$$
$$Pr\,(M) = M/N$$

$$N = AB/M$$

N = total population of violations (limited)
A = reported violations from project A
B = reported violations from project B
M = double reported violations

Figure 7.6 Different reporting of human rights violations and multiple systems estimation.

in B to the total number of violations (N), such that: $M/A = B/N$. Transforming this ratio and solving for N algebraically means that N (i.e. the true population of violations) $= AB/N$. This general ratio forms the basis for the way in which MSE can be used to calculate the total number of human rights violations using multiple sources of information, each of which is organized into the 'who did what to whom' model of database design.

In a classic illustration of statistical estimation, MSE is using information about violations that are known to calculate information about violations that are not known, much like the way in which public opinion surveys use information they *do know* about the public to calculate information that they *do not know* about the public. The key difference between the statistical estimations used in public opinion research and MSE is that where public opinion research uses random samples of the population, MSE uses multiple non-random samples of the population. Both forms of analysis produce statistical estimates with associated margins of error, where public opinion research typically calculates the percentage of the population expressing some sort of preference for something (plus or minus some margin of error), while MSE in truth commissions calculates the total number of particular types of human rights violations during a given time period (plus or minus some margin of error).

This general form of MSE is the same for two or more sources of data on human rights violations. Consider a human rights project with three sources of data (A, B, and C), each of which do or do not have violations reported to them (0,1). Figure 7.7 represents the resulting matrix of possibilities for violations being reported to the various sources. Since violations can either be reported or not be reported, and there are three sources, there are 2^3 (or 8) total possibilities. Each of the eight cells in the matrix reports the combination of possibilities of both separate and joint reporting of human rights violations, since it is entirely possible for the same individual to report violations to two different organizations. Cell VIII is the only one with absolutely unknown information, since it represents the combination where all three sources have not recorded any violations (see

		Yes		No	
	C>	Yes	No	Yes	No
A Yes		I	II	III	IV
		(1, 1, 1)	(1, 1, 0)	(1, 0, 1)	(1, 0, 0)
No		V	VI	VII	VIII
		(0, 1, 1)	(0, 1, 0)	(0, 0, 1)	(0, 0, 0)

Figure 7.7 Matrix of possibilities for human rights violations being reported to three sources.

Source: A general form of this matrix presented in Bishop, Feinberg and Holland (1975: 237).

Bishop, Feinberg and Holland 1975: 237). MSE uses information across matching cells to calculate the expected values in this empty cell using different fit assumptions (independent or overlapping sources of information) and a log linear model of estimation (see Bishop, Fienberg and Holland 1975: 237–246), which is a modified version of the basic multivariate regression technique discussed in Chapter 6.

The use of multiple samples and MSE overcome most of the residual sources of systematic error associated with non-random convenience samples, *such as those found in most truth commissions*. Heterogeneous sources of bias can be controlled through stratifying the data according to the geographical features of the country under investigation. Endogenous sources of bias such as lying, timidity, and political mobilization of testimony can be controlled through analysis of the reporting densities and the resulting 'shape' of the data across the different samples. Systematic lies will show up as large flat areas within the data, while political mobilization of testimonies will show up as a lump in the reporting densities. Both features look suspicious to the data analyst. After having controlled for these possible sources of bias, the results of MSE can produce the following generic analytical statements about human rights violations:

1. There are N ($\pm$ SE) instances of detention for the period t_1–t_n;
2. There are N ($\pm$ SE) instances of torture for the period t_1–t_n;
3. There are N ($\pm$ SE) instances of assassination for the period t_1–t_n;
4. There have been a total of N ($\pm$ SE) violations for the period t_1–t_n;
5. There is a statistically significant difference between the number of killings committed by perpetrator P_1 and by perpetrator P_2;
6. There is a statistically significant difference between the number of killings committed in rural departments and urban departments;
7. There is a statistically significant difference between the number of killings committed during period t_1–t_2 and period t_3–t_4.

Such statements represent a very close approximation of the kinds of 'truth findings' found in the legal mandates of truth commissions, where inferences drawn on statistically significant differences between victims, violations, and perpetrators, as well as time and space provide the necessary patterns and macro-historical pictures of the nature of human rights violations that have taken place during any period of conflict, authoritarian rule, and/or foreign occupation. But beyond these technical statistical discussions, how has MSE been applied in the field? Guatemala, Peru, and East Timor are excellent cases to illustrate how MSE has been used to estimate the true nature and extent of human rights violations, and why MSE presented crucial evidence for the truth commissions in these countries that simply would not have been possible had they used only one source of human rights information.

The case of Guatemala

CEH (the Commission to Clarify Past Human Rights Violations and Acts of Violence that Have Caused the Guatemalan People to Suffer) was established in 1994, but did not begin its work until 1997 (Hayner 2002: 45). It was set up to (1) clarify human rights violations and incidents of violence related to the armed confrontation that took place between 1962 and 1996; (2) make recommendations to preserve the memory of the victims and to foster respect and observance of human rights, and to strengthen the democratic process; and (3) analyse the factors and circumstances that have a bearing on the incidents. It collected what it considered to be 7,517 verifiable statements (or *casos registrados*), which identified 24,910 killings (Ball 2000b: 260). These statements were complemented by 5,465 statements collected by the Recovery of Historic Memory Project (REMHI), which identified 21,200 killings, and 5,000 statements collected by the International Centre for Human Rights Investigations (CIIDH) (Ball, Kobrak and Spirer 1999: 5; Spirer 2000: 176), which identified 8,533 killings (Ball 2000b: 260).

As part of its overall system of information management, CEH combined its data with the data collected by REMHI and CIIDH. By using the three sources of data, multiple systems estimation showed that conflict between 1978 and 1996 was responsible for between 119,300 and 145,000 deaths, with the most likely figure being 132,000 (CEH 1999: 72; Ball 2000b: 261). Since the two additional organizations (REMHI and CIIDH) were ideologically quite distant from one another, they collected human rights violation information that had very little overlap in the coverage of cases with one another or with the information collected by CEH. In technical terms, M was small relative to N (see Figure 7.6), which means the estimate had a relatively large margin of error. If the two additional organizations had more overlap in their information on human rights violations, the estimate would have remained approximately 132,000, but the range of values on either side of the estimate would have been smaller. Despite the small overlap among the three sources, MSE showed the degree to which the conflict had such a large impact on such a small country.

The case of Peru

In 2001, through an official Decree (No. 065-2001-PCM), President Alejandro Toledo established the *Comisión de Verdad y Reconciliación* (Truth and Reconciliation Commission, CVR) in Peru to investigate human rights violations that occurred as part of the armed conflict between 1980 and 2000.[4] The conflict took place during the prolonged democratic transition that had begun in 1980 and was challenged by a return to authoritarianism during President Fujimori's administration (1990–2000). The main actors involved in the conflict were *Sendero Luminoso* ('Shining Path', a Maoist revolutionary movement), the *Movimiento Revolucionário Tupac Amaru* (Revolutionary Movement of Tupac Amaru, or MRTA), and the government. Article 3 of the decree law gave the CVR a mandate to investigate assassinations, kidnappings, forced disappearances, torture, violation of collective rights in Andean and indigenous communities, and other crimes and serious human rights violations.

The CVR collected 16,917 statements, conducted 120 elite interviews with key actors from the main sectors involved in the conflict, carried out public hearings, and conducted *estudios en profundidad* (in-depth studies) across thirty typical cases that characterized the period, and published its final report on 28 August 2003 (www.cverdad.org.pe/ingles/ifinal/index.php). The work of the CVR was accompanied by separate databases that had been prepared by the *Defensoria del Pueblo* (Defence of the People) and a combination of depositions taken by four NGOs. These four NGOs included the National Coalition of Human Rights (CNDDHH), the Agricultural Development Centre (CEDAP), the Human Rights Commission (COMISEH), and the International Committee of the Red Cross (ICRC). The CVR received testimonies on 23,969 dead or disappeared people for the period of the conflict, where 18,397 victims could be identified by their full names (CVR Final Report, Statistical Annex; Ball, Asher, Sulmont and Manrique 2003: 3).

The final report combined the data from these sources and used MSE to estimate that a total of 69,280 people were killed or disappeared during the conflict, with a 12 per cent margin of error that ranges from a lower limit of 61,007 to an upper limit of 77,552 (ibid.: 2). Figure 7.8 shows the three sources of data and the three cells with 'unknown' data that MSE was used to estimate. Figure 7.9 shows the final estimates of killings broken down by the main categories of perpetrator, and found that *Sendero Luminoso* committed 46 per cent of these killings and disappearances, 30 per cent were committed by state agents, and the remaining 24 per cent by other perpetrators. The largest number of killings and disappearances occurred in Ayacucho, a remote highland region, followed by the Centre, Northeast, South Andes, Huancavelica, Lima, and others. These results were further broken down by examining violations by perpetrator and region. While *Sendero Luminoso* was found to be the main perpetrator in the highlands, state

Perú 1980–2000: Reported numbers of deaths, by responsible party, by the presence or absence of each of the sources of data

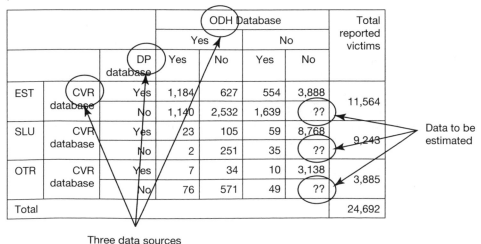

			ODH Database				Total reported victims
			Yes		No		
		DP database	Yes	No	Yes	No	
EST	CVR database	Yes	1,184	627	554	3,888	11,564
		No	1,140	2,532	1,639	??	
SLU	CVR database	Yes	23	105	59	8,768	9,243
		No	2	251	35	??	
OTR	CVR database	Yes	7	34	10	3,138	3,885
		No	76	571	49	??	
Total							24,692

Data to be estimated

Three data sources

Figure 7.8 Three separate sources of data and the blank cells to be estimated by MSE.

Source: Adapted from Ball, Asher, Sulmont and Manrique (2003: 16).

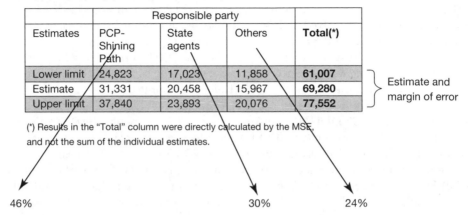

Perú 1980–2000: Estimates and confidence interval limits of the total number of deaths caused by the armed internal conflict, by responsible party (confidence level: 95%)

Estimates	Responsible party			Total(*)
	PCP-Shining Path	State agents	Others	
Lower limit	24,823	17,023	11,858	61,007
Estimate	31,331	20,458	15,967	69,280
Upper limit	37,840	23,893	20,076	77,552

(*) Results in the "Total" column were directly calculated by the MSE, and not the sum of the individual estimates.

46%   30%   24%

Figure 7.9 The final estimates for the number of people killed in Peru, 1980–2000.

Source: Adapted from Ball, Asher, Sulmont and Manrique (2003: 7).

agents were found to be the main perpetrators in and around metropolitan Lima. The MSE calculations controlled for biases through the use of multiple sources, where the information was further stratified according to political and geographic regions, and corroborated through comparison with demographic analysis. Figure 7.10 shows the number of killings by geographical department, where nearly half of all the documented deaths were known to have occurred in the highland region of Ayacucho. Interestingly, this figure resembles that which Greer (1935) produced for the Reign of Terror in France (see Figure 5.4).

The case of East Timor

In East Timor, the United Nations Transitional Administration (UNTAET) established the Commission for Reception, Truth and Reconciliation (CAVR) in July 2001. The late Sergio Vieira de Mello, Transition Administrator, swore in its seven national commissioners on 21 January 2002. The CAVR is mandated to investigate the human rights violations that occurred between 25 April 1974 and 25 October 1999, the years of conflict and Indonesian occupation of East Timor. The work of CAVR comprises truth telling for victims and perpetrators, a programme of community reconciliation for lesser crimes, and making recommendations to the government for further activities and policies related to reconciliation and the promotion of human rights. The CAVR used the 'who did what to whom' data model, but unlike the cases of Guatemala and Peru, did not have additional sources of data made available by human rights NGOs. Rather, in seeing the value of multiple sources, it created two additional sources of information. The first source was the result of conducting a retrospective mortality survey of 1,396 households that were randomly selected from a total of 180,000 households, which collected data on residence patterns and deaths of household members and relatives during the period of Indonesian occupation. The second source was the product of a graveyard census, where the name, date of birth, and date of death were recorded for every grave with available

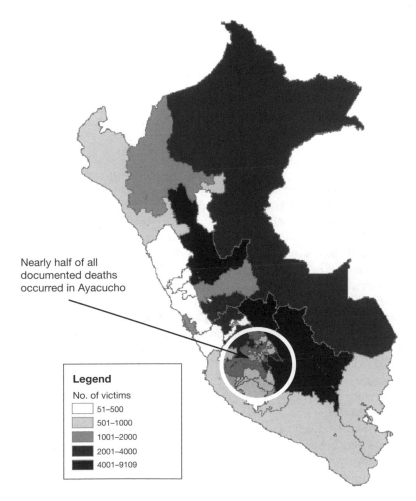

Nearly half of all
documented deaths
occurred in Ayacucho

Legend

No. of victims

	51–500
	501–1000
	1001–2000
	2001–4000
	4001–9109

Figure 7.10 Geographical distribution of political killings in Peru, 1980–2000.

Source: Adapted from the CVR Final Report.

information, a process that produced 250,000 unique entries. MSE has then been used to match the information across these three sources of data in order to provide an overall estimate of the total number of killings. While the CAVR has yet to publish its findings, its experience demonstrates how, in the absence of previously available data, multiple sources of data can be created using different collection techniques.

More than 'getting the number right'

It is clear that these statistical techniques as applied to the narrative accounts of human rights violations have in many ways provided a valuable solution to the fundamental problem facing all truth commissions. In practice, there have been significant processes of learning both across and within truth commissions such that the 'who did what to whom' model for analysing large-scale human rights violations has developed into what Kuhn (1970) has called a 'normal science'. Its practices are well documented and can be replicated, and its overall framework of analysis remains flexible enough to adapt to the cultural specificities of the variety of contexts in which it has been applied. The model uses the violation as the basic unit of analysis, which preserves the complex structure of a human rights event and allows for various degrees of subsequent secondary analysis that examines the nature and extent of violations by providing statistical estimates of violation types, victim types, and perpetrator types as well as the relationships between these main variables. The use of multiple sources in the cases of Guatemala, Peru, and East Timor has been able to harness the full value of statistical estimation to the true population of violations, while controlling for possible sources of systematic bias.

But the analysis of the social science of truth commissions presented in this chapter goes well beyond 'getting the number right', where the findings of the various truth commissions have challenged preconceived ideas and dominant myths that had developed within these countries about the true nature and extent of the human rights violations committed. Indeed, the MSE can establish the degree to which specific sub-populations have been targeted by perpetrators, such as the indigenous communities that were targeted by the security forces in Guatemala and the highland peasant communities targeted by *Sendero Luminoso* in Peru. For example, the CEH findings show that across all six regions in Guatemala, there were a disproportionate number of deaths among the indigenous people, and in two of the regions the ratio of indigenous deaths to non-indigenous deaths reached five to one, supporting the notion that security forces were committing genocide (see Ball 2000b: 277). Such analysis in theory could be carried out in Darfur, which could test Colin Powell's assertion that the Sudanese government was allowing genocide to be committed (BBC 2004).

In Peru, the estimations in the report challenged a number of dominant myths that had characterized previous assessments of the government's conflict with *Sendero Luminoso*. First, the results showed the violence was almost three times as severe as previous calculations had suggested. Domestic and international NGOs, human rights activists, and commentators had long believed that 'only' 22,000 people had died in the conflict, while the findings suggest that the number was closer to 70,000. Second, the report showed that despite popular perceptions about the nature of the violence, *Sendero Luminoso* and not the military was the primary perpetrator during the period under investigation. Third, as in Guatemala, the violence disproportionately affected the Andean and indigenous populations of Peru, who had suffered in isolation and ignorance from metropolitan Lima. These challenges to the popular political imaginary of post- (and mid-) authoritarian Peru would not have been possible without the application of statistical techniques reviewed here. In this way, the process of estimation provides additional insights about the patterns of violations that are not readily apparent to the truth commission and help in generating plausible explanations for the patterns that have been determined.

Beyond these main contributions, the estimated population of human rights violations and its many dimensions (e.g. time, space, demography, social, economic, political, ethnic) is then filtered and interpreted through the lenses and explanatory paradigms that dominate the membership of a truth commission in order to provide a full explanation for what happened, why it happened, and how it happened. As Chapters 3 and 4 outlined, such explanatory paradigms can range from formal nomothetic and deductive approaches to deep hermeneutic and thick descriptive approaches, where this range of paradigms suggests that the combination of different disciplines within truth commissions will have an impact on what the commission looks for and how it explains what it sees. Wilson (1997: 153) argues that legal epistemology leads to a focus on the 'legal facts which could stand up a court of law . . . and [t]hat which matters is that which is universal, documentable through reference to "hard" facts and relevant to rationalist legal inquiry' (see also Chapman and Ball 2001: 21–23).

Since the number of victims, violations, and perpetrators is so vast, much of the work in truth commissions is not building case files for prosecution in the ways that criminal proceedings take place in bodies such as the ICTY, the ICTR, and the International Criminal Court. But a significant membership of truth commissions comprises lawyers, whose epistemological position has a direct bearing on the ways in which the truth will be uncovered, represented, and explained. In contrast, the social sciences are equally interested in single cases, not in and of themselves, but as they relate to other cases, and how they fit into the larger context and patterns of events that are uncovered. Overemphasis of legal analysis and explanation can miss the forest for the trees, and can lead to the 'eradication of subjectivity' (Wilson 1997: 155) essential in providing a full picture of what happened to victims as they form part of larger social and political structures of interaction. While both sides of this relatively crude disciplinary divide seek out systematically gathered information, they see its accumulation as serving different purposes. Thus, in the abstract, the way in which a truth commission dominated by lawyers approaches the question of estimating and explaining the population of human rights violations differs dramatically from one dominated by social scientists.

Suggestions for further reading

Ball, P. B., Asher, J., Sulmont, D. and Manrique, D. (2003) *How Many Peruvians Have Died?*, Washington, DC: American Association for the Advancement of Science (AAAS), http://shr.aaas.org/hrdag/peru/aaas_peru_5.pdf.

Ball, P. B., Spirer, H. F. and Spirer, L. (eds) (2000) *Making the Case: Investigating Large Scale Human Rights Violations Using Information Systems and Data Analysis*, Washington DC: American Association for the Advancement of Science.

Hayner, P. B. (1994) 'Fifteen Truth Commissions – 1974–1994: A Comparative Study', *Human Rights Quarterly*, 16: 597–655.

Hayner, P. B. (2002) *Unspeakable Truths: Facing the Challenges of Truth Commissions*, New York: Routledge.

Skaar, E. (1999) 'Truth Commissions, Trials – or Nothing? Policy Options in Democratic Transitions', *Third World Quarterly*, 20 (6): 1109–1128.

Skaar, E., Gloppen, S. and Surhke, A. (eds) (2005) *Roads to Reconciliation*, Lexington, MA: Lexington Books.

Wilson, R. A. (2001) *The Politics of Truth and Reconciliation in South Africa: Legitimizing the Post-Apartheid State*, Cambridge University Press, Cambridge.

8 Human rights impact assessment

In 1976, Jimmy Carter was elected President of the United States and he pledged to re-orient American foreign policy to one that placed a primacy on the promotion and protection of human rights. In 1986, the Foreign Ministers of the then European Community signed a Declaration on Human Rights and Foreign Policy. After the 1997 General Election in the United Kingdom, the late Robin Cook, who was then the new Foreign Secretary, announced that Britain would pursue an ethical foreign policy, which included upholding the rule of law, the promotion of democracy, and the protection of human rights. Throughout the latter half of the 20th century, the main aims and objectives of international and domestic human rights NGOs were to protect all or some of the human rights found in the Universal Declaration of Human Rights through a variety of strategies, including setting international standards, lobbying governments and inter-governmental organizations, providing legal opinion and legal advice, carrying out programmes to help affected groups, and providing direct assistance to victims of human rights violations (see Welch 2001a; Landman and Abraham 2004). These examples of pronouncements from governments, inter-governmental organizations, and non-governmental organizations all share the common theme that some form of 'purposive social action' (Merton 1936) will lead to a positive outcome for human rights or have a positive *impact* on human rights.

But how do we know if such foreign policies by governments and inter-governmental organizations, funding programmes by donor agencies, as well as the many activities carried out by NGOs actually ever make a difference to human rights? How can we harness the analytical leverage and logic of inference from the social sciences to assess whether such policies and activities have an impact on human rights? Human rights impact assessment is a relatively new field of research and practice that seeks to provide answers to these crucial questions facing the human rights community. The human rights community wants to know what works and what does not work in the field in an effort to promote the full realization of human rights. Impact assessment draws on the systematic nature of social scientific analysis and work in the substantive fields of development studies, monitoring and evaluation, environmental sciences, business administration and public policy, while it is in many ways a response to the new funding environment where governments, inter-governmental organizations, and donor agencies want to know the 'added value' of the multitude of human rights activities they fund. Indeed, at a conference on human rights impact assessment in Brussels, representatives of the European Commission wanted to know how they could judge the tangible outcomes and impact of the programmes, organizations, and projects that they had funded (see Radstaake and Bronkhurst 2002). In the area of development, the World Bank claims that, 'Donors want evidence that funds provided by their taxpayers achieve results, and the recipients of funds want to see tangible improvements in their living conditions'.[1] Finally, domestic and international human rights NGOs want to know if their activities in 'a particular target country cause an improvement in the human rights practices of the government of the target country' (Cingranelli and Richards 2001: 225).

In light of these developments and observations, the main aim of human rights impact assessment is to determine the degree to which a 'set of directed human activities' (Mohr 1995) has an impact on human rights, which are represented by some form of indicator (either qualitative or quantitative). Such a set of human activities can be *intentional* and have a *direct impact* on the human rights situation (e.g. the policies and activities in the examples above), or they can be *unintentional* and have either a *direct* or *indirect* impact on the human rights situation (e.g. large-scale development projects that displace indigenous communities such as the Plan Puebla Panama in the Lacandon jungle in Chiapas in Mexico). This volume has already shown how social scientific methods can be applied to human rights problems in general (Chapter 4), at the global level of analysis (Chapter 6), and in the single-country work of truth commissions (Chapter 7), all of which require some form of human rights measurement (Chapter 5). In building on the arguments, methods, and evidence from these chapters, this current chapter shows how the same logic of inference found in social scientific analysis can provide a foundation for human rights impact assessment. The chapter argues that the theories and methods of the social sciences are most suited to *ex post* assessments of *direct* and *indirect* impact, while the results of such assessments are useful when governments, inter-governmental organizations, and NGOs consciously include the human rights impact into their *ex ante* planning and programme formulation processes. To this end, the chapter outlines the main dimensions of human rights impact assessment and explains how quantitative and qualitative analytical techniques can be used to carry out human rights impact assessments using hypothetical examples and real cases from the field of human rights.

Types of human rights impact assessment

Impact assessments fall into four different categories that are the result of the combination of their different forms (*direct* and *indirect*) and their timing (*ex ante* and *ex post*). Figure 8.1 shows these two dimensions and the resulting categories of impact assessment. Impact assessments in Cell I involve the kind of *ex ante* planning carried out by organizations that *intentionally* want to change the human rights situation through a series of targeted activities designed to achieve a variety of objectives. In such planning processes, the impact assessment ideally would need a baseline assessment of the human rights situation before the implementation of a particular project, strategy, policy, or programme and some way of collecting human rights indicators to monitor the degree to which the main aims and objectives will be met. In this way, impact assessments in Cell I anticipate the likely effects (or observable implications) of a set of activities that have been designed to improve the human rights situation and consciously incorporate human rights indicators. Such assessments are future-oriented and build monitoring of human rights and the collection of human rights indicators into all stages of the project cycle.

Impact assessments in Cell II involve the kind of *ex ante* planning carried out by organizations pursuing aims and objectives that are indirectly related to the promotion and protection of human rights, such as large-scale development projects financed by the World Bank, the implementation of structural adjustment programmes, general overseas

Forms

	Direct	Indirect
	I	II
Ex ante	Intentional planning to change the human rights situation	Awareness of impact of other and/or unrelated activities
	III	IV
Ex post	Evaluation and assessment of policies, strategies, and programmes for changing the human rights situation	Evaluation and assessment of outcomes of policies, strategies, and programmes that were not intended for changing the human rights situation

(Timing)

Figure 8.1 Categories of human rights impact assessment.

development assistance, direct foreign investment and the activities of multinational corporations, and any other kind of third-party assistance where the impact on human rights is initially seen as *unintentional*. The goals of these activities are primarily to build infrastructure, improve the allocation of goods and resources in the economy, extract resources, assemble goods, or make textiles, and promote general levels of growth and development. Human rights may not be seen as important to those planning these activities, but outside organizations can nonetheless carry out a human rights impact assessment of the likely consequences of such activities for the human rights of the affected population and use the results of their analysis to lobby those organizations wishing to carry out such programmes in an effort to build attention to human rights into the project cycle. For example, would the development of the infrastructure displace a community and destroy its ancestral land? Will the full implementation of an IMF structural adjustment programme lead to greater social inequalities, social exclusion and limited forms of justice? Will the extractive, manufacturing, and textile activities violate international labour standards? These and many other unintended consequences for human rights can be assessed and fed back into the planning process.

Examples of *ex ante* impact assessments in the field of development studies have begun to take on more explicit references to human rights, where so-called 'rights-based' approaches to development seek to mainstream human rights into all aspects of the planning and project cycle across a variety of development projects, including those poverty reduction strategy papers (PRSPs) submitted by governments (Human Rights Council of Australia 1995; UNDP 2000; OHCHR 2002; Gosling and Edwards 2003). This approach asks serious questions about the degree to which affected communities have been consulted about a potential development project, whether the community wants the project to be implemented, whether the community has had access to the planning process, whether it has taken part in the formal decision-making process concerning its implementation, and whether and how it will benefit from its successful completion. These types of impact assessment draw on the insights from strategic environmental assessments (Verheem 2000) and social impact assessments (IAIA 2003) where the likely environmental and broader social consequences of any project are fed into the planning and development phase of large-scale projects.

But since social science methodology is limited in its ability to see into the future, many impact assessments are *ex post* analyses of changes over time or comparative analyses of similar projects, programmes, and policies that have been carried out, the results of which inform *ex ante* impact assessments of new activities. With rigorous research design and the application of systematic methods, important lessons can be learned from the inferences that are drawn from the analysis of previous activities. Thus, in Cell III human rights impact assessment examines the ways in which specific sets of activities whose explicit aims and objectives were to improve the human rights situation have fared. As part of the funding process, many organizations are now required to have in place some form of *ex post* impact assessment to see whether the main aims and objectives have been met through the pursuit of specific sets of activities. Other organizations are finding that they now have to demonstrate to key donors what they have achieved in the field of human rights and whether they achieved what they claimed they would achieve in their planning documents and public statements issued before particular projects commenced.

For example, after years of funding several prominent human rights NGOs, the Ministry of Foreign Affairs of the Netherlands sought to evaluate the degree to which these NGOs had achieved their broad aims and the aims of their specific programmes (Landman and Abraham 2004). The NGOs included Anti-Slavery International (London), Article 19 (London), International Federation of Human Rights Leagues (Paris), International Commission of Jurists (Geneva), International Helsinki Federation for Human Rights (Vienna), International Service for Human Rights (Geneva), Minority Rights Group International (London), World Organisation Against Torture (Geneva), and Penal Reform International (Paris and London). Part of the evaluation assessed the international advocacy strategies adopted by each of these organizations. They were able to document the degree to which their international advocacy activities had a role in the adoption of new international and domestic standards for the protection of human rights (e.g. minority rights, new definitions of modern forms of slavery); new or enhanced international mechanisms for the protection of a subset of human rights (e.g. the Special Representative to the Secretary General on human rights defenders and the Special Unit in the Inter-American Commission for Human Rights, the Working Group on Minority Rights); direct support for the functioning of new human rights mechanisms (e.g. the Special Rapporteur on Prisons and Conditions of Detention in the African Commission for People's and Human Rights); and in some cases, the release of victims of human rights abuses through urgent appeals and direct campaigning (e.g. the World Organization Against Torture) (Landman and Abraham 2004: 3).

Despite a successful demonstration of a link between their advocacy activities and real outcomes, all the organizations in the evaluation were conscious that their activities alone did not contribute solely to the outcomes, but that in combination with many other factors, they acknowledged their role in bringing about such positive change (Landman and Abraham 2004: 3). This distinction between *attribution* and *contribution* is crucial in *ex post* impact assessments of human rights programmes, policies, and strategies meant to have a direct impact on a particular human rights situation. As the discussion in the next section of this chapter will show, demonstrating pure attribution of an organization's activities to achieving an improvement in the human rights situation is a huge challenge for human rights impact assessment. But multivariate quantitative and qualitative analytical techniques can examine questions of organizational *contribution* to a particular outcome, since they can control for other possible factors that may account for the outcome alongside those specified as being explicitly related to the outcome.

Finally, Cell IV shows those cases of *ex post* impact assessments carried out on a set of activities that are not intentionally designed to have an impact on human rights. Here it seems the list of possible activities for analysis is virtually endless, including the impact of particular practices of multinational corporations (see Chapter 6); the impact of large-scale infrastructure projects such as dams, roads, airports, and clean water systems; the impact of large-scale industrial and agricultural developments such as power plants, deforestation, oil exploration and pipeline construction, and mining and other extractive activities; the impact of bilateral and multilateral trade agreements, and/or trade-related intellectual property rights (TRIPS) agreements; the impact of World Bank/IMF structural adjustment and macro-stabilization programmes; and the impact of poverty reduction strategies, and health-related policies and programmes. In these cases, it is possible to conduct an *ex post* assessment of the human rights impact of these activities, which relies on a clear specification of which particular rights may have been affected, operationalization of relevant human rights indicators, and the specification of a plausible set of relationships and testable propositions about the link between the activities that were carried out and the human rights situation.

Theories of change and impact complexity

The discussion of these four types of impact assessment shows the variety of ways in which we can think about the direct and indirect impact that certain sets of activities may have on a human rights situation, whether that assessment is part of the planning process or is an *ex post* analysis of activities that have already been carried out. Underlying all these types of impact assessment is a general model of change, which seeks to identify a significant relationship between some form of single intervention and multiple interventions on the one hand, and human rights on the other. Such a general model is complex for any impact assessment, and human rights impact assessments are no different, where questions of time, causation, and spuriousness affect any assessment's ability to draw inferences about the true impact of a set of activities.

Figure 8.2 illustrates some of these aspects of a human rights impact assessment through a hypothetical example. The vertical axis shows a measure of human rights protection that ranges from low to high. The horizontal axis depicts time, and the upward-rising line shows an increasing protection of human rights over time. The vertical 'interruptions' are possible policy interventions from third parties in the affairs of the state in question. Such interventions could be aid allocation, development projects, and/or specific programmes carried out by human rights NGOs. Early intervention at time t_1 may lead to a gradual improvement in rights protection. Intervention at time t_2 just precedes a dramatic improvement in rights protection, while intervention at time t_3 directly follows such a dramatic improvement. There is also a fourth possibility: human rights protection would have improved without such interventions in the first place. This *counterfactual* situation is an important and often neglected idea in human rights impact assessment, since it is entirely possible that human rights situations improve without explicit interventions. Finally, it is possible that factors other than the intervention may have an effect on the human rights situation. Such a logic of impact analysis and its problems can be illustrated with two real-world examples: (1) US foreign policy during the Pinochet years in Chile 1973–1990 and (2) European Union human rights policy for applicant states.

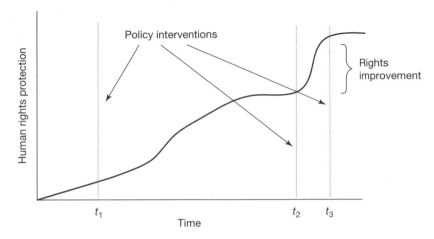

Figure 8.2 Varieties of intervention and human rights impact assessment.

US foreign policy and the Pinochet regime in Chile

In the years that immediately followed the military *coup d'état* of 11 September 1973, the military regime engaged in a counter-offensive against civil society and committed gross violations of human rights. By 1976, Chile had passed a series of Constitutional Acts that institutionalized the regime and made General Pinochet the President of the Republic. Alongside these developments, the regime created the National Intelligence Directorate (DINA), which was responsible for internal security and, arguably, committed most of the human rights abuses for the remainder of the Pinochet years (see Valenzuela and Valenzuela 1986; Constable and Valenzuela 1991; Foweraker and Landman 1997; Foweraker, Landman and Harvey 2003). As noted above, Jimmy Carter was elected President of the United States in 1976, and shortly thereafter declared that US foreign policy would be guided by a concern for human rights. Diplomatic pressure, public pronouncements, and a congressional amendment cutting US foreign economic and military assistance to the regime (see Kornbluh 2003) may have led to the promulgation of the 1980 Chilean Constitution, which gave a further institutional legitimacy to the regime and was accompanied by an easing in repressive tactics. The arrival of the Reagan Administration in the US led to a policy shift away from a concern for human rights, and Chile plunged back into a highly repressive period through the mid-1980s, and then experienced an unsuccessful plebiscite for Pinochet in 1988, followed by a rapid transition to democracy. In the event, the Reagan Administration claimed that its policy of lukewarm support for the Pinochet regime led to Chile's eventual return to democracy (see Kornbluh 2003: 419–420).

In this brief account it is possible to see how both the Carter and the Reagan policies could be viewed as having a positive impact on human rights protection, even though ideologically and in practical terms, the policies were diametrically opposed to one another. An easing of repression followed Carter's human rights policy pronouncements, while Reagan's support for Pinochet was ultimately followed by a democratic transition. Judging the impact of human rights policy in either case is difficult from this kind of anecdotal evidence without examining important dynamic relationships over time, and it also ignores the possibility of other factors that may explain the regime's eventual transformation, including the international and domestic pressure from human rights groups and splits within the regime itself between 'rule-oriented' and more hard-line factions (see Risse, Ropp and Sikkink 1999; Hawkins 2002).

EU enlargement

The second example involves European Union enlargement, which integrates 'old' and 'new' states of Europe, a process made more acute with the collapse of the Soviet Union and the consequent proliferation of independent nation states in the region. Through a variety of policies, the EU lowered trade barriers to these new countries and extended through its PHARE programme significant resources to reform and rebuild their economies. Through its 1993 Copenhagen principles, the EU has had additional economic and political criteria for membership that include the promotion and protection of human rights. It appears that any nation state wishing to join the EU is subject to both significant 'push' and 'pull' factors. On the one hand, increased economic benefit from a common market, with its pool of labour and capital offers an attractive set of incentives for nations to join the EU, particularly small and economically underdeveloped states. On the other hand, the EU can insist on certain conditions for membership that make nation states reform their domestic institutional, political, and economic arrangements to promote sustainable economic progress, democracy, and human rights.

There are two important considerations that make this relationship between policy intervention and nation-state practice difficult to assess. First, it is not clear whether states improve their promotion of human rights before or after entering into negotiations with the EU (t_2 vs. t_3 in Figure 8.2). It is possible for states to engage in a process of 'anticipatory adaptation' (Haggard, Levy, Moravscik and Niolaides 1993: 182; Keohane 2002: 74; Landman 2005b) in their practices and improve their rights protections well before the negotiations, or they may improve these protections during their period of negotiation. There is thus a complex temporal relationship between policy intervention and nation-state behaviour. Second, it is not clear whether the proliferation of new countries seeking entry has led the EU to formulate new policies on the promotion and protection of human rights that would not have been formulated in the absence of such new states. Indeed, the origin of the European Community was to protect vital resources and promote healthy economies within a liberal-democratic framework, where the original members were all broadly speaking, liberal-democratic capitalist states. Thus, the development of the European Union's political criteria for entry may be seen as a reaction to developments in the wider Europe following the collapse of the Soviet Union or as a proactive measure to promote a larger policy of democracy and human rights.

Analytical techniques for impact assessment

The abstract example depicted in Figure 8.1 and the examples of US foreign policy toward Chile and EU enlargement show that human rights impact assessment faces a series of significant methodological challenges, some of which have been addressed through quantitative and qualitative social scientific techniques. First, there are statistical techniques for analysing time-series measures of human rights that may be better able to estimate the possible impact of these policy interventions while controlling for other factors, and there are certain qualitative methods for examining more holistic assessments that take into account the necessary and sufficient conditions for a change in human rights (see also Chapter 4 this volume). Each of these strategies is considered in turn.

Statistical methods

The discussion thus far has argued that at a fundamental level, impact assessment examines the degree to which some form of intervention makes a difference for a particular human rights situation. Figure 8.3 depicts the four logical possibilities for this relationship between intervention and outcome. It is possible that there is no effect between the intervention and improvement in the human rights situation (Figure 8.3a). It is possible that there is a 'slope effect' for the intervention, where during the time period directly following an intervention, the human rights situation improves dramatically (Figure 8.3b). It is possible that there is an 'intercept effect' for the intervention, where immediately following the intervention, the human rights situation improves dramatically like a 'step' and then continues along its previous course of improvement (Figure 8.3c). Finally, it is possible that there are slope and intercept effects for the intervention, where there is both a jump in the human rights situation and a new rate of change following the intervention (Figure 8.3d).

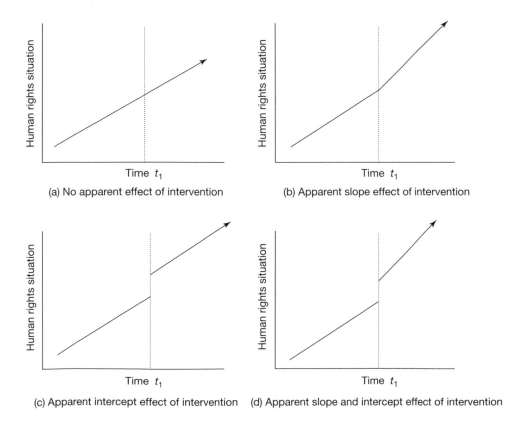

Figure 8.3 Possible effects of an intervention on the human rights situation.

One popular statistical solution for estimating these different effects is to use time-series regression analysis of the kind outlined in Chapter 6, where the unit of analysis is time and the purpose of the regression is to estimate the significance of an intervention on a change in the time trend of the human rights situation that has been measured. This kind of analysis has been used in social scientific research to estimate the effects of public policies, such as social security, coal mine safety measures, and civil rights legislation; the effects of specific laws, such as traffic and gun control measures; the influence of major political shifts such as reform or revolution (Lewis-Beck 1979, 1986); the effects of Latin American elections on macroeconomic performance (Remmer 1993); the effects of NATO bombing and Kosovo Liberation Army actions on killings in Kosovo (Ball and Asher 2002; and Chapter 5); and the relationship between citizenship rights and social movement through time (Foweraker and Landman 1997: 194–214). The standard form of the regression equation shown in Chapter 6 is modified to take into account the structure of a time-interrupted trend, where the 'interruption' is the intervention that was meant to improve the human rights situation. The intervention is represented through a dichotomous, or dummy variable I_t, which is coded 0 for every year preceding the intervention and 1 for every year starting from the intervention. Coding in this way acts as a 'switch' that stays 'on' once the intervention has taken place. The model also has a time trend variable T_t, which is coded 1 for the first time observation (e.g. day, month, year), 2 for the second, and then consecutively through the remainder of the overall time period being examined (see Mohr 1995: 209; Landman and Foweraker 1997). Like the standard regression equation in Chapter 6, this modified equation has an intercept term α_t and an error term μ_t (specified with a subscript for time), and appears as follows:

$$\hat{Y}_t = \alpha_t + \beta T_t + \beta_t I_t + \mu_t \tag{1}$$

In this case, $\hat{Y}_t$ represents the human rights situation over time and is predicated on the availability of some relevant and measurable aspect of human rights (see Chapter 5 and discussion below). This kind of regression analysis estimates the magnitude, direction, and statistical significance of the intervention (i.e. β_t), as well as the significance of the trend itself (i.e. β) and is therefore appropriate for assessing the kind of impact depicted in Figure 8.3c. If the regression analysis finds that β_t is positive and significant, the intervention at the specific point in time is associated with a significant shift in the human rights situation. Adding a variable that captures the interaction effect between the time trend and the intervention (i.e. $T_t \times I_t$) changes the equation into the following form:

$$\hat{Y}_t = \alpha_t + \beta T_t + \beta_t I_t + \beta_2 T_t I_t + \mu_t \tag{2}$$

Here, regression analysis produces separate estimates for the slope and intercept shifts in the trend, and is therefore most appropriate for assessing the kind of impact depicted in Figures 8.5b and 8.5d. If the analysis finds that β_t and β_2 are positive and significant, then the intervention at that particular time is associated with a 'jump' in the trend and a new slope to that trend.

This type of analysis can incorporate two additional factors important in human rights impact assessment. First, there may be repeated interventions over time that may have an effect on the human rights situation, in which case the statistical analysis can include multiple dummy variables representing these time interruptions (see Foweraker and Landman 1997: 195–214). Second, such modelling needs to include additional explanatory factors that may account for the change in the human rights situation, thereby controlling for 'third forces' unrelated to the policy intervention itself. Thus, alongside the time trend, time interruption, and time interaction variables, it is entirely possible to include variables that are relevant to the human rights situation that is being analysed, such as socio-economic conditions, political regime type, international influences, among others.

But despite the ability for these techniques to incorporate multiple interventions and additional explanatory factors, several significant challenges remain in using these techniques for human rights impact assessment. First, it is rare indeed that a human rights situation exhibits such an even and linear form of improvement. Rather, human rights situations tend to fluctuate over time with noticeable 'peaks' and 'troughs' in the trend across the time period that is being investigated, such that identifying discernible trends and modelling them statistically is made more difficult. Second, this whole style of analysis is predicated on the availability of discrete time-series data on particular dimensions and categories of human rights, which in many areas of human rights work may not yet be available. Third, simple forms of interrupted time-series analysis are susceptible to problems of autocorrelation (i.e. correlations in error terms over time), possible non-comparability of pre- and post-intervention time periods, arbitrary selection of the starting point in the time series, and ambiguities in the underlying matrix of the data (see Huitema 2004). For these reasons more sophisticated 'autoregressive integrated moving average' (ARIMA) models are recommended (Mohr 1995; Huitema 2004). Finally, such impact analysis will also come up against the 'fundamental problem of causal inference' (Holland 1986), where even if there are statistically significant estimates for slope and intercept shifts, the most a statistical human rights impact assessment could assert is that there is a 'realized causal effect' for the intervention, where a state of affairs after the intervention appears to be significantly different from the state of affairs before the intervention (King, Keohane and Verba 1994: 76–85).

Qualitative analysis

For reasons of data availability and the limitations to statistical methods outlined above, many efforts at human rights impact assessment may want to consider qualitative methods exclusively or as complementary forms of analysis. Standards-based human rights data are available for global quantitative analysis (see Chapters 5 and 6) and events-based data are available for a limited number of countries that have experienced periods of conflict, authoritarian rule, or foreign occupation (see Chapter 7), but there is still a significant dearth of high-quality, discrete time-series data that could be used in human rights impact assessments in particular areas of human rights work. Rather, governments, inter-governmental organizations, and human rights organizations tend to have patchy, incomplete, and problematic statistical data and narrative accounts, reports, ephemera, media reports, and other forms of documentation on human rights events, outcomes, and developments from which they seek to draw inferences about the relative impact of their own work in the field. But combining these sources of information with reasonable judgements about what have been likely developments and outcomes can begin to establish a compilation of useful information that can be analysed in systematic fashion alongside more rigorously collected data.

Many of the nine human rights NGOs evaluated by the Dutch government provided many different examples of macro- and micro-indicators of impact in their particular line of human rights work, where those organizations with more 'service delivery' functions were better able to collect meaningful indicators on their impact. For example, in its Rwanda Programme to help the over 130,000 prisoners awaiting trials since the 1994 genocide, Penal Reform International cited as examples of its own impact new community justice legislation, the development of biogas facilities that convert human waste into energy, increasing numbers of prisoners obtaining agricultural and construction skills (including brick and bed making), and prison management enhancement and training of prison staff (Landman and Abraham 2004: 119–120). These sorts of tangible outcomes had a direct impact on the lives of the prisoners and by extension addressed a number of significant human rights problems, even though the proportion of the prison population that benefited from these projects remained low.

In another example, Minority Rights Group (MRG) was able to provide a variety of indicators of impact for its Roma programme, which sought to raise the capacity and visibility of the Roma community and promote greater protection of their rights throughout the countries of Southeastern Europe (Landman and Abraham 2004: 93–98). The aims and objectives for the Roma Programme were articulated in such a way as to provide tangible indicators for success and impact. First, they supplied evidence of increased capacity and sustainability of partners (e.g. 32 Roma organizations were direct beneficiaries). Second, networks of Roma NGOs and others have been set up within specific countries, while links were formed with international, regional, and local authorities. Third, the beneficiaries have increased their skills and confidence, have gained valuable expertise in specific areas, have gained other skills such as English and computing, and have found employment in the NGOs with whom they worked. Fourth, MRG's methodology within the region has been adopted in other programmes. Fifth, some of the country-specific products, such as research on education policy, have been disseminated within the country, while there has been impact in the media. Finally, the Roma Programme has generally increased the knowledge of human rights and advocacy skills, and has shifted the discourse within the young Roma and extended community in being able to claim their rights more forcefully (Landman and Abraham 2004: 97).

These examples suggest that in the absence of discrete time-series data, limited forms of human rights impact assessment are still possible, where the aims and objectives of programmes are linked to key indicators that demonstrate the tangible benefits of a set of activities for a selected group of beneficiaries. But in what ways can such material provided by human rights NGOs and other actors in the field of human rights be used to build a more comprehensive picture, contribute to systematic *ex post* impact assessments whose findings could inform *ex ante* assessments carried out during the project and programme planning stage? A final strategy for harnessing the information collected by such human rights actors is to use qualitative comparative analysis (see Chapter 4) to gauge the degree to which concerted human rights activities can actually make a difference. The key difference in this method is that it does not look for independent effects of separate interventions or explanatory factors but the combinations of necessary and sufficient conditions for particular outcomes (Ragin 1987, 1994; Ragin, Berg-Schlosser and de Meur 1996).

Rather than rely on discrete time-series data on the human rights situation, qualitative comparative analysis in the first instance requires outcomes to be specified in dichotomous terms (e.g. no improvement vs. significant improvement) and it requires the set of possible causal conditions also to be specified in dichotomous terms (e.g. absence of causal condition vs. presence of causal condition). An organization carrying the impact assessment would have to specify a set of criteria matched across its various indicators of success to first judge in which cases it feels that significant human rights improvements have been made. The validity and reliability of such an exercise would be strengthened through a very public and transparent declaration of the set of criteria and judgements that have been made. The organization would have to be equally up-front about the ways in which it selected the causal conditions and determined their presence or absence. The result of these determinations would be the construction of a Boolean 'truth table' (Ragin 1987), which listed all the cases that were being examined and the configuration of both the casual conditions and the outcomes of interest.

Table 8.1 is a hypothetical truth table that could be constructed for a typical human rights NGO that seeks to improve the human rights situation through capacity building of local NGOs relevant to the specific rights problem that is being addressed. The organization has criteria for when it judges a significant improvement in the human rights situation has taken place and compares them to the various indicators that it has collected. The combination of criteria and indicators allows it to classify across its case whether there has been a significant improvement in the human rights situation. It also specifies a series of five causal conditions that it feels are the main factors that may account for an improvement in the human rights situation. This list of causal factors includes the effect of the capacity building activities that the organization has carried out and four factors that are exogenous to the organization. Taken together, the five causal conditions

Table 8.1 Hypothetical truth table for human rights impact assessment

Cases	Causal conditions					Outcome
	A	B	C	D	E	F
1	A	b	c	d	e	f
2	A	b	c	d	e	f
3	A	b	c	d	E	f
4	A	B	C	D	e	F
5	A	B	C	D	E	F
6	A	B	C	D	e	F
7	A	b	c	d	E	f
8	A	b	c	d	e	f
9	A	B	C	D	e	F
10	A	B	C	D	E	F

Key to table:

A = establishment of an international human rights standard
B = domestic implementation of the international standard
C = capacity building of local NGOs
D = supportive domestic political environment
E = supportive supranational environment
F = improvement in human rights situation

Capital letter = presence of condition or outcome
Lower-case letter = absence of condition or outcome

included in the truth table are the establishment of an international standard (A), domestic implementation of the international standard (B), capacity building of local NGOs (C), supportive domestic political environment (D), and a supportive supra-national environment (E), while the outcome is an improvement in the human rights situation (F).

The table shows that across the ten cases (let us assume they are countries) for which information has been collected and judged using the organization's own criteria there is a complex set of combinations for the presence or absence of the causal conditions and the presence or absence of the outcome. The purpose of the truth table and subsequent analysis is to determine if there are any discernible patterns across the causal conditions and the different outcomes. In this example, the shaded region in the table shows that across cases 4, 5, 6, 9 and 10 there is the same combination of factors and outcome. Formally, Boolean analysis would list this set of matches as a preliminary causal combination (A + B + C + D = F), where the combination of the presence of an international standard, the domestic implementation of the standard, successful capacity building of local NGOs, and supportive international and domestic political environments is related to an improvement in the human rights situation.

Closer examination of the table reveals more insights for this impact assessment. First, the international standard (A) is always present, which means that all the cases have been 'exposed' to this new international standard at the time of the assessment. The assessment in many ways can eliminate this factor from its preliminary combination and argue that the remaining combination is domestic implementation, capacity building, and a supportive domestic environment (B + C + D). Second, the obverse of the successful combination is also true, that is, the absence of a combination of domestic implementation, capacity building, and a supportive domestic environment means that an improvement in the human rights situation has not occurred (b + c + d = f). Third, a supportive supranational environment does not appear to be a necessary or sufficient condition for an improvement in the human rights situation. There are cases with a supportive supranational environment and an improvement in the human rights situation (5 and 10); cases with a supportive environment and no improvement (3 and 7); cases with no supportive environment and an improvement (4, 6, and 9); and cases with no supportive environment and no improvement (1, 2, and 8).

This example of a Boolean truth table demonstrates that qualitative comparative analysis is a powerful tool for human rights impact assessment for four main reasons. First, it allows for the inclusion of information that has not been measured precisely, but that is represented through reasonable judgements and the application of criteria that are defensible. Second, it uses the combinatory logics of binary variables found in Boolean algebra to simplify the complexity of the world in order to tease out the set of necessary and sufficient conditions for improving the human rights situation within a specific area of work for human rights organizations. Third, it allows for an assessment to demonstrate how the activities of an organization *contribute* to an improvement of the human rights situation, and how such a contribution needs to take place alongside the presence of other important factors that are largely outside the control and influence of the organization. Fourth, beyond identifying this set of necessary and sufficient conditions, the technique also allows the assessment to determine the reasons for why the human rights situation *did not* improve in certain cases. The general insight from social science that the explanation and assessment of failures, or 'negative' cases is vital in improving our understanding of social phenomena (see Skocpol 1979; Wickham-Crowley 1992: 320–326; Landman

2003; Mahoney and Goertz 2004), is equally vital in contributing to our understanding of what 'works' in the field of human rights.

From past experiences to future planning

It is clear from this chapter that insights from social science methodology have much to offer to human rights scholars and practitioners who wish to carry out human rights impact assessments of any kind. Developing impact assessment tools will help organizations respond to a general trend in the donor-driven world of 'logical frame analysis', the rise of the audit culture, and the concern from the human rights community over whether various planned interventions on behalf of human rights actually make a difference. Great claims continue to be made by governments, inter-governmental organizations and non-governmental organizations about their impact on human rights. Human rights impact assessment is meant to find systematic ways to test such claims and to provide the links between sets of activities and real improvements on the ground. It is clear that carrying out such tests is a complex task and involves difficult-to-collect indicators on particular human rights problems, judgements about the degree to which improvements in a human rights situation have actually taken place, and the specification of a research design that is appropriate to the assessment that is taking place.

This chapter has argued that the social sciences are probably best equipped to carry out *ex post* forms of impact assessment, the results of which can then be fed back into the planning phase of any organization wishing to make a difference for human rights, and any organization concerned about the potential human rights impact of their activities, or as an important advocacy tool to show organizations that are not necessarily conscious of human rights, the potential impact of their activities. Maximizing the rigour of a human rights impact assessment can only help to strengthen the types of inferences that are drawn and add weight to the types of human rights arguments that are made. The underlying logic of impact assessment is straightforward but is vulnerable to a number of methodological challenges that if not adequately addressed may lead to making insecure inferences about impact, and ultimately undermine the kinds of human rights arguments that we make. Such insecure inferences can either result in under-estimating impact that does exist or over-estimating impact that does not exist, either of which may prove harmful in the struggle for human rights.

Suggestions for further reading

Cingranelli, D. and Richards, D. (2001) 'Measuring the Impact of Human Rights Organizations', in C. E. Welch, Jr. (ed.), *NGOs and Human Rights: Promise and Performance*, Philadelphia: University of Pennsylvania Press, 225–237.

International Association of Impact Assessment, IAIA (2003) 'Social Impact Assessment: International Principles', *IAIA Special Publications Series No. 2*, Fargo, ND: International Association of Impact Assessment (www.iaia.org).

Mohr, L. B. (1995) *Impact Analysis for Programme Evaluation*, 2nd edn, Thousand Oaks, CA: Sage.

Radstaake, M. and Bronkhurst, D. (2002) *Matching Practice with Principles, Human Rights Impact Assessment: EU Opportunities*, Utrecht, Netherlands: Humanist Committee on Human Rights (HOM).

Ragin, C. (1987) *The Comparative Method: Moving beyond Qualitative and Quantitative Strategies*, Berkeley: University of California Press.

9 Theory and method in studying human rights

This book has organized its main set of discussions around the general categories of theory, method and substance. Its substantive discussion on the content of human rights was based less on debates within extant normative theory, and more on the accumulation of international human rights law, which in many ways has established an agreed set of international standards to which it is hoped all countries aspire in their efforts to promote and protect human rights. Rather than being mired in debates about the metaphysical basis for the existence of human rights or the debates between strict legal positivists and legal proceduralists on the origins and functions of international law, the book started from a more *pragmatic* and *sociological* stance by focusing on real-world observable practices of state and non-state actors that the international community has defined as 'violations' to an increasing set of agreed international standards. This orientation is *pragmatic* since it sidesteps the ongoing philosophical debates on human rights and sees their protection as important means to obtaining the fundamental human ends of freedom, autonomy, and dignity (see Mendus 1995). It is *sociological* since it is grounded in the idea that we now speak about human rights precisely because over the centuries, as human communities have struggled against all forms of oppression, they have increasingly framed those struggles using the discourse of rights (see Marshall 1963; Bobbio 1996; Foweraker and Landman 1997; Woodiwiss 2005).

In this way, rights are 'made' through social, political, and economic actions and choices, which are in turn mediated through different cultural understandings and structural contexts, all of which are susceptible to systematic social science analysis of the kinds outlined and developed in this book. Social science analysis addresses this 'making' of human rights through the systematic application of theory and methods to substantive human rights problems. It is hoped that the book has gone some way in setting out the main theoretical, methodological, and substantive issues associated with this question of application in the field in an effort to move this particular research and practical agenda forward, as well as to provide a useful set of tools for scholars and practitioners to continue in their own struggles to improve the protection of human rights. This final chapter reviews the main thrust of the book across the categories of theory, method and substance, and then looks forward to a future research agenda that must address significant remaining challenges for the full development of a social science of human rights.

Reviewing the main thrust of the book

The treatment of theory in this book showed that individual and collective actions relevant to human rights should be seen as being embedded in larger cultural understandings and structural limitations, even if we conceive of those actions as otherwise being rational. Such rational actions are carried out by individuals, states, and/or organizations and are subject to significant influences of culture and structure, where the domestic idea of the 'socially embedded unit act' (Lichbach 1997) and the international idea of 'embedded liberalism' (Ruggie 1982) capture the essence of constrained action that characterizes the social world. Within such conceptions of constrained action, human rights are meant to be a significant constraint on state and non-state actors, who are generally free to pursue their ends if and only if they do not violate the fundamental human rights and freedoms protected through the various international human rights instruments. And it is the international human rights regime comprising these instruments and their associated mechanisms, albeit weak, that uses inter-state agreements and treaty mechanisms to constrain the actions of states towards their own populations while at the same time establishing the core content of human rights that can be operationalized for systematic social science analysis. Both the set of actions and the ways they are understood in human rights terms form the basic objects of enquiry covered in this book.

The book has demonstrated further that systematic social scientific analysis is predicated on the development of qualitative and quantitative indicators and measures of human rights as state commitments *in principle*, as state and non-state *practices*, and as outcomes of public *policies* (see Chapter 5; and Landman 2004). Data collection efforts in the field of human rights are useful in and of themselves for providing rich and systematic contextual descriptions and the mapping of national and cross-national patterns and variation in human rights protection. But for a social science of human rights that seeks the larger goals of *explanation* and *understanding* (see von Wright 1971; King, Keohane and Verba 1994; Flyvberg 2001; Brady and Collier 2004), qualitative and quantitative human rights information must be subjected to 'second-order' analysis that establishes empirical relationships and generalizations, identifies significant exceptions to these generalizations, and provides useful prescriptions to enhance our ability to improve the protection of human rights around the world. Only through linking *evidence* and *inference* in a systematic fashion can social science research make a valuable and lasting contribution to the struggle for human rights.

Secondary analysis of human rights problems combines the insights and testable propositions from empirical theories with different methods at different levels of analysis. Throughout such analysis, the research design that is established should provide the best 'fair test' of the empirical observations within the given time and resource constraints of a project or research programme. For this volume, such a fair test is predicated on the use of empirical information on human rights violations, the derivation of hypotheses and observable implications from empirical theories, and the systematic analysis of the empirical material through 'publicly known procedures to infer from evidence whether what the theory implied is correct' (King, Keohane and Verba 1995: 476). This means that regardless of the method or level of analysis, any research project in human rights should be able to answer the following three questions: (1) What does the research seek to find out? (2) How will it find it out? And (3) how does the researcher know if the answer to the question is correct? (King, Keohane and Verba 1995: 475). These three crucial questions are addressed in turn.

Identifying a research question

The first question simply asks the researcher to identify a research question that is significant, interesting, and relevant to the field of enquiry and is specified in such a way *that an answer can be discovered*. In other words, research questions should address something that is important in the real world and should make some contribution to the extant social scientific literature (King, Keohane and Verba 1994: 14–18). There is virtually an infinite supply of research questions in the field of human rights, many of which have been discussed at length in this volume. For example, the research questions have ranged from general questions about what explains the global variation in the protection of personal integrity rights to questions about local understandings of rights and citizenship in the Bolivian town of Villa Pagador. Across all the empirical examples used in this book, the research question was well specified and the rules of enquiry were more or less public and open to scrutiny, either for querying the substantive inferences that were drawn or for replicating and building on extant findings.

Good research questions are specified in such a way that an answer can be investigated through the application of theory and method, where some sort of puzzle or paradox is in need of explanation and understanding (e.g. why countries have such differing human rights records, or why and to what purpose public lynching is being carried out in Villa Pagador). In addition, with the possible exception of *ex ante* human rights impact assessments, research questions should not be speculative, but grounded in an empirical record from the past or immediate present from which certain inferences are made possible. Only then can the assumptions of the analysis be varied to predict likely scenarios. For example, in Poe and Tate's (1994: 862–866) seminal study of the global variation of human rights violations, the analysis shows the projected effects on human rights violations over time based on the estimates of the real effects from the existing record. In stochastic and probabilistic models of social phenomena, the extant empirical record is examined to model that which is observed in order to make predictive statements about what is likely to occur in the event of similar or different antecedent conditions (see Cioffi-Revilla 1998). But the initial research questions in such studies (such as the onset of war or the collapse of societies) are grounded in the empirical record that already exists (see Cioffi-Revilla and Landman 1999).

The method of analysis

The second question asks the researcher how the research question will be addressed. For example, will the research use qualitative methods, quantitative methods, or some mixture of both? Will the research be grounded in the cultural specificities of one country or will it compare evidence across a larger selection of countries? If the research compares evidence from a small number of countries, has it addressed problems of selection bias, variance in the outcome that is to be explained, and the use of most similar and most different methods of comparison? As Chapter 4 made clear, such decisions tend to reflect the epistemological orientation of the researcher and the way in which he or she thinks that knowledge about the world can be established. If the analysis emphasizes understanding over explanation, then the research design may reflect a need for more in-depth qualitative methods. If the analysis emphasizes explanation over understanding, then the research design may reflect the need for more rigorous methods that compare and contrast positive and negative instances of something, the presence or absence of key factors that may be related to the presence or absence of particular outcomes of interest that are to be explained.

Knowing how to be wrong

Finally, the third question addresses the fundamental problem of research design. Namely, what sort of evidence should the research uncover if the observable implications of theory were not obtained? Is there the presence of something that should be absent or is there the absence of something that should be present? A proper research design should anticipate such results and know *a priori* how they are related to the theory that has been used to address the question. For expository and interpretative analysis, has the empirical record that has been used presented any surprises, unexpected results, or counter-intuitive understandings? Has the researcher successfully distanced himself or herself from the subject population to provide the kind of independent interpretation and evaluation of what has taken place? How does the researcher know if his or her particular interpretation has been correct? What rules governed the choice of the subject population? How was the archival record accessed and used? For explanatory analysis, has the researcher correctly specified a series of testable propositions? Is there a null hypothesis? Based on the empirical record, have dominant hypotheses been supported, weakened, not supported, or rejected completely? What rules governed the collection of evidence? Did the model specification or analytical framework include relevant alternative explanatory factors?

These questions and the ways that they have been variously answered by those who have produced a significant collection of social science research on human rights to date were all evident in one form or another across the substantive discussions in the book and in particular across the chapters on global comparative analysis, the truth commissions, and human rights impact assessment. Global comparative analysis has examined the ways in which human rights are related to a series of possible explanatory variables on the one hand, and how human rights are related to a series of dependent variables on the other. The search for the determinants of human rights violations has moved beyond the socio-political variables such as economic development, democracy, and warfare to consider the role for foreign investment and international law, while human rights have been examined as important conditions for the allocation of foreign aid. Through the open specification of their research questions and research design, these studies are open to public scrutiny, debate, and criticism, all of which can contribute to building our general knowledge about human rights conditions as well as the conditions for a greater protection of human rights in the world.

Within and across truth commissions around the world, significant learning has taken place on the best ways to represent complex and controversial information on human rights violations collected through inherently biased means. Developments in social scientific and statistical methods as well as 'borrowing' from other disciplines and fields of enquiry have meant that such inherently biased 'convenience' samples of narrative accounts of atrocities given to truth commissions are far less vulnerable when their data are combined with data from other sources and collected through other means. The Guatemalans and Peruvians overcame their selection problems with multiple sources of narrative data, while the East Timorese found ways to complement their narrative statements with alternative types of information such as data from a retrospective household survey and a census of all the graveyards in the country. Such lateral thinking and development of networks of practitioners in a given field of enquiry to solve particularly tricky problems, capture the essence of the progressive accumulation of knowledge that lies at the heart of the social sciences.

Finally, in the newest and therefore still developing field of human rights impact assessment, the theories, methods, and measures from extant social science have proven valuable for devising systematic ways of judging the impact of policies, interventions, and strategies carried out by governments, inter-governmental organizations, and non-governmental organizations on particular human rights situations. The same logic of inference and attention to research design are critical for maximizing the ability of any impact assessment to reach the kind of useful conclusions that can be fed into the planning and policy-making cycle for human rights activities. Human rights impact assessment confronts the same challenges of causal inference, measurement, and research design as other areas of human rights research. There have been qualitative case studies of specific human rights organizations and some comparative analysis of broad patterns of impact for human rights NGOs (see Forsythe 1976; Tolley 1989; Risse, Ropp and Sikkink 1999; Clark 2001), but there have not been systematic, comparative, quantitative analyses of the impact of human rights NGOs (Cingranelli and Richards 2001: 225; see also Chapter 6 this volume). The relative dearth of qualitative research and the absence of quantitative research do not mean that such research is impossible or that it represents a social scientific chimera. Rather, like the development of solutions to the problems confronted by truth commissions, the tools, measures, and methods outlined in this book are available for new lateral thinking in this new area of analysis.

Remaining challenges for a social science of human rights

It is clear from the discussions throughout all the chapters in this book that the social sciences have grappled with and have in many ways overcome significant ontological, epistemological, and methodological challenges of carrying out systematic human rights research. The field has developed systematized definitions of human rights and operationalized many of these into comparable measures. Various 'ways of knowing' in the social sciences have been brought to bear on significant human rights problems. And there are numerous examples of social scientific human rights research using a variety of different methods. But despite these many achievements, it is equally clear that significant lacunae remain. Improvements and enhancements to a social science of human rights can be made across theoretical, methodological, and substantive dimensions, including the need for more regional and small-N analysis, more quantitative single-case studies, greater attention to human rights measurement issues, the use of disaggregated primary data, and greater attention to the empirical theories.

The global comparisons on human rights protection have set an important precedent for trying to explain the patterns, regularities, and variation in the violation of a very narrow set of human rights. Chapter 6 made the limits of such studies clear, but their underlying logic of inference can frame enquiries using lower levels of analysis and qualitative human rights information. Case selection and the comparative framework that is adopted will have a direct bearing on the type of answers that researchers get from their analyses (see Geddes 1990). More careful attention to this basic methodological rule would have strengthened many existing studies on human rights, where too often the focus has been on countries in which particular outcomes were obtained and not on the variation of the outcome of interest. Human rights research could benefit through new comparative studies using regional and small-N comparisons that are conscientious of method. Indeed, areas studies scholars are effectively using a most similar systems design in explaining different outcomes within Western Europe, Eastern Europe, Latin America, Africa, or Asia. In adopting a most different systems design, cross-regional comparisons could identify different countries that have had similar outcomes or have undergone similar processes. A social science of human rights that remains attentive to questions of method can help explain how societies have achieved greater protection of human rights, the lessons from which can help other societies in achieving similar outcomes.

In addition, the classic methodological problem of 'too many variables, not enough cases' (Collier 1991) can be overcome through the adoption of most similar or most different systems design (or their variants) (Faure 1994), and through raising the number of observations within the countries under comparison by collecting evidence at lower levels of aggregation. For example, federal systems such as Mexico, the United States, Brazil, and Germany offer excellent opportunities for raising the number observations through the collection of evidence from the different states that comprise these countries. The work on truth commissions has shown that the time-series data on violations can also be disaggregated across space, type of perpetrator, type of victim, and type of violation, all of which enrich and deepen our understanding of crimes against humanity. While not yet available, similar disaggregated data on the violations of the right to food, the right to health, and the right to adequate housing could show the gender, class, and occupational differentiation in the enjoyment of these rights. Small-N comparisons over time can comprise enough observations for quantitative analysis or qualitative comparative analysis of the kind outlined in Chapter 4 and Chapter 8 (see Jones 1995; Landman 1999, 2005e).

Moreover, comparative historical approaches can focus on 'critical junctures' 'path dependency', and other factors over the *longue durée* that may help explain the variation in human rights protection across different countries and regions (Collier and Collier 1991; Steinmo, Thelen and Longstreth 1992; Mahoney and Rueschemeyer 2003; Brady and Collier 2004; Pierson 2004). For example, Brockett (2005) uses comparative historical analysis and time-series data on social protest and patterns of state repression in the cases of El Salvador and Guatemala in order to examine the dynamic relationship between political movements and state violence. His study examines the paradox of cycles of protest under extreme threat from agents of the state, where progressive activists participated in strikes, demonstrations, factory and farm occupations, and sit-ins in public offices. The study is an example of a comparison of two similar countries, in the same geographic region, with similar levels of state violence, and yet in Guatemala, state repression virtually eliminates a popular rural movement, while in El Salvador, an urban movement 'persists in the face of great risk' (Brockett 2005: 3).

Beyond these issues of method and more grounded analysis of fewer countries, there are additional issues concerning the development and availability of human rights measures. Chapter 5 showed that these include events-based, standards-based, and survey-based measures, but that there is still the tendency to use standardized scales that focus on the violation of political and civil rights. Part of this bias is explained by the traditional concerns of political science (the discipline most responsible for the development of these scales) over political institutions, democracy, state–citizen relations, and the so-called 'negative' rights of liberty. Part of the bias is explained by the relative intractability of economic, social, and cultural rights to quantitative measurement. The 'minorities at risk' project has developed indicators for the mobilization of, discrimination against, and violence against 284 minority and communal groups worldwide (www.cidcm.umd.edu/inscr/mar), and Cingranelli and Richards have developed standards-based scales for worker rights, and women's economic and social rights (www.humanrightsdata.com). But there remains a dearth of efforts to provide other types of data and measures on economic and social rights. Future research in the social sciences needs to move beyond an exclusive focus on political and civil rights, while efforts at measurement should pay closer attention to the existence of primary data on human rights violations. Moreover, both Chapters 1 and 5 made clear that all rights have positive and negative dimensions such that the social science community must develop more measures for the positive dimensions of civil and political rights and more measures for the negative dimensions of economic and social rights.

Thus, social scientists need to *broaden* the scope of rights that ought to be measured and *deepen* their sources of information. As Chapter 7 showed, parts of the human rights NGO community have taken the measurement agenda on board and have responded by providing rich sets of data on patterns of human rights abuses that remain very close to the actual victims of such abuse. These sources of data tend to focus on gross violations of human rights and also need to broaden their attention to include the violation of economic, social, and cultural rights. Efforts at surveying 'at-risk' populations have proved fruitful in producing individual-level data on human rights violations, but these efforts could also broaden their focus to include data beyond gross human rights violations. Any such attempts to deepen sources of data and to remain closer to the ground, as it were, will necessarily trade off against the ability to make larger inferences about the nature, extent, and reasons for human rights violations across the world. But the global comparisons have answered one set of important questions, while more studies at lower levels of analysis using more primary data could help fill the numerous remaining lacunae in the field.

Finally, social science research on human rights ought to engage more forcefully with the dominant empirical theories outlined in Chapter 3. The extant global studies on human rights, much like their behavioural predecessors, are thin on theory and thick on statistical analysis. Indeed, they occupy the theoretical 'messy centre' common to much comparative political science (Kohli *et al.* 1995), and tend not to engage explicitly with rationalist, structuralist, or culturalist theories at the domestic and international levels. Human rights violations are common everyday experiences for millions of people around the world. They are therefore not an aberration, but form typical patterns of social, political, and economic interaction. It thus seems paramount that the social sciences marshal the insights and analytical leverage from rationalist, structuralist, and culturalist perspectives in an effort to explain and understand why such patterns of abuse persist even though the world has witnessed a significant proliferation of human rights norms since the 1948 Universal Declaration and the 'precarious triumph' of human rights at the turn of the 21st century (Reiff 1999).

Notes

Chapter 5

1 Portions of this chapter have appeared in Landman (2004), but have been updated to include developments at the Office of the High Commissioner for Human Rights, my own participation in a European Commission-funded meeting of international experts in the use of indicators in the work of the UN Human Rights Treaty Bodies (Åbo Akademi, Finland, 11–13 March 2005), a one-day workshop on human rights measurement organized by the Human Rights Section of the American Political Science Association (Chicago, 1 September 2004), and developments in the non-governmental sector with respect to work on processing and analysis of human rights violations data for truth commissions, in particular, the work of Dr Patrick Ball and the Human Rights Data Analysis Group (HRDAG) at Benetech (www.benetech.org).

Chapter 6

1 A small portion of this chapter has appeared in my previous work (Landman 2003: 206–208; Landman 2005a: 556–560) and has benefited greatly from discussion with my MA students who have taken my course 'The Comparative Politics of Human Rights', where they have queried the appropriateness of global comparative analysis to some of the human rights problems discussed in this chapter.
2 'Anocracy' refers to a mixed regime with democratic and autocratic features that make it particularly unstable.

Chapter 7

1 This chapter benefited greatly from my work on a project for the International Centre for Transitional Justice (ICTJ), which assessed and evaluated the use of information management systems in truth commissions. I would like to thank the key individuals at the ICTJ and the American Association for the Advancement of Science (AAAS) for their openness and candid discussions with me and my research assistant, Ms Diana Morales. These individuals include Alex Boraine, Priscilla Hayner, Lisa Margarell, Rebecca Lichtenfeld, Mariecke Wierda, and Vasuki Nesiah at the ICTJ, and Patrick Ball and Kristen Cibelli at the AAAS. We are also grateful to many other people across the world who kindly responded to our questions, especially all those involved in the Peruvian *Comisión de Verdad y Reconciliación* (CVR), who received us in Lima in November 2003 with generous hospitality and open discussions about their work. The opinions and interpretations expressed throughout this chapter are entirely my own.
2 The Human Rights Data Analysis Group (HRDAG) at the American Association for the Advancement of Science is now located at the Benetech Initiative, a non-profit organization dedicated to using information technology in the service of human rights, and has been developing a variety of software packages for analysing human rights data and technical assistance to truth commissions (www.benetech.org).
3 The probability statements come from interviews with Patrick Ball (4–5 September 2003) at the American Association for the Advancement of Science in Washington DC, and can be found in Ball, Asher, Sulmont and Manrique (2003: 19–24).

4 There were four elected governments during the period of conflict: Fernando Belaunde (1980–1985), Alan Garcia (1985–1990), and Albert Fujimori (1990–2000). In 1992 President Fujimori carried out an 'autogolpe' in which the Congress was shut down and the President ruled single-handedly until his exile in 2000. While academic opinion sees this period as a democratic reversal or an example of 'delegative' democracy (see Foweraker, Landman and Harvey 2003), the CVR's final report refers to the period as a dictatorship and sees the year 2000 as marking a new democratic transition (2003 Volume 1: 19; see also Youngers 2003: 304–363).

Chapter 8

1 This quotation comes from the World Bank's web page on impact assessment, accessed on Friday, 13 May 2005: http://web.worldbank.org/WBSITE/EXTERNAL/EXTABOUTUS/ 0,,contentMDK:20103866~menuPK:250989~pagePK:51123644~piPK:329829~theSiteP K:29708,00.html.

References

Abbott, K. W., Keohane, R. O., Moravscik, A., Slaughter, A. and Snidal, D. (2000) 'The Concept of Legalization', *International Organization*, 54 (3): 401–419.

Abouharb M. R. and Cingranelli, D. L. (2004) 'Human Rights and Structural Adjustment: The Importance of Selection', in S. C. Carey and S. C. Poe (eds), *Understanding Human Rights Violations: New Systematic Studies*, Aldershot: Ashgate, 127–141.

Adcock, R. and Collier, D. (2001) 'Measurement Validity: A Shared Standard for Qualitative and Quantitative Research', *American Political Science Review*, 95 (3): 529–546.

Adler, E. (2002) 'Constructivism and International Relations', in W. Carlsnaes, T. Risse and B. Simmons (eds), *Handbook of International Relations*, London: Sage, 95–118.

Almond, G. (1996) 'Political Science: The History of the Discipline', in R. E. Goodin and H. Klingemann (eds), *The New Handbook of Political Science*, Oxford: Oxford University Press, 50–96.

Almond, G. with Genco, S. (1977) 'Clouds, Clocks and the Study of Politics', *World Politics*, 29 (4): 489–522.

Almond, G. and Verba, S. (1963) *The Civic Culture: Political Attitudes and Democracy in Five Nations*, Princeton, NJ: Princeton University Press.

Alston, P. (1997) 'Making Economic and Social Rights Count: A Strategy for the Future', *The Political Quarterly*, 68 (2): 188–195.

Alston, P. (2002) 'Resisting the Merger and Acquisition of Human Rights by Trade Law: A Reply to Petersmann', *European Journal of International Law*, 13 (4): 815–844.

Alston, P. and Crawford, J. (eds) (2000) *The Future of UN Human Rights Monitoring*, Cambridge: Cambridge University Press.

Amowitz, L. L., Reis, C., Lyons, K. H., Vann, B., Mansaray, B., Akinsulure-Smith, A., Taylor, L. and Iacopino, V. (2002) 'Prevalence of War-Related Sexual Violence and Other Human Rights Abuses among Internally Displaced Persons in Sierra Leone', *Journal of the American Medical Association*, 23/30 January, 287 (4): 513–521.

Anderson, O. W. (1976) 'Comments on Snyder, Hermann, and Lasswell, "A Global Monitoring System"', *International Studies Quarterly*, 20 (3): 493–494.

Arat, Z. F. (1991) *Democracy and Human Rights in Developing Countries*, Boulder, CO: Lynne Rienner Publishers.

Archer, M. (1995) *Realist Social Theory: The Morphogenetic Approach*, Cambridge: Cambridge University Press.

Avruch, K. and Vejarano, B. (2001) 'Truth and Reconciliation Commissions: A Review Essay and Bibliography', *Social Justice: Anthropology, Peace, and Human Rights*, 21 (1–2): 47–108.

Axelrod, R. (1984) *The Evolution of Cooperation*, New York: Basic Books.

Ball, P. B. (2000a) 'The Salvadoran Human Rights Commission: Data Processing, Data Representation, and Generating Analytical Reports', in P. B. Ball, H. F. Spirer and L. Spirer (eds), *Making the Case: Investigating Large Scale Human Rights Violations Using Information Systems and Data Analysis*, Washington DC: American Association for the Advancement of Science, 15–26.

Ball, P. B. (2000b) 'The Guatemalan Commission for Historical Clarification: Generating Analytical Reports, Inter-Sample Analysis', in P. B. Ball, H. F. Spirer and L. Spirer (eds), *Making the Case: Investigating Large Scale Human Rights Violations Using Information Systems and Data Analysis*, Washington DC: American Association for the Advancement of Science, 259–286.

Ball, P. B. with Cifuentes, R., Dueck, J., Gregory, R., Salcedo, D. and Saldarriaga, C. (1994) *A Definition of Database Design Standards for Human Rights Agencies*, Washington, DC: American Association for the Advancement of Science, http://shr.aaas.org/DBStandards/cover.html.

Ball, P. B. and Asher, J. (2002) 'Statistics and Slobodan: Using Data Analysis and Statistics in the War Crimes Trial of Former President Milosevic', *Chance*, 15 (4): 17–24.

Ball, P. B., Asher, J., Sulmont, D. and Manrique, D. (2003) *How Many Peruvians Have Died?*, Washington, DC: American Association for the Advancement of Science (AAAS), http://shr.aaas.org/hrdag/peru/aaas_peru_5.pdf.

Ball, P. B., Kobrak, P. and Spirer, H. (1999) *State Violence in Guatemala 1960–1996: A Quantitative Reflection*, Washington DC: American Association for the Advancement of Science.

Ball, P. B., Spirer, H. F. and Spirer, L. (eds) (2000) *Making the Case: Investigating Large Scale Human Rights Violations Using Information Systems and Data Analysis*, Washington DC: American Association for the Advancement of Science.

Banaszak, L. A. (1996) *Why Movements Succeed or Fail: Opportunity, Culture, and the Struggle for Woman Suffrage*, Princeton, NJ: Princeton University Press.

Banks, A. S. (1994) *Cross-Polity Time-Series Data Archive*, Binghamton, NY: State University of New York at Binghamton.

Baran, P. (1975) *The Political Economy of Neo-Colonialism*, London: Heinemann.

Barbalet, J. M. (1988) *Citizenship: Rights, Struggle and Class Inequality*, Milton Keynes: Open University Press.

Barratt, B. (2004) 'Aiding or Abetting: British Foreign Aid Decisions and Recipient Country Human Rights', in S. C. Carey and S. C. Poe (eds), *Understanding Human Rights Violations: New Systematic Studies*, Aldershot: Ashgate, 43–62.

Bates, R. H. (2001) *Prosperity and Violence: The Political Economy of Development*, New York: W. W. Norton.

BBC (2004) 'Powell Declares Genocide in Sudan', http://news.bbc.co.uk/go/pr/fr/-/2/hi/africa/3641820.stm, published: 2004/09/09 19:37:44 GMT.

Beck, N. and Katz, J. N. (1995) 'What to Do (and Not to Do) with Time-Series Cross-Section Data', *American Political Science Review*, 89 (3): 634–647.

Beetham, D. (1999) *Democracy and Human Rights*, Cambridge: Polity Press.

Bell, D. (1976) *The Coming of the Post-Industrial Society: A Venture in Social Forecasting*, New York: Basic Books.

Bendix, R. (1964) *Nation Building and Citizenship: Studies of our Changing Social Order*, New York: Wiley.

Bendix, R. (1978) *Kings or People: Power and the Mandate to Rule*, Berkeley: University of California Press.

Bhaskar, R. (1975) *A Realist Theory of Science*, Brighton: Harvester Wheatsheaf.

Bhaskar, R. (1986) *Scientific Realism and Human Emancipation*, London: Verso.

Bishop, Y. M. M., Fienberg, S. E. and Holland, P. W. (1975) *Discrete Multivariate Analysis: Theory and Practice*, Cambridge, MA: MIT Press.

Bobbio, N. (1996) *The Age of Rights*, Cambridge: Polity Press.

Bohrnstedt, G. W. and Knoke, D. (1988) *Statistics for Social Data Analysis*, Itasca, IL: F. E. Peacock.

Boix, C. (2003) *Democracy and Redistribution*, Cambridge: Cambridge University Press.

Boix, C. and Stokes, S. (2003) 'Endogenous Democratization', *World Politics*, 55 (July): 517–549.

Boli, J. and Thomas, G. (eds) (1999) *Constructing World Culture*, Stanford, CA: Stanford University Press.

Bollen, K. A. (1992) 'Political Rights and Political Liberties in Nations: An Evaluation of Rights

Measures, 1950 to 1984', in T. B. Jabine and R. P. Claude (eds), *Human Rights and Statistics: Getting the Record Straight*, Philadelphia: University of Pennsylvania Press, 188–215.

Booth, K. and Dunne, T. (eds) (2002) *Worlds in Collision: Terror and the Future of Global Order*, London: Palgrave.

Boyle, K. (1995) 'Stock-taking on Human Rights: The World Conference on Human Rights, Vienna 1993', *Political Studies*, 43: 79–95.

Brady, H. E. and Collier, D. (2004) *Rethinking Social Inquiry: Diverse Tools, Shared Standards*, Lanham, MD: Rowman and Littlefield.

Bratton, M. and van de Walle, N. (1997) *Democratic Experiments in Africa: Regime Transitions in Comparative Perspective*, Cambridge: Cambridge University Press.

Brockett, C. (2005) *Political Movements and Violence in Central America*, Cambridge: Cambridge University Press.

Brohman, J. (1996) *Popular Development: Rethinking the Theory and Practice of Development*, Oxford: Blackwell.

Brownlie, I. (2003) *Principles of Public International Law*, 6th edn, Oxford: Oxford University Press.

Buergenthal, T. (1995) *International Human Rights in a Nutshell*, St. Paul, MN: West Publishing Co.

Burkhart, R. E. and Lewis-Beck, M. (1994) 'Comparative Democracy, the Economic Development Thesis', *American Political Science Review*, 88 (4): 903–910.

Campbell, B. B. and Brenner, A. D. (2002) *Death Squads in Global Perspective: Murder with Deniability*, London: Palgrave.

Campbell, T. and Miller, S. (eds) (2004) *Human Rights and the Moral Responsibilities of Corporate and Public Sector Organizations*, New York: Springer-Verlag.

Cardoso, F. H. and Faletto, E. (1979) *Dependency and Development in Latin America*, Berkeley: University of California Press.

Carey, S. and Poe, S. (2004) *Understanding Human Rights Violations: New Systematic Studies*, Aldershot: Ashgate.

Carlsnaes, W., Risse, T. and Simmons, B. (eds) (2002) *Handbook of International Relations*, London: Sage.

CEH (Comisión para el Easclarecimiento Histórico) (1999) *Guatemala Memoria del Silencio: Informe de la Comisión para el Easclarecimiento Histórico*, vol. I, New York: UNOPS.

Chapman, A. R. (1996) 'A "Violations Approach" for Monitoring the International Covenant on Economic, Social, and Cultural Rights', *Human Rights Quarterly*, 18 (1): 23–66.

Chapman, A. R. and Ball, P. (2001) 'The Truth of Truth Commissions: Comparative Lessons from Haiti, South Africa, and Guatemala', *Human Rights Quarterly*, 23 (1): 1–43.

Cingranelli, D. (1988) *Human Rights: Theory and Measurement*, Basingstoke: Macmillan.

Cingranelli, D. and Richards, D. (2001) 'Measuring the Impact of Human Rights Organizations', in C. E. Welch, Jr. (ed.), *NGOs and Human Rights: Promise and Performance*, Philadelphia: University of Pennsylvania Press, 225–237.

Cioffi-Revilla, C. (1998) *Politics and Uncertainty: Theory, Models, and Applications*, Cambridge: Cambridge University Press.

Cioffi-Revilla, C. and Landman, T. (1999) 'Evolution of Maya Polities in the Ancient Mesoamerican System', *International Studies Quarterly*, 43 (December): 559–598.

Clague, C., Keefer, P., Knack, S. and Olson, M. (1996) 'Property and Contract Rights in Autocracies and Democracies', *Journal of Economic Growth*, 1 (2): 243–276.

Clague, C., Keefer, P., Knack, S. and Olson, M. (1997) 'Democracy, Autocracy, and the Institutions Supportive of Economic Growth', in C. Clague (ed.), *Institutions and Economic Development: Growth and Governance in Less-Developed and Post-Socialist Countries*, Baltimore: Johns Hopkins University Press.

Clapham, C. (ed.) (1982) *Private Patronage and Public Power: Political Clientelism in the Modern State*, London: Pinter.

Clark, A. M. (2001) *Diplomacy of Conscience: Amnesty International and Changing Human Rights Norms*, Princeton, NJ: Princeton University Press.

Claude, R. P. (1976) 'The Classical Model of Human Rights Development', in R. P. Claude (ed.), *Comparative Human Rights*, Baltimore: Johns Hopkins University Press, 6–49.

Claude, R. P. and Jabine, T. B. (1992) 'Exploring Human Rights Issues with Statistics', in T. B. Jabine and R. P. Claude (eds), *Human Rights and Statistics: Getting the Record Straight*, Philadelphia: University of Pennsylvania Press, 5–34.

Clohesy, A. (2000) 'Provisionalism and the (Im)possibility of Justice in Northern Ireland', in D. Howarth, A. J. Norval and Y. Stavrakakis (eds), *Discourse Theory and Political Analysis: Identities, Hegemonies, and Social Change*, Manchester: Manchester University Press, 70–85.

Clohesy, A. (2005) 'The Human Rights Act: Politics, Power, and the Law', in D. Howarth and J. Torfing (eds), *Discourse Theory in European Politics: Identity, Policy, and Governance*, London: Palgrave, 170–189.

Cohen, Y. (1994) *Radicals, Reformers, and Reactionaries: The Prisoner's Dilemma and the Collapse of Democracy in Latin America*, Chicago: University of Chicago Press.

Collier, D. (ed.) (1979) *The New Authoritarianism in Latin America*, Princeton, NJ: Princeton University Press.

Collier, D. (1991) 'New Perspectives on the Comparative Method', in D. A. Rustow and K. P. Erickson (eds), *Comparative Political Dynamics: Global Research Perspectives*, New York: HarperCollins, 7–31.

Collier, D. (1993) 'The Comparative Method', in A. Finifter (ed.), *Political Science: The State of the Discipline*, Washington, DC: The American Political Science Association, 105–119.

Collier, D. (1995) 'Translating Quantitative Methods for Qualitative Researchers: The Case of Selection Bias', *American Political Science Review*, 89 (June): 461–466.

Collier, R. B. and Collier, D. (1991) *Shaping the Political Arena: Critical Junctures, The Labour Movement, and Regime Dynamics in Latin America*, Princeton, NJ: Princeton University Press.

Colomer, J. (1991) 'Transitions by Agreement: Modelling the Spanish Way', *American Political Science Review*, 85 (4): 1283–1302.

Colomer, J. M. and Pascual, M. (1994) 'The Polish Games of Transition', *Communist and Post-Communist Studies*, 27 (3): 275–294.

Compa, L. and Diamond, S. (eds) (1996) *Human Rights, Labour Rights, and International Trade*, Philadelphia: University of Pennsylvania Press.

CONADEP (1984) *Nunca Más (Never Again): A Report by Argentina's National Commission on Disappeared People*, Buenos Aires: CONADEP.

Constable, P. and Valenzuela, A. (1991) *A Nation of Enemies: Chile under Pinochet*, New York: W. W. Norton.

Couvalis, G. (1997) *The Philosophy of Science: Science and Objectivity*, London: Sage.

CVR (Comisión de Verdad y Reconciliación de Perú) (2003) *Informe Final*, Lima: Comisión de Verdad y Reconciliación.

Dahl, R. A. (1971) *Polyarchy: Participation and Opposition*, New Haven, CT: Yale University Press.

Dalton, R. and Kuechler, M. (1999) *Challenging the Political Order: New Social Movements in Western Democracies*, Cambridge: Polity Press.

Dassin, J. (ed.) (1986) *Torture in Brazil, A Report by the Archdiocese of São Paulo*, New York: Vintage Books.

Davenport, C. (1995) 'Multi-dimensional Threat Perception and State Repression', *American Journal of Political Science*, 39 (3): 683–713.

Davenport, C. (1999) 'Human Rights and the Democratic Proposition', *Journal of Conflict Resolution*, 43 (1): 92–116.

Davenport, C. (2000) *Paths to State Repression: Human Rights Violations and Contentious Politics*, Lanham, MD: Rowman and Littlefield.

Davenport, C. and Armstrong, D. A. (2004) 'Democracy and the Violation of Human Rights: A Statistical Exploration from 1976 to 1996', *American Journal of Political Science*, 48 (3): 538–554.

Davidson, S. (1993) *Human Rights*, Buckingham: Open University Press.

De Brito, A., González-Enríquez, C. and Aguilar, P. (2001) *The Politics of Memory: Transitional Justice in Democratizing Societies*, Oxford: Oxford University Press.

Della Porta, D. and Diani, M. (1999) *Social Movements: An Introduction*, Oxford: Blackwell.

de Meur, G. and Berg-Schlosser, D. (1994) 'Comparing Political Systems: Establishing Similarities and Dissimilarities', *European Journal of Political Research*, 26: 193–219.

de Soto, H. (2000) *The Mystery of Capital*, London: Black Swan Books.

Deutsch, K. (1960) 'Toward an Inventory of Basic Trends and Patterns in Comparative and International Politics', *American Political Science Review*, 54 (1): 34–57.

Devine, F. (1995) 'Qualitative Analysis', in D. Marsh and G. Stoker (eds), *Theories and Methods in Political Science*, London: Macmillan, 137–153.

Devine, F. and Heath, S. (1999) *Sociological Research Methods in Context*, Basingstoke: Macmillan.

Diamond, L. (1999) *Developing Democracy: Toward Consolidation*, Baltimore: Johns Hopkins University Press.

Di Maggio, P. and Powell, W. W. (1983) 'The Iron Cage Revisited: Institutional Isomorphism and Collective Rationality in Organizational Fields', *American Sociological Review*, 48 (April): 147–160.

Dogan, M. and Pelassy, D. (1990) *How to Compare Nations: Strategies in Comparative Politics*, 2nd edn, Chatham, NJ: Chatham House.

Domínguez, J. I. (1979) 'Assessing Human Rights Conditions: International Human Rights Norms', in J. I. Domínguez, N. S. Rodley, B. Wood and R. Falk (eds), *Enhancing Global Human Rights*, New York: McGraw Hill, 25–47.

Domínguez, J. I., Rodley, N. S., Wood, B. and Falk, R. (1979) *Enhancing Global Human Rights*, New York: McGraw-Hill.

Donnelly, J. (1986) 'International Human Rights: A Regime Analysis', *International Organization*, 40: 599–642.

Donnelly, J. (1989) *Universal Human Rights in Theory and Practice*, Ithaca, NY: Cornell University Press.

Donnelly, J. (1994) 'Post-Cold War Reflections on the Study of Human Rights', *Ethics and International Affairs*, 8: 97–117.

Donnelly, J. (1998) *International Human Rights*, 2nd edn, Boulder, CO: Westview.

Donnelly, J. (1999a) 'Democracy, Development, and Human Rights', *Human Rights Quarterly*, 21 (3): 608–632.

Donnelly, J. (1999b) 'The Social Construction of Human Rights', in T. Dunne and N. Wheeler (eds), *Human Rights in Global Politics*, Cambridge: Cambridge University Press, 71–102.

Donnelly, J. (2000) *Realism and International Relations*, Cambridge: Cambridge University Press.

Donnelly, J. (2003) *Universal Human Rights in Theory and Practice*, 2nd edn, Ithaca, NY: Cornell University Press.

Downs, A. (1957) *An Economic Theory of Democracy*, New York: Harper.

Drazen, A. (2000) *Political Economy in Macroeconomics*, Princeton, NJ: Princeton University Press.

Dueck, J. (1992) 'HURIDOCS Standard Formats as a Tool in the Documentation of Human Rights Violations', in T. B. Jabine and R. P. Claud (eds), *Human Rights and Statistics: Getting the Record Straight*, Philadelphia: University of Pennsylvania Press, 127–158.

Duvall, R. and Shamir, M. (1980) 'Indicators from Errors: Cross-National, Time Serial Measures of the Repressive Disposition of Government', in C. L. Taylor (ed.), *Indicator Systems for Political, Economic, and Social Analysis*, Cambridge, MA: Oelgeschlager, Gunn and Hain, Publishers, Inc.

Duverger, M. (1951) *Political Parties: Their Organization and Activity in the Modern State*, London: Methuen.

Eckstein, H. (1975) 'Case-study and Theory in Political Science', in F. I. Greenstein and N. S. Polsby (eds), *Handbook of Political Science, Vol. 7: Strategies of Inquiry*, Reading, MA: Addison-Wesley, 79–137.

Eckstein, S. and Wickham-Crowley, T. (eds) (2003) *Struggles for Social Rights in Latin America*, New York: Routledge.

Eulau, H. (1996) *Micro-Macro Dilemmas in Political Science: Personal Pathways through Complexity*, Norman, OK: University of Oklahoma Press.

European Commission (2001) *The European Union's Role in Promoting Human Rights and Democratization in Third Countries*, Brussels: European Commission.

Executive Board, American Anthropological Association (1947) 'Statement on Human Rights Submitted to the Commission on Human Rights, United Nations', *American Anthropology*, 49: 539–543.

Falk, R. (2000) *Human Rights Horizons*, London: Routledge.

Faure, A. M. (1994) 'Some Methodological Problems in Comparative Politics', *Journal of Theoretical Politics*, 6 (3): 307–322.

Fay, B. (1975) *Social Theory and Political Practice*, London: Allen & Unwin.

Fearon, J. and Wendt, A. (2002) 'Rationalism v. Constructivism: A Skeptical View', in W. Carlsnaes, T. Risse and B. Simmons, B. (eds), *Handbook of International Relations*, London: Sage, 52–72.

Feyerabend, P. (1993) *Against Method*, London: Verso Press.

FIDH-OMCT (2003) *Human Rights Defenders on the Front Line*, Annual Report 2002, Paris and Geneva.

Finnis, J. (1980) *Natural Law and Natural Rights*, Oxford: Oxford University Press.

Flyvberg, B. (2001) *Making Social Science Matter: Why Social Inquiry Fails and How It Can Succeed Again*, Cambridge: Cambridge University Press.

Forsythe, D. P. (1976) 'The Red Cross as a Transnational Movement: Conserving and Changing the Nation State System', *International Organization*, 30: 607–630.

Forsythe, D. P. (2000) *Human Rights in International Relations*, Cambridge: Cambridge University Press.

Foweraker, J. (1995) *Theorizing Social Movements*, London: Pluto Press.

Foweraker J. and Krznaric, R. (2001) 'Measuring Liberal Democratic Performance: A Conceptual and Empirical Critique', *Political Studies*, 45 (3): 759–787.

Foweraker J. and Krznaric, R. (2003) 'Differentiating the Democratic Performance of the West', *European Journal of Political Research*, 42: 313–340.

Foweraker, J. and Landman, T. (1997) *Citizenship Rights and Social Movements: A Comparative and Statistical Analysis*, Oxford: Oxford University Press.

Foweraker, J. and Landman, T. (2002) 'Constitutional Design and Democratic Performance', *Democratization*, 9 (Summer): 43–66.

Foweraker, J. and Landman, T. (2004) 'Economic Development and Democracy: Revisited: Why Depdendency Theory Is Not Yet Dead', *Democratization*, 11 (1): 1–21.

Foweraker, J., Landman, T. and Harvey, N. (2003) *Governing Latin America*, London: Polity Press.

Fox, J. (1997) *Applied Regression Analysis, Linear Models, and Related Methods*, London: Sage.

Francioni, F. (2001) *The Environment, International Trade and Human Rights*, Oxford: Hart Publishing.

Francisco, R. (2004) 'After the Massacre: Mobilization in the Wake of Harsh Repression', *Mobilization* 9 (2) (June): 107–126.

Franck, T. M. (1990) *The Power of Legitimacy among Nations*, New York: Oxford University Press.

Franzosi, R. (1990) 'Computer-assisted Coding of Textual Data: An Application to Semantic Grammarrs', *Sociological Methods and Research*, 19 (2): 225–257.

Franzosi, R. (2004) *From Words to Numbers: Narrative, Data and Social Science*, Cambridge: Cambridge University Press.

Fraser, A. S. (1999) 'Becoming Human: The Origins and Development of Women's Human Rights', *Human Rights Quarterly*, 21 (4): 853–906.

Freeman, M. (2001) 'Is a Political Science of Human Rights Possible?', *The Netherlands Quarterly of Human Rights*, 19 (2): 121–137.

Freeman, M. (2002a) 'Anthropology and the Democratisation of Human Rights', *The International Journal of Human Rights*, 6 (3): 37–54.

Freeman, M. (2002b) *Human Rights: An Interdisciplinary Approach*, Cambridge: Polity.

Gallie, W. B. (1956) Essentially Contested Concepts, *Proceedings of the Aristotelian Society*, 51: 167–198.

Galtung, J. (1977) *Methodology and Ideology*, Copenhagen: Christian Ejlers.

Gastil, R. D. (1978), *Freedom in the World: Political Rights and Civil Liberties, 1978*, Boston: G. K. Hall.

Gastil, R. D. (1980), *Freedom in the World: Political Rights and Civil Liberties*, Westport, CT: Greenwood Press.

Gastil, R. D. (1988) *Freedom in the World: Political and Civil Liberties, 1986–1987*, New York: Freedom House.

Gastil, R. D. (1989) *Freedom in the World: Political and Civil Liberties, 1988–1989*, New York: Freedom House.

Gastil, R. D. (1990) 'The Comparative Survey of Freedom: Experiences and Suggestions', *Studies in Comparative International Development*, 25: 25–50.

Gates, S. and Humes, B. D. (1997) *Games, Information and Politics: Applying Game Theoretic Models to Political Science*, Ann Arbor: University of Michigan Press.

Gautier, D. (1986) *Morals by Agreement*, Oxford: Clarendon Press.

Geddes, B. (1990) 'How the Cases You Choose Affect the Answers You Get: Selection Bias in Comparative Politics', *Political Analysis*, 2: 131–150.

Geddes, B. (1991) 'A Game Theoretic Model of Reform in Latin American Democracies', *American Political Science Review*, 85 (June): 371–392.

Geddes, B. (1994) *Politician's Dilemma: Building State Capacity in Latin America*, Berkeley: University of California Press.

Geddes, B. (1999) 'What Do We Know about Democratization after Twenty Years?', *Annual Review of Political Science*, 2: 115–144.

Geddes, B. (2003) *Paradigms and Sand Castles: Theory Building and Research Design in Comparative Politics*, Ann Arbor: University of Michigan Press.

Geertz, C. (1973) 'Thick Description: Toward an Interpretative Theory of Culture', in *The Interpretation of Cultures*, New York: Basic Books, 3–30.

Gerner, D. J., Schrodt, P. A., Francisco, R. A. and Weddle, J. (1994) 'The Analysis of Political Events Using Machine Coded Data', *International Studies Quarterly* 38 (March): 91–119.

Ghandhi, P. R. (2002) *Blackstone's International Human Rights Documents*, 3rd edn, Oxford: Oxford University Press.

Gibney, M. and Dalton, M. (1996) 'The Political Terror Scale', in D. L. Cingranelli (ed.), *Human Rights and Developing Countries*, Greenwich, CT: JAI Press, 73–84.

Gibney, M. and Stohl, M. (1998) 'Human Rights and US Refugee Policy', in M. Gibney (ed.), *Open Borders? Closed Societies?: The Ethical and Political Issues*, Westport, CT: Greenwood Press.

Gibson, J. S. (1996) *Dictionary of International Human Rights Law*, Lanham, MD: Scarecrow Press.

Giddens, A. (1976) *New Rules of Sociological Method*, London: Hutchinson.

Giddens, A. (1979) *Central Problems in Social Theory*, London: Macmillan.

Giddens, A. (1981) *A Contemporary Critique of Historical Materialism*, London: Macmillan.

Giffard, C. (2002), *Torture Reporting Handbook*, Colchester, UK: Human Rights Centre, University of Essex.

Gilbert, P. (2003) *New Terror, New Wars*, Edinburgh: Edinburgh University Press.

Gillies, D. (1993) *Human Rights, Democracy and 'Good Governance': Stretching the World Bank's Policy Frontiers*, Montreal: International Centre for Human Rights and Democratic Development.

Gloppen, S. (2005) 'Roads to Reconciliation: A Conceptual Framework', in E. Skaar, S. Gloppen and A. Surhke (eds), *Roads to Reconciliation*, Lexington, MA: Lexington Books, 17–50.

Goldstein, D. (2003) 'In Our Own Hands: Lynching, Justice, and the Law in Bolivia', *American Ethnologist*, 30 (1): 22–43.

Goldstein, D. (2004) *The Spectacular City: Violence and Performance in Urban Bolivia*, Durham, NC: Duke University Press.

Goldstein, J. (1992) 'A Conflict–Cooperation Scale for WEIS Events Data', *Journal of Conflict Resolution*, 36 (2): 369–385.

Gómez, M. (2003) *Human Rights in Cuba, El Salvador and Nicaragua: A Sociological Perspective on Human Rights Abuse*, London: Routledge.

Gordon, S. (1991) *The History and Philosophy of Social Science*, London: Routledge.

Gosling, L. and Edwards, M. (2003) *Toolkits: A Practical Guide to Planning, Monitoring, Evaluation and Impact Assessment*, London: Save the Children.

Gourevitch, P. (2002) 'Domestic Politics and International Relations', in W. Carlsnaes, T. Risse and B. Simmons, B. (eds), *Handbook of International Relations*, London: Sage, 309–328.

Gray, C. (2002) 'World Politics as Usual after September 11: Realism Vindicated', in K. Booth and T. Dunne (eds), *Worlds in Collision: Terror and the Future of Global Order*, London: Palgrave, 226–241.

Gray, J. (1998) *False Dawn: The Delusions of Global Capitalism*, London: Granta.

Green, D. (ed.) (2002) *Constructivism and Comparative Politics*, Armonk, NY: M. E. Sharpe.

Green, D. and Shapiro, I. (1994) *Pathologies of Rational Choice Theory: A Critique of Applications in Political Science*, New Haven, CT: Yale University Press.

Green, M. (2001) 'What We Talk about When We Talk about Indicators: Current Approaches to Human Rights Measurement', *Human Rights Quarterly*, 23: 1062–1097.

Greenberg, K. J., Dratel, J. L. and Lewis, A. (eds) (2005) *The Torture Papers: The Road to Abu Ghraib*, Cambridge: Cambridge University Press.

Greer, D. (1966) *The Incidence of Terror during the French Revolution: A Statistical Interpretation*, Gloucester, MA: Peter Smith Publisher Inc.

Griggs, S. and Howarth, D. (2000) 'New Environmental Movements and Direct Action Protest: The Campaign against Manchester Airport's Second Runway', in D. Howarth, A. J. Norval and Y. Stavrakakis (eds), *Discourse Theory and Political Analysis: Identities, Hegemonies, and Social Change*, Manchester: Manchester University Press, 52–69.

Gurr, T. R. (1968) 'A Causal Model of Civil Strife', *American Political Science Review*, 62: 1104–1124.

Gurr, T. R. (1970) *Why Men Rebel*, Princeton, NJ: Princeton University Press.

Gurr, T. R. (1993) 'Why Minorities Rebel: A Cross National Analysis of Communal Mobilization and Conflict Since 1945', *International Political Science Review*, 14 (2): 161–201.

Haggard, S., Levy, M. A., Moravscik, A. and Niolaides, K. (1993) 'Integrating the Two Halves of Europe: Theories of Interests, Bargaining and Institutions', in R. O. Keohane, J. Nye and S. Hoffman (eds), *After the Cold War: International Institutions and State Strategies in Europe, 1989–1991*, Cambridge, MA: Harvard University Press, 182–202.

Hague, R., Harrop, M. and Breslin, S. (1992) *Political Science: A Comparative Introduction*, New York: St Martin's Press.

Hamm, B. (2001) 'FoodFirst Information and Action Network', in C. E. Welch, Jr. (ed.), *NGOs and Human Rights: Promise and Performance*, Philadelphia: University of Pennsylvania Press, 167–181.

Hansclever, A., Mayer. P. and Rittberger, V. (1997) *Theories of International Regimes*, Cambridge: Cambridge University Press.

Harris, D. (1998) 'Regional Protection of Human Rights: The Inter-American Achievement', in D. Harris and S. Livingstone (eds), *The Inter-American System of Human Rights*, Oxford: Oxford University Press, 1–29.

Harris, D. and Livingstone, S. (eds) (1998) *The Inter-American System of Human Rights*, Oxford: Oxford University Press.

Harvey, N. and Halverson, C. (2000) 'The Secret and the Promise: Women's Struggles in Chiapas', in D. Howarth, A. J. Norval and Y. Stavrakakis (eds), *Discourse Theory and Political Analysis: Identities, Hegemonies, and Social Change*, Manchester: Manchester University Press, 151–167.

Hathaway, O. (2002) 'Do Treaties Make a Difference? Human Rights Treaties and the Problem of Compliance', *Yale Law Journal*, 111: 1932–2042.

Hawkins, D. (2002) *International Human Rights and Authoritarian Rule in Chile*, Lincoln: University of Nebraska Press.

Hawkins, D. (2004) 'Explaining Costly International Institutions: Persuasion and Enforceable Human Rights Norms', *International Studies Quarterly*, 48: 779–804.

Hay, C. (1995) 'Structure and Agency', in D. Marsh and G. Stoker (eds), *Theories and Methods in Political Science*, London: Macmillan, 189–206.

Hay, C. (2002) *Political Analysis*, London: Palgrave.

Hayner, P. B. (1994) 'Fifteen Truth Commissions – 1974–1994: A Comparative Study', *Human Rights Quarterly*, 16: 597–655.

Hayner, P. B. (2002) *Unspeakable Truths: Facing the Challenges of Truth Commissions*, New York: Routledge.

Haynes, J. (2002) *Politics in the Developing World: A Concise Introduction*, Malden, MA: Blackwell.

Helliwell, J. F. (1994) 'Empirical Linkages between Democracy and Economic Growth', *British Journal of Political Science*, 24: 225–248.

Henderson, C. (1993) 'Population Pressures and Political Repression', *Social Science Quarterly*, 74: 322–333.

Hendricks, J. W. (1976) 'The Problem of Outcome Evaluation: A Comment on the Proposed Global Monitoring System', *International Studies Quarterly*, 20 (4): 621–628.

Hibbs, D. (1973) *Mass Political Violence: A Cross-National Causal Analysis*, New York: Wiley.

Higgins, R. (1994) *Problems and Process: International Law and How We Use It*, Oxford: Oxford University Press.

Higley, J. and Gunther, R. (eds) (1992) *Elites and Democratic Consolidation in Latin America and Southern Europe*, Cambridge: Cambridge University Press.

Hirschman, A. (1970) 'The Search for Paradigms as a Hindrance to Understanding', *World Politics*, 22: 329–343.

Holland, P. W. (1986) 'Statistics and Causal Inference', *Journal of the American Statistical Association*, 81 (396): 945–960.

Holmes, S. and Sunstein, C. R. (1999) *The Cost of Rights: Why Liberty Depends on Taxes*, New York: W. W. Norton.

Holston, J. and Appadurai, A. (1999) 'Introduction: Cities and Citizenship', in J. Holston (ed.), *Cities and Citizenship*, Durham, NC: Duke University Press, 1–18.

Home Office of the United Kingdom (2003) *2001 Home Office Citizenship Survey: People, Families, and Communities*, Home Office Research Study 270, London: Home Office of the United Kingdom.

Howard, R. (1988) 'The Full-Belly Thesis: Should Economic Rights Take Priority over Civil and Political Rights? Evidence from Sub-Saharan Africa', *Human Rights Quarterly*, 5 (4): 467–490.

Howarth, D. (1995) 'Discourse Theory', in D. Marsh and G. Stoker (eds), *Theories and Methods in Political Science*, London: Macmillan, 115–136.

Howarth, D. (2000a) *Discourse*, Buckingham: Open University Press.

Howarth, D. (2000b) 'The Difficult Emergence of a Democratic Imaginary: Black Consciousness and Non-Racial Democracy in South Africa', in D. Howarth, A. J. Norval and Y. Stavrakakis (eds), *Discourse Theory and Political Analysis: Identities, Hegemonies, and Social Change*, Manchester: Manchester University Press, 168–192.

Howarth, D. (2005) 'Applying Discourse Theory: The Method of Articulation', in D. Howarth and J. Torfing (eds), *Discourse Theory in European Politics: Identity, Policy, and Governance*, London: Palgrave, 316–349.

Howarth, D. and Norval, A. J. (eds) (1998) *South Africa in Transition: New Theoretical Perspectives*, Basingstoke: Macmillan.

Howarth, D., Norval, A. J. and Stavrakakis, Y. (eds) (2000) *Discourse Theory and Political Analysis: Identities, Hegemonies, and Social Change*, Manchester: Manchester University Press.

Huggins, M. K. (2000) 'Legacies of Authoritarianism: Brazilian Torturers' and Murderers' Reformulation of Memory', *Latin American Perspectives*, 27 (2): 57–78.

Huggins, M. K., Haritos-Fatouros, M. and Zimbardo, P. G. (2002) *Violence Workers: Police Torturers and Murderers Reconstruct Brazilian Atrocities*, Berkeley: University of California Press.

Huitema, B. E. (2004) 'Analysis of Interrupted Time-Series Experiments Using ITSE: A Critique', *Understanding Statistics*, 3(1): 27–46.

Human Rights Council of Australia (1995) *The Rights Way to Development: A Human Rights Approach to Development Assistance*, Marrickville, NSW: Human Rights Council of Australia.

Huntington, S. P. (1991) *The Third Wave: Democratization in the Late Twentieth Century*, Norman: University of Oklahoma Press.

Hurrell, A. (1999) 'Power, Principle and Prudence: Protecting Human Rights in a Deeply Divided World', in T. Dunne and N. Wheeler (eds), *Human Rights in Global Politics*, Cambridge: Cambridge University Press, 277–302.

IAIA (International Association of Impact Assessment) (2003) 'Social Impact Assessment: International Principles', *IAIA Special Publications Series No. 2*, Fargo, ND: International Association of Impact Assessment (www.iaia.org).

Ignatieff, M. (2001) *Human Rights as Politics and Idolatry*, Princeton, NJ: Princeton University Press.

Inglehart, R. (1977) *The Silent Revolution: Changing Values and Political Styles among Western Publics*, Princeton, NJ: Princeton University Press.

Inglehart, R. (1990) *Culture Shift in Advanced Industrial Societies*, Princeton, NJ: Princeton University Press.

Inglehart, R. (1997) *Modernization and Postmodernization*, Princeton, NJ: Princeton University Press.

Inglehart, R. (1998) 'Political Values', in J. W. van Deth (ed.), *Comparative Politics: The Problem of Equivalence*, London: Routledge, 61–85.

Ingram, A. (1994) *A Political Theory of Rights*, Oxford: Oxford University Press.

Innes, J. E. (1992) 'Human Rights Reporting as a Policy Tool: An Examination of the State Department Country Reports', in T. B. Jabine and R. P. Claude (eds), *Human Rights and Statistics: Getting the Record Straight*, Philadelphia: University of Pennsylvania Press, 235–257.

International Institute for Democracy and Electoral Assistance (IDEA) (2004) 'Reconciliation Lessons Learned from United Nations Peacekeeping Missions: Case Studies – Sierra Leone and Timor L'Este', *Report Prepared by International IDEA for the Office of the High Commissioner for Human Rights (OHCHR) Annual of Field Presences (HOFP) Meeting, Geneva*, Stockholm: International IDEA.

Interorganizational Committee on Principles and Guidelines for Social Impact Assessments (2003) 'Principles and Guidelines for Social Impact Assessment in the USA', *Impact Assessment and Project Appraisal*, 21 (3): 231–250.

Ishay, M. (2004) *The History of Human Rights: From Ancient Times to the Globalization Era*, Berkeley: University of California Press.

Jabine, T. B. and Claude, R. P. (eds) (1992) *Human Rights and Statistics: Getting the Record Straight*, Philadelphia: University of Pennsylvania Press.

Jaggers, K. and Gurr, T. R. (1995) 'Tracking Democracy's Third Wave with the Polity III Data', *Journal of Peace Research*, 32 (4): 469–482.

James, W. and van de Vijver, L. (eds) (2000) *After the TRC: Reflections on Truth and Reconciliation in South Africa*, Athens, OH: Ohio University Press.

Jessop, B. (2002) *The Future of the Capitalist State*, Cambridge: Polity Press.

Jones, B., Gray, A., Kavanagh, D., Moran, M., Norton, P. and Seldon, A. (1998) *Politics UK*, 3rd edn, London: Prentice Hall.

Jones, M. P. (1995) *Electoral Laws and the Survival of Presidential Democracies*, Notre Dame, IN: University of Notra Dame Press.

Jones, P. (1994) *Rights*, London: Macmillan.

Kaase, M. and Newton, K. (1995) *Beliefs in Government, Vol. V: Beliefs*, Oxford: Oxford University Press.

Kaldor, M. (1999) *New and Old Wars: Organized Violence in a Global Era*, Cambridge: Polity Press.

Karl, T. L. (1990) 'Dilemmas of Democratization in Latin America', *Comparative Politics*, 23: 1–21.

Katznelson, I. (1997) 'Structure and the Configuration in Comparative Politics', in M. Lichbach and A. Zuckerman (eds), *Comparative Politics: Rationality, Culture, and Structure*, Cambridge: Cambridge University Press, 81–112.

Kaufmann, D., Kraay, A. and Mastruzzi, M. (2003) *Governance Matters III: Governance Indicators for 1996–2002*, Draft for Comment, Washington DC: World Bank.

Kaufmann, D., Kraay, A. and Zoido-Lobaton, P. (1999a), *Aggregating Governance Indicators*, Policy Research Working Paper No. 2195, Washington DC: World Bank.

Kaufmann, D., Kraay, A. and Zoido-Lobaton, P. (1999b), *Governance Matters*, Policy Research Working Paper No. 2196, Washington DC: World Bank

Kaufmann, D., Kraay, A. and Zoido-Lobaton, P. (2000) 'Governance Matters: From Measurement to Action', *Finance and Development*, 37 (2), Washington DC: International Monetary Fund.

Kaufmann, D., Kraay, A. and Zoido-Lobaton, P. (2002) *Governance Matters II: Updated Indicators for 2000–01*, Policy Research Working Paper No. 2772, Washington DC: World Bank.

Keck, M. and Sikkink, K. (1998) *Activists beyond Borders: Advocacy Networks in International Politics*, Ithaca, NY: Cornell University Press.

Keith, L. C. (1999) 'The United Nations International Covenant on Civil and Political Rights: Does it Make a Difference in Human Rights Behavior?', *Journal of Peace Research*, 36 (1): 95–118.

Keith, L. C. (2004) 'National Constitutions and Human Rights Protection: Regional Differences and Colonial Influences', in S. Carey and S. C. Poe (eds), *Understanding Human Rights Violations: New Systematic Studies*, Aldershot: Ashgate, 162–185.

Kendall, S. and Staggs, M. (2005) 'From Mandate to Legacy: The Special Court for Sierra Leone as a Model for "Hybrid Justice"', *Interim Report on the Special Court for Sierra Leone*, Berkeley: War Crimes Study Center, University of California Berkeley (April).

Kennan, G. (1951) *American Diplomacy, 1900–1950*, Chicago: University of Chicago Press.

Keohane, R. (1984) *After Hegemony: Cooperation and Discord in World Political Economy*, Princeton, NJ: Princeton University Press.

Keohane, R. O. (2001) 'Governance in a Partially Globalized World', *American Political Science Review*, 951 (1): 1–13.

Keohane, R. O. (2002) *Governance in a Partially Globalized World*, London: Routledge.

Keyssar, A. (2000) *The Right to Vote: The Contested History of Democracy in the United States*, New York: Basic Books.

King, G., Keohane, R. O. and Verba, S. (1994) *Designing Social Inquiry: Scientific Inference in Qualitative Research*, Princeton, NJ: Princeton University Press.

King, G., Keohane, R. O. and Verba, S. (1995) 'The Importance of Research Design in Political Science', *American Political Science Review*, 89 (2): 475–481.

Knack, S. and Keefer, P. (1995), 'Institutions and Economic Performance: Cross-Country Tests Using Alternative Institutional Measures', *Economics and Politics*, 7: 207–227.

Knight, J. (2003) 'Statistical Model Leaves Peru Counting the Cost of Civil War', *Nature*, 425: 6.

Kohli, A., Evans, P., Katzenstein, P. J., Przeworski, A., Rudolph, S. H., Scott, J. C. and Skocpol, T. (1995) 'The Role of Theory in Comparative Politics: A Symposium', *World Politics*, 48: 1–49.

Korey, W. (1998) *NGOs and the Universal Declaration of Human Rights: A Curious Grapevine*, London: Palgrave.

Kornbluh, P. (2003) *The Pinochet File: A Declassified Dossier on Atrocity and Accountability*, New York: The New Press.

Krasner, S. D. (1997) 'Sovereignty, Regimes, and Human Rights', in V. Rittberger (ed.), *Regime Theory and International Relations*, Oxford: Clarendon Press, 139–167.

Krasner, S. D. (1999) *Sovereignty: Organized Hypocrisy*, Princeton, NJ: Princeton University Press.

Kriesi, H. (1996) 'The Organizational Structure of New Social Movements in a Political Context', in D. McAdam, J. D. McCarthy and M. N. Zald (eds), *Comparative Perspectives on Social Movements: Political Opportunities, Mobilizing Structures, and Cultural Framings*, Cambridge: Cambridge University Press, 152–184.

Kriesi, H., Koopmans, R., Dyvendak, J. W. and Giugni, M. G. (1995) *New Social Movements in Western Europe: A Comparative Analysis*, London: University College of London Press.

Kritz, N. J. (ed.) (1995) *Transitional Justice: How Emerging Democracies Reckon with Former Regimes*, United States Institute of Peace Press, Washington D.C.

Kuhn, T. S. (1970) *The Structure of Scientific Revolutions*, 2nd edn, Chicago: University of Chicago Press.

Landman, T. (1999) 'Economic Development and Democracy: The View from Latin America', *Political Studies*, 47 (4): 607–626.

Landman, T. (2000a) *Issues and Methods in Comparative Politics: An Introduction*, London: Routledge.

Landman, T. (2000b) *Agents of Change: The Comparative Impact of Social Movements*, unpublished PhD manuscript, Colchester: University of Essex.

Landman, T. (2001) 'Measuring the International Human Rights Regime', paper presented at the 97th Annual Meeting of the American Political Science Association, 30 August–2 September, San Francisco.

Landman, T. (2002) 'Comparative Politics and Human Rights', *Human Rights Quarterly*, 24 (4): 890–923.

Landman, T. (2003) *Issues and Methods in Comparative Politics: An Introduction*, 2nd edn, London: Routledge.

Landman, T. (2004) 'Measuring Human Rights: Principle, Practice, and Policy', *Human Rights Quarterly*, 26 (November): 906–931.

Landman, T. (2005a) 'Review Article: the Political Science of Human Rights', *British Journal of Political Science*, 35 (3): 549–572.

Landman, T. (2005b) *Protecting Human Rights: A Global Comparative Study*, Washington DC: Georgetown University Press.

Landman, T. (2005c) *Protecting Human Rights: A Cross-national Time-Series Dataset*, Colchester: University of Essex.

Landman, T. (2005d) 'Democracy Analysis', in *International IDEA 10th Anniversary Handbook*, Stockholm: International IDEA, 19–27.

Landman, T. (2005e) 'Development, Democracy, and Human Rights in Latin America', in J. Dine and A. Fagan (eds), *Capitalism and Human Rights*, Cheltenham: Edward Elgar Publishers, 330–357.

Landman, T. and Abraham, M. (2004) *Evaluation and Assessment of Nine Human Rights NGOs*, The Hague: Ministry of Foreign Affairs of the Netherlands.

Landman, T. (2006) 'Holding the Line: Human Rights Defenders in the Age of Terror', *British Journal of Politics and International Relations*.

Landman, T. and Häusermann, J. (2003) *Map-Making and Analysis of the Main International Initiatives on Developing Indicators on Democracy and Good Governance*, Report to the European Commission.

Lasswell, H. (1941) 'The Technique of Symbol Analysis', *Experimental Division for the Study of War Time Communications*, Washington DC: Library of Congress.

Laver, M., Benoit, K. and Garry, J. (2003) 'Extracting Policy Positions from Political Texts Using Words as Data', *American Political Science Review*, 97 (May): 311–331.

Lawyers Committee for Human Rights (1993) *The World Bank: Governance and Human Rights*, New York: Lawyers Committee for Human Rights.

Lee, R. M. and Fielding, N. G. (2004) 'Tools for Qualitative Data Analysis', in M. Hardy and A. Bryman (eds), *Handbook of Data Analysis*, London: Sage, 529–546.

Levy, J. (2002) 'War and Peace', in W. Carlsnaes, T. Risse and B. Simmons (eds), *Handbook of International Relations*, London: Sage, 350–368.

Lewellen, T. C. (1995) *Dependency and Development: An Introduction to the Third World*, Westport, CT: Bergin and Garvey.

Lewis-Beck, M. S. (1979) 'Some Economic Effects of Revolution: Models, Measurement, and the Cuban Evidence', *American Journal of Sociology*, 84: 1127–1149.

Lewis-Beck, M. S. (1980) *Applied Regression: An Introduction*, London: Sage.

Lewis-Beck, M. S. (1986) 'Interrupted Time-Series', in W. D. Berry and M. Lewis-Beck (eds), *New Tools for Social Scientists*, Beverly Hills, CA: Sage.

Li, Q. and Reuveny, R. (2003) 'Economic Globalization and Democracy: An Empirical Analysis', *British Journal of Political Science*, 33: 29–54.

Lichbach, M. I. (1984) 'The International News About Governability: A Comparison of the *New York Times* and Six News Wires', *International Interactions* 10: 311–340.

Lichbach, M. (1987) 'Deterrence or Escalation? The Puzzle of Aggregate Studies of Repression and Dissent', *Journal of Conflict Resolution*, 31 (June): 266–297.

Lichbach, M. (1994) 'What Makes Rational Peasants Revolutionary? Dilemma, Paradox, and Irony in Peasant Collective Action', *World Politics*, 46 (April): 383.

Lichbach, M. (1995) *The Rebel's Dilemma*, Ann Arbor: University of Michigan Press.

Lichbach, M. (1997) 'Social Theory and Comparative Politics', in M. Lichbach and A. Zuckerman (eds), *Comparative Politics: Rationality, Culture, and Structure*, Cambridge: Cambridge University Press, 239–276.

Lichbach, M. (2003) *Is Rational Choice Theory All of Social Science?*, Ann Arbor: University of Michigan Press.

Lichbach, M. and Zuckerman, A. (eds) (1997) *Comparative Politics: Rationality, Culture, and Structure*, Cambridge: Cambridge University Press.

Lijphart, A. (1971) 'Comparative Politics and Comparative Method', *The American Political Science Review*, 65 (3): 682–693.

Lijphart, A. (1975) 'The Comparable Cases Strategy in Comparative Research', *Comparative Political Studies*, 8 (2): 158–177.

Linz, J. J. (1964) 'An Authoritarian Regime: Spain', in E. Allardt and S. Rokkan (eds), *Mass Politics*, New York: Free Press, 251–283.

Linz, J. J. and Stepan, A. (1996) *Problems of Democratic Transition and Consolidation: South America, Southern Europe, and Post-Communist Europe*, Baltimore: Johns Hopkins University Press.

Lipset, S. M. (1959) 'Some Social Requisites for Democracy: Economic Development and Political Legitimacy', *The American Political Science Review*, 53: 69–105.

Luebbert, G. (1991) *Liberalism, Fascism, or Social Democracy: Social Classes and the Political Origins of Regimes in Inter-war Europe*, New York: Oxford University Press.

Lustick, I. (1996) 'History, Historiography, and Political Science: Multiple Historical Records and the Problem of Selection Bias', *American Political Science Review*, 90 (3): 605–618.

McAdam, D., McCarthy, J. D. and Zald, M. N. (eds) (1996) *Comparative Perspectives on Social Movements: Political Opportunities, Mobilizing Structures, and Cultural Framings*, Cambridge: Cambridge University Press.

McBarnet, D. (2004) 'Human Rights, Corporate Responsibility and the New Accountability', in T. Campbell and S. Miller (eds), *Human Rights and the Moral Responsibilities of Corporate and Public Sector Organisations*, New York: Springer-Verlag, 63–80.

McCamant, J. F. (1981) 'Social Science and Human Rights', *International Organization*, 35 (3): 531–552.

McClelland, C. (1983) 'Let the User Beware', *International Studies Quarterly*, 27: 169–177.

MacIntyre, A. (1971) 'Is a Science of Comparative Politics Possible?', *Against the Self-Images of the Age*, London: Duckworth, 260–279.

MacIntyre, A. (1984) *After Virtue*, 2nd edn, South Bend, IN: University of Notre Dame Press.

Mahoney, J. and Goertz, G. (2004) 'The Possibility Principle: Choosing Negative Cases in Comparative Research', *American Political Science Review*, 98 (4): 653–699.

Mahoney, J. and Rueschemeyer, D. (eds) (2003) *Comparative Historical Analysis in the Social Sciences*, Cambridge: Cambridge University Press.

Mair, P. (1996) 'Comparative Politics: An Overview', in R. E. Goodin and H. Klingemann (eds), *The New Handbook of Political Science*, Oxford: Oxford University Press, 309–335.

Malanczuk, P. (1997) *Akehurst's Modern Introduction to International Law, Seventh Revised Edition*, London: Routledge.

Mann, M. (1993) *The Sources of Social Power, II, The Rise of Classes and Nation States 1760–1914*, Cambridge: Cambridge University Press.

March, J. G. and Olsen, J. P. (1984) 'The New Institutionalism: Organizational Factors in Political Life', *American Political Science Review*, 78: 734–749.

March, J. G. and Olsen, J. P. (1998) 'The Institutional Dynamics of International Political Orders', *International Organization*, 52 (4): 943–969.

Marshall, T. H. (1963) 'Citizenship and Social Class', in *Sociology at the Crossroads and Other Essays*, London: Heinemann, 67–127.

Marx, K. (1978a) 'On the Jewish Question', in R. C. Tucker (ed.), *The Marx-Engels Reader*, 2nd edn, New York: Norton, 26–52.

Marx, K. (1978b) 'The Eighteenth Brumaire of Louis Bonaparte', in R. C. Tucker (ed.), *The Marx-Engels Reader*, 2nd edn, New York: Norton, 594–617.

Mazariegos, O. (2000a) 'The Recovery of Historical Memory Project of the Human Rights Office of the Archbishop of Guatemala', in P. B. Ball, H. F. Spirer and L. Spirer (eds), *Making the Case: Investigating Large Scale Human Rights Violations Using Information Systems and Data Analysis*, Washington DC: American Association for the Advancement of Science, 151–174.

Mazariegos, O. (2000b) 'The International Center for Human Rights Investigations: Generating Analytical Reports', in P. B. Ball, H. F. Spirer and L. Spirer (eds), *Making the Case: Investigating Large Scale Human Rights Violations Using Information Systems and Data Analysis*, Washington DC: American Association for the Advancement of Science, 175–204.

Mearsheimer, J. J. (2001) *The Tragedy of Great Power Politics*, New York: W. W. Norton.

Méndez, J. E., O'Donnell, G. and Pinheiro, P. S. (eds) (1999) *The (Un) Rule of Law and the Underprivileged in Latin America*, South Bend, IN: Notre Dame University Press.

Mendus, S. (1995) 'Human Rights in Political Theory', *Political Studies*, 43 (Special Issue): 10–24.

Merton, R. K. (1936) 'The Unanticipated Consequences of Purposive Social Action', *American Sociological Review*, 1 (6): 894–904.

Messer, E. (1993) 'Anthropology and Human Rights', *Annual Review of Human Rights*, 22: 221–249.

Meyer, W. H. (1996) 'Human Rights and MNCs: Theory vs. Quantitative Evidence', *Human Rights Quarterly*, 18 (2): 368–397.

Meyer, W. H. (1998) *Human Rights and International Political Economy in Third World Nations: Multinational Corporations, Foreign Aid, and Repression*, Westport, CT: Praeger.

Meyer, W. H. (1999a) 'Confirming, Infirming, and Falsifying Theories of Human Rights: Reflections on Smith, Bolyard, and Ippolito Through the Lens of Lakatos', *Human Rights Quarterly*, 21 (1): 220–228.

Meyer, W. H. (1999b) 'Human Rights and International Political Economy in Third World Nations: Multinational Corporations, Foreign Aid, and Repression', *Human Rights Quarterly*, 21 (3): 824–830.

Michels, R. (1959) *Political Parties: A Sociological Study of the Oligarchical Tendencies of Modern Democracy* (tr. E. and C. Paul), New York: Dover.

Mill, J. S. (1843) *A System of Logic*, London: Longman.

Miller, W. L. (1995) 'Quantitative Analysis', in D. Marsh and G. Stoker (eds), *Theories and Methods in Political Science*, London: Macmillan, 154–172.

Minow, M. (1998) *Between Vengeance and Forgiveness: Facing History after Genocide and Mass Violence*, Boston: Beacon Press.

Mitchell, C., Stohl, M., Carleton, D. and Lopez, G. (1986) 'State Terrorism: Issues of Concept and Measurement', in M. Stohl and G. Lopez, *Government Violence and Repression: An Agenda for Research*, Westport, CT: Greenwood Press.

Mitchell, N. (2004) *Agents of Atrocity: Leaders, Followers, and the Violation of Human Rights in Civil War*, London: Palgrave.

Mitchell, N. J. and McCormick, J. M. (1988) 'Economic and Political Explanations of Human Rights Violations', *World Politics*, 40: 476–498.

Mohr, L. B. (1995) *Impact Analysis for Programme Evaluation*, 2nd edn, Thousand Oaks, CA: Sage.

Moore, B. (1966) *The Social Origins of Dictatorship and Democracy: Lord and Peasant in the Making of the Modern World*, Boston: Beacon Press.

Moore, B. (1978) *Injustice: The Social Bases of Obedience and Revolt*, London: Macmillan.

Moran, T. (ed.) (1985) *Multinational Corporations: The Political Economy of Foreign Direct Investment*, Lexington, MA: Lexington Books.

Moran, T. (1998) *Foreign Direct Investment and Development: The New Policy Agenda for Developing Countries and Economies-in-Transition*, Washington DC: Institute for International Economics.

Morgenthau, H. J. (1961) *Politics among Nations: The Struggle for Power and Peace*, 3rd edn, New York: Alfred A. Knopf.

Munck, G. (2001) 'Game Theory and Comparative Politics: New Perspectives and Old Concerns', *World Politics*, 53 (January): 173–204.

Munck, G. and Verkuilen, J. (2002) 'Conceptualizing and Measuring Democracy: Evaluating Alternative Ideas', *Comparative Political Studies*, 35 (1): 5–34.

Münkler, H. (2005) *The New Wars*, Cambridge: Polity Press.

Mutua, M. (2001) 'Human Rights International NGOs: A Critical Evaluation', in C. E. Welch (ed.) *NGOs and Human Rights: Promise and Performance*, Philadelphia: University of Pennsylvania Press, 151–163.

Norval, A. (1996) *Deconstructing Apartheid Discourse*, London: Verso.

O'Donnell, G. (1973) *Economic Modernization and Bureaucratic Authoritarianism*, Berkeley, CA: Institute of International Studies.

OHCHR (2002) Draft Guidelines: A Human Rights Approach to Poverty Reduction Strategies, Geneva: Office of the High Commissioner for Human Rights (www.unhchr.ch/development/povertyfinal.html).

Olson, M. (1965) *The Logic of Collective Action: Public Goods and the Theory of Groups*, Cambridge, MA: Harvard University Press.

Otto, D. (1996) 'Nongovernmental Organizations in the United Nations System: The Emerging Role of International Civil Society', *Human Rights Quarterly*, 18 (1): 107–141.

Parr, S. F. (2002) 'Indicators of Human Rights and Human Development: Overlaps and Differences', in M. Radstaake and D. Bronkhurst *Matching Practice with Principles, Human Rights Impact Assessment: EU Opportunities*, Utrecht, Netherlands: Humanist Committee on Human Rights (HOM), 31–32.

Parsons, T. (1937) *The Structure of Social Action*, New York: Free Press.

Payne, L. (2000) *Uncivil Movements: The Armed Right Wing and Democracy in Latin America*, Baltimore: Johns Hopkins University Press.

Petersmann, E. U. (2002) 'Time for a United Nations "Global Compact" for Integrating Human Rights into the Law of Organizations: Lessons from European Integration', *European Journal of International Law*, 13 (3): 621–650.

Peterson, C. G. J. (1896) 'The Yearly Immigration of Young Plaice into the Limfjord from the German Sea', *Report of the Danish Bioloigical Station to the Ministry of Fisheries*, 6: 1–48.

Physicians for Human Rights (2002a) *Maternal Mortality in Herat Province, Afghanistan*, Boston: Physicians for Human Rights.

Physicians for Human Rights (2002b) *War-related Sexual Violence in Sierra Leone: A Population-based Assessment*, Boston: Physicians for Human Rights.

Physicians for Human Rights (2002c) *A Survey of Human Rights Abuses among New Internally Displaced Persons Herat, Afghanistan*, A Briefing Paper, Boston: Physicians for Human Rights.

Physicians for Human Rights (2003) *Southern Iraq: Reports of Human Rights Abuses and Views on Justice, Reconstruction and Government*, A Briefing Paper, Boston: Physicians for Human Rights.

Pierson, P. (2004) *Politics in Time: History, Institutions, and Social Analysis*, Princeton, NJ: Princeton University Press.

Piven, F. F. and Cloward, R. A. (1977) *Poor People's Movements: Why They Succeed, How They Fail*, New York: Vintage.

Poe, S. (1990) 'Human Rights and Foreign Aid: A Review of Quantitative Studies and Suggestions for Future Research', *Human Rights Quarterly*, 12: 499–509.

Poe, S. C. (1991) 'Human Rights and the Allocation of US Military Assistance', *Journal of Peace Research*, 28: 205–216.

Poe, S. C. (1992) 'Human Rights and Economic Aid Allocation', *American Journal of Political Science*, 36: 147–167.

Poe, S. C. (2004) 'The Decision to Repress: An Integrative Theoretical Approach to the Research on Human Rights and Repressoin', in S. Carey and S. C. Poe (eds), *Understanding Human Rights Violations: New Systematic Studies*, Aldershot: Ashgate, 16–42.

Poe, S. C. and Keith, L. C. (2002) 'Personal Integrity Abuse during Domestic Crises', Paper Prepared for the 98th Annual Meeting of the American Political Science Association, Boston.

Poe, S. C. and Meernik, J. (1995) 'US Military Aid in the 1980s: A Global Analysis', *Journal of Peace Research*, 32 (4): 399–411.

Poe, S. C. and Sirirangsi, R. (1993) 'Human Rights and US Economic Aid to Africa', *International Interactions*, 18 (4): 1–14.

Poe, S. C. and Sirirangsi, R. (1994) 'Human Rights and Economic Aid', *Social Science Quarterly*, 75 (3): 494–509.

Poe, S. and Tate, C. N. (1994) 'Repression of Human Rights to Personal Integrity in the 1980s: A Global Analysis', *American Political Science Review*, 88: 853–872.

Poe, S. C., Tate, C. N. and Keith, L. C. (1999) 'Repression of the Human Right to Personal Integrity Revisited: A Global Cross-National Study Covering the Years 1976–1993', *International Studies Quarterly*, 43: 291–313.

Poe, S. C., Wendel-Blunt, D. and Ho, K. (1997) 'Global Patterns in the Achievement of Women's Human Rights to Equality', *Human Rights Quarterly*, 19: 813–835.

Pogge, T. (2002) *World Poverty and Human Rights: Cosmopolitan Responsibilities and Reforms*, Malden, MA: Blackwell.

Popkin, M. and Bhuta, N. (1999). 'Latin American Amnesties in Comparative Perspective: Can the Past Be Buried', *Ethics & International Affairs*, 13: 99–122.

Popper, K. (1959) *The Logic of Scientific Discovery*, London: Hutchinson.

Popper, K. (1972) 'Of Clouds and Clocks: An Approach to the Problem of Rationality and Freedom in Man', in K. Popper, *Objective Knowledge: An Evolutionary Approach*, Oxford: Clarendon Press, 210–255.

Pritchard, K. (1989) 'Political Science and the Teaching of Human Rights', *Human Rights Quarterly*, 11 (3): 459–475.

Przeworski, A. (1985) 'Marxism and Rational Choice', *Politics and Society*, 14 (4): 379–409.

Przeworski, A. (1991) *Democracy and the Market*, Cambridge: Cambridge University Press.

Przeworski, A. and Teune, H. (1970) *The Logic of Comparative Social Inquiry*, New York: Wiley.

Przeworski, A., Alvarez, M. E., Cheibub, J. A. and Limongi, F. (2000) *Democracy and Development: Political Institutions and Well-Being in the World, 1950–1990*, Cambridge: Cambridge University Press.

Putnam, R. (1988) 'Diplomacy and Domestic Politics: The Logic of Two-Level Games', *International Organization*, 42 (3): 427–460.

Putnam, R. (1993) 'Diplomacy and Domestic Politics: The Logic of Two-Level Games', in P. B. Evans, H. K. Jacobson and R. D. Putnam (eds), *Double-Edged Diplomacy: International Bargaining and Domestic Politics*, Los Angeles: University of California Press, 431–468.

Putnam, R. (ed.) (2002) *Democracies in Flux: The Evolution of Social Capital in Contemporary Society*, Oxford: Oxford University Press.

Radstaake, M. and Bronkhurst, D. (2002) *Matching Practice with Principles, Human Rights Impact Assessment: EU Opportunities*, Utrecht, Netherlands: Humanist Committee on Human Rights (HOM).

Ragin, C. (1987) *The Comparative Method: Moving beyond Qualitative and Quantitative Strategies*, Berkeley: University of California Press.

Ragin, C. (1994) 'Introduction to Qualitative Comparative Analysis', in T. Janoski and A. Hicks (eds), *The Comparative Political Economy of the Welfare State*, Cambridge: Cambridge University Press, 299–320.

Ragin, C. (2000) *Fuzzy Set Social Science*, Chicago: University of Chicago Press.

Ragin, C., Berg-Schlosser, D. and de Meur, G. (1996) 'Political Methodology: Qualitative Methods', in R. E. Goodin and H. Klingemann (eds), *The New Handbook of Political Science*, Oxford: Oxford University Press, 749–768.

Reiff, D. (1999) 'The Precarious Triumph of Human Rights', *New York Times Magazine*, 8 August, 36–41.

REMHI (Recovery of Historical Memory Project) (1999) *Guatemala Never Again! The Official Report of the Human Rights Office, Archdiocese of Guatemala*, Maryknoll, NY: Orbis Books.

Remmer, K. (1993) 'The Political Economy of Elections in Latin America, 1980–1991', *American Political Science Review*, 87 (2): 393–407.

Renteln, A. D. (1988) 'Relativism and the Search for Human Rights', *American Anthropologist*, New Series, 90 (1): 56–72.

Risse, T. (2002) 'Transnational Actors and World Politics', in W. Carlsnaes, T. Risse and B. Simmons, B. (eds), *Handbook of International Relations*, London: Sage, 255–274.

Risse, T., Ropp, S. C. and Sikkink, K. (1999) *The Power of Human Rights: International Norms and Domestic Change*, Cambridge: Cambridge University Press.

Rittberger, V. (1997) *Regime Theory and International Relations*, Oxford: Clarendon Press.

Ritzer, G. and Smart, B. (eds) (2001) *Handbook of Social Theory*, Thousand Oaks, CA: Sage.

Roberts, L., Lafta, R., Garfield, R., Khudhairi, J. and Burnham, G. (2004) 'Mortality before and after the 2003 Invasion of Iraq: Cluster Sample Survey', *The Lancet*, 29 October, http://image.thelancet.com/extras/04art10342web.pdf.

Robertson, A. H. and Merrills, J. G. (1996) *Human Rights in the World: An Introduction to the Study of the International Protection of Human Rights*, 4th edn, Manchester: Manchester University Press.

Rodley, N. S. (1979) 'Monitoring Human Rights in the 1980s', in J. I. Domínguez, N. S. Rodley, B. Wood and R. Falk (eds), *Enhancing Global Human Rights*, New York: McGraw-Hill, 117–154.

Roniger, L. and Sznajder, M. (1999) *The Legacy of Human Rights Violations in the Southern Cone: Argentina, Chile, and Uruguay*, Oxford: Oxford University Press.

Rorty, R. (1993) 'Human Rights, Rationality, and Sentimentality', in S. Shute and S. Hurley (eds), *On Human Rights: The Oxford Amnesty Lectures*, New York: Basic Books, 112–134.

Ross, M. H. (1997) 'Culture and Identity in Comparative Political Analysis', in M. Lichbach and A. Zuckerman (eds), *Comparative Politics: Rationality, Culture, and Structure*, Cambridge: Cambridge University Press, 42–80.

Rotberg, R. (2004) *When States Fail: Causes and Consequences*, Princeton, NJ: Princeton University Press.

Rubin, B. R. and Newberg, P. R. (1980) 'Statistical Analysis for Implementing Human Rights Policy', in P. R. Newberg (ed.), *The Politics of Human Rights*, New York: New York Press, 268–284.

Rueschemeyer, D., Stephens, E. H. and Stephens, J. (1992) *Capitalist Development and Democracy*, Cambridge: Polity Press.

Ruggie, J. G. (1982) 'International Regimes, Transactions, and Change: Embedded Liberalism in the Postwar Economic Order', *International Organization*, 36 (2): 379–415.

Russett, B. and Oneal, J. R. (2001) *Triangulating Peace: Democracy, Interdependence, and International Organizations*, New York: Norton.

Sadasivam, B. (1997) 'The Impact of Structural Adjustment on Women: A Governance and Human Rights Agenda', *Human Rights Quarterly*, 19 (3): 630–665.

Sartori, G. (1970) 'Concept Misinformation in Comparative Politics', *American Political Science Review*, 64: 1033–1053.

Sartori, G. (1994) 'Compare Why and How: Comparing, Miscomparing and the Comparative Method', in M. Dogan and A. Kazancigil (eds), *Comparing Nations: Concepts, Strategies, Substance*, Oxford: Basil Blackwell, 14–34.

Schabas, W. (2005) 'The Sierra Leone Truth and Reconciliation Commission', in E. Skaar,

S. Gloppen and A. Surhke (eds), *Roads to Reconciliation*, Lexington, MA: Lexington Books, 129–156.

Schmitter, P. C. and Lehmbruch, G. (eds) (1979) *Trends toward Corporatist Intermediation*, London: Sage.

Schmitz, H. P. and Sikkink, K. (2002) 'International Human Rights', in W. Carlsnaes, T. Risse and B. Simmons (eds), *Handbook of International Relations*, London: Sage, 517–537.

Scott, J. (2000) *Social Network Analysis: A Handbook*, London: Sage.

Scott, T. J. (2001) 'Evaluating Development-Oriented NGOs', in C. E. Welch, Jr. (ed.), *NGOs and Human Rights: Promise and Performance*, Philadelphia: University of Pennsylvania Press, 204–221.

Shapiro, M. and Stone Sweet, A. (2002) *On Law, Politics, and Judicialization*, Oxford: Oxford University Press.

Shue, H. (1980) *Basic Rights: Subsistence, Affluence and US Foreign Policy*, Princeton, NJ: Princeton University Press.

Simmons, B. and Martin, L. L. (2002) 'International Organizations and Institutions', in W. Carlsnaes, T. Risse and B. Simmons (eds), *Handbook of International Relations*, London: Sage, 192–211.

Skaar, E. (1999) 'Truth Commissions, Trials – or Nothing? Policy Options in Democratic Transitions', *Third World Quarterly*, 20 (6): 1109–1128.

Skaar, E. (2005) 'Argentina: Truth, Justice, and Reconciliation', in E. Skaar, S. Gloppen and A. Surhke (eds), *Roads to Reconciliation*, Lexington, MA: Lexington Books, 157–176.

Skaar, E., Gloppen, S. and Surhke, A. (eds) (2005) *Roads to Reconciliation*, Lexington, MA: Lexington Books.

Skocpol, T. (1979) *States and Social Revolutions: A Comparative Analysis of France, Russia, and China*, Cambridge: Cambridge University Press.

Skocpol, T. and Somers, M. (1980) 'The Uses of Comparative History in Macrosocial Inquiry', *Comparative Studies in Society and History*, 22: 174–197.

Smelser, N. (1962) *Theory of Collective Behavior*, New York: The Free Press.

Smith, J., Bolyard, M. and Ippolito, A. (1999) 'Human Rights and the Global Economy: A Response to Meyer', *Human Rights Quarterly*, 21: 207–219.

Smith, J., Pagnucco, R. and Lopez, G. A. (1998) 'Globalizing Human Rights: The Work of Transnational Human Rights NGOs in the 1990s', *Human Rights Quarterly*, 20 (2): 379–412.

Snidal, D. (2002) 'Rational Choice and International Relations', in W. Carlsnaes, T. Risse and B. Simmons (eds), *Handbook of International Relations*, London: Sage, 73–94.

Snyder, R. C., Hermann, C. F. and Lasswell, H. D. (1976) 'A Global Monitoring System: Appraising the Effects of Government on Human Dignity', *International Studies Quarterly*, 20 (2): 221–260.

Sorell, T. (2004) 'Business and Human Rights', in T. Campbell and S. Miller (eds), *Human Rights and the Moral Responsibilities of Corporate and Public Sector Organisations*, New York: Springer-Verlag, 129–144.

Sorell, T. and Landman, T. (2005) 'Justifying Human Rights" The Roles of Domain, Audience and Constituency', unpublished paper.

Speed, S. and Reyes, A. (2002) '"In Our Own Defense": Rights and Resistence in Chiapas', *Political and Legal Anthropology Review*, 25 (1): 69–89.

Spirer, H. (1990) 'Violations of Human Rights: How Many?', *American Journal of Economics and Sociology*, 49 (2): 199–210.

Spirer, J. (2000) 'The International Center for Human Rights Investigations: Generating Analytical Reports', in P. B. Ball, H. F. Spirer and L. Spirer (eds), *Making the Case: Investigating Large Scale Human Rights Violations Using Information Systems and Data Analysis*, Washington DC: American Association for the Advancement of Science, 175–185.

Steinberg, R., Barton, J., Goldstein, J. and Josling, T. (2005) *The Evolution of the Trade Regime: Economics, Law, and Politics of the GATT/WTO*, Princeton, NJ: Princeton University Press.

Steinmo, S., Thelen, K. and Longstreth, F. (1992) *Structuring Politics: Historical Institutionalism in Comparative Analysis*, Cambridge: Cambridge University Press.

Stiglitz, J. (2002) *Globalization and its Discontents*, London: Allen Lane.

Stimson, J. (1985) 'Regression in Space and Time: A Statistical Essay', *American Political Science Review*, 29: 914–947.

Stone Sweet, A. (1999) 'Judicialization and the Construction of Governance', *Comparative Political Studies*, 32 (2): 147–184.

Strawson, J. (ed.) (2002) *Law after Ground Zero*, Sydney: Glasshouse Press.

Strouse, J. C. and Claude, R. P. (1976) 'Empirical Comparative Rights Research: Some Preliminary Tests of Development Hypotheses', in R. P. Claude (ed.), *Comparative Human Rights*, Baltimore: Johns Hopkins University Press, 51–67.

Tarrow, S. (1989) *Democracy and Disorder: Protest and Politics in Italy 1966–1973*, Oxford: Clarendon Press.

Tarrow, S. (1994) *Power in Movement: Social Movements, Collective Action and Politics*, Cambridge: Cambridge University Press.

Tashakkori, A. and Teddlie, C. (1998) *Mixed Methodology: Combining Qualitative and Quantitative Approaches*, London: Sage.

Taylor, C. L. and Hudson, M. (1972) (eds) *World Handbook of Political and Social Indicators*, 2nd edn, New Haven, CT: Yale University Press.

Taylor, C. L. and Jodice, D. A. (1983) (eds) *World Handbook of Political and Social Indicators: Political Protest and Government Change, Vol. II*, 3rd edn, New Haven, CT: Yale University Press.

Thelen, K. and Steinmo, S. (1992) 'Historical Institutionalism in Comparative Perspective', in S. Steinmo, K. Thelen and F. Longstreth (eds), *Structuring Politics: Historical Institutionalism in Comparative Analysis*, Cambridge: Cambridge University Press, 1–32.

Thomas, C. (2000) *Global Governance, Development and Human Security: The Challenge of Poverty and Inequality*, London: Pluto Press.

Thompson, K. and Giffard, C. (2002) *Reporting Killings as Human Rights Violations*, Colchester, UK: Human Rights Centre, University of Essex.

Tilly, C. (1978) *From Mobilization to Revolution*, Englewood Cliffs, NJ: Prentice-Hall.

Tilly, C., Tilly, L. and Tilly, R. (1975) *The Rebellious Century 1830–1930*, Cambridge, MA: Harvard University Press.

Todaro, M. (1997) *Economic Development*, 7th edn, Reading, MA: Addison-Wesley.

Tolley, H. (1989) 'Popular Sovereignty and International Law: ICJ Strategies for International Standard Setting', *Human Rights Quarterly*, 11: 561–585.

Travers, M. (2001) *Qualitative Research through Case Studies*, London: Sage.

Tsebelis, G. (1990) *Nested Games: Rational Choice in Comparative Politics*, Berkeley: University of California Press.

Turner, B. S. (1993) 'Outline of a Theory of Human Rights', *Sociology*, 27 (3): 489–512.

United Nations (1998) *Declaration on the Right and Responsibility of Individuals, Groups and Organs of Society to Promote and Protect Universally Recognized Human Rights and Fundamental Freedoms*, General Assembly resolution 53/144.

United Nations (2003) Interim report of the Special Rapporteur of the Commission on Human Rights on the right to everyone to enjoy the highest attainable standard of physical and mental health, Mr. Paul Hunt, New York: United Nations, A/58/427.

United Nations (2004) Interim report of the Special Rapporteur of the Commission on Human Rights on the right to everyone to enjoy the highest attainable standard of physical and mental health, Mr. Paul Hunt, New York: United Nations, A/59/422.

United Nations Development Programme (1999) *Human Development Report*, New York: UNDP.

United Nations Development Programme (2000) *Human Development Report*, New York: UNDP.

United Nations Global Compact Office and the Office of the High Commissioner for Human Rights (2004) *Embedding Human Rights in Business Practice*, New York: United Nations. www.unglobalcompact.org.

United Nations Office of the High Commissioner for Human Rights (2002) *Draft Guidelines: Human Rights Approach to Poverty Reduction Strategies*, Geneva: United Nations Office of the High Commissioner for Human Rights.

USAID (1998a) *Democracy and Governance: A Conceptual Framework*, Washington, DC: Center for Democracy and Governance, Technical Publications Series, USAID, www.usaid.gov/democracy/pubsindex.html.

USAID (1998b) *Handbook of Democracy and Governance Program Indicators*, Washington, DC: Center for Democracy and Governance, Technical Publications Series, USAID, www.usaid.gov/democracy/pubsindex.html.

Valenzuela, J. S. and Valenzuela, A. (1986) *Military Rule in Chile: Dictatorship and Oppositions*, Baltimore: Johns Hopkins University Press.

van Maarseveen H. and van der Tang, G. (1978), *Written Constitutions: A Computerized Comparative Study*, New York: Oceana Publications.

Verheem, R. (2000) *A Short Introduction on Strategic Environmental Impact Assessment*, Commission for EIA in the Netherlands, www.iaia.org.

Villa-Vicencio, C. and Verwoerd, W. (eds) (2000) *Looking Back, Reaching Forward: Reflections on the Truth and Reconciliation Commission of South Africa*, Cape Town: University of Cape Town Press and London: Zed Books.

Viotti, P. R. and Kauppi, M. V. (1999) *International Relations Theory: Realism, Globalism, and Beyond*, Boston: Allyn and Bacon.

Vogt, W. P. (1999) *Dictionary of Statistics and Methodology: A Nontechnical Guide for the Social Sciences*, London: Sage.

Von Wright, G. H. (1971) *Explanation and Understanding*, London: Routledge & Kegan Paul.

Waldron, J. (1984) *Theories of Rights*, Oxford: Oxford University Press.

Waldron, J. (ed.) (1987) *'Nonsense upon Stilts': Bentham, Burke, and Marx on the Rights of Man*, London: Methuen.

Waltz, K. (1979) *Theory of International Politics*, Reading, MA: Addison-Wesley.

Wantchekon, L. and Healy, A. (1999) 'The "Game" of Torture', *Journal of Conflict Resolution*, 43 (5): 569–609.

Ward, H. (1995) 'Rational Choice Theory', in D. Marsh and G. Stoker (eds), *Theories and Methods in Political Science*, London: Macmillan, 76–93.

Ward, K. (2000) 'The United Nations Mission for the Verification of Human Rights in Guatemala: Database Representation', in P. B. Ball, H. F. Spirer and L. Spirer (eds), *Making the Case: Investigating Large Scale Human Rights Violations Using Information Systems and Data Analysis*, Washington DC: American Association for the Advancement of Science, 137–150.

Weber, M. (1968) *Economy and Society*, Berkeley: University of California Press.

Weber, M. (1991a) 'Politics as a Vocation', in H. H. Gerth and C. W. Mills (eds), *From Max Weber: Essays in Sociology*, London: Routledge, 77–128.

Weber, M. (1991b) 'Science as a Vocation', in H. H. Gerth and C. W. Mills (eds), *From Max Weber: Essays in Sociology*, London: Routledge, 129–156.

Weiss, T. (2000) 'Governance, Good Governance and Global Governance: Conceptual and Actual Challenges', *Third World Quarterly*, 21 (5): 795–814.

Weissbrodt, D. and Bartolomei, M. L. (1991) 'The Effectiveness of International Human Rights Pressures: The Case of Argentina, 1976–1983', *Minnesota Law Review*, 75: 1009–1035.

Welch, C. E., Jr. (ed.) (2001a) *NGOs and Human Rights: Promise and Performance*, Philadelphia: University of Pennsylvania Press.

Welch, C. E., Jr. (2001b) 'Introduction', in C. E. Welch, Jr. (ed.), *NGOs and Human Rights: Promise and Performance*, Philadelphia: University of Pennsylvania Press, 1–22.

Wendt, A. (1999) *Social Theory of International Politics*, Cambridge: Cambridge University Press.

Whiteley, P. (1999) 'The Origins of Social Capital', in J. Van Deth, M. Maraffi, K. Newton and P. Whiteley, *Social Capital and European Democracy*, London: Routledge, 25–44.

Whiteley, P. (2000) 'Economic Growth and Social Capital', *Political Studies*, 48: 443–466.

Wickham-Crowley, T. (1992) *Guerrillas and Revolution in Latin America*, Princeton, NJ: Princeton University Press.

Wilensky, H. (2002) *Rich Democracies: Political Economy, Public Policy, and Performance*, Berkeley: University of California Press.

Wilson, R. A. (1997) 'Representing Human Rights Violations: Social Context and Subjectivities', in R. A. Wilson (ed.), *Human Rights, Culture, and Context: Anthropological Approaches*, London: Pluto Press, 134–160.

Wilson, R. A. (2001) *The Politics of Truth and Reconciliation in South Africa: Legitimizing the Post-Apartheid State*, Cambridge University Press, Cambridge.

Wilson, R. A. and Mitchell, J. P. (2003) *Human Rights in Global Perspective: Anthropological Studies of Rights, Claims and Entitlements*, London: Routledge.

Wolf, E. (1969) *Peasant Wars of the Twentieth Century*, New York: Harper Torchbooks.

Woodiwiss, A. (2005) *Human Rights*, London: Routledge.

World Bank (1992) *Development and Good Governance*, Washington DC: World Bank.

Wright, S. (2001) *International Human Rights, Decolonisation and Globalisation: Becoming Human*, London: Routledge.

Young, R. A. (1976) 'Toward a Global Monitoring System: Some Comments and Suggestions', *International Studies Quarterly*, 20 (4): 629–634.

Youngers, C. (2003) *Violencia Política y Sociedad Civil en el Perú*, Lima: Instituto de Estudios Peruanos.

Zagare, F. C. (1984) *Game Theory: Concepts and Applications*, London: Sage.

Zakaria, F. (2003) *The Future of Freedom: Illiberal Democracy at Home and Abroad*, New York: W. W. Norton.

Zald, M. N. and Ash, R. (1966) 'Social Movement Organizations: Growth, Decay, and Change', *Social Forces*, 44: 327–341.

Zanger, S. C. (2000a) 'A Global Analysis of the Effect of Regime Changes on Life Integrity Violations, 1977–1993', *Journal of Peace Research* 37 (2): 213–233.

Zanger, S. C. (2000b) 'Good Governance and European Aid: The Impact of Political Conditionality', *European Union Politics*, 1 (3): 293–317.

Zeller, R. and Carmines, E. (1980) *Measurement in the Social Sciences: The Link between Theory and Data*, London: Cambridge University Press.

Zürn, M. (2002) 'From Independence to Globalization', in W. Carlsmaes, T. Risse and B. Simmons (eds), *Handbook of International Relations*, London: Sage, 235–254.

Index